THE COMPLETE

JOHN LENNON SONGS

Published in 2020 in the United States by Weldon Owen International
1150 Brickyard Cove Road
Richmond, CA 94801
www.weldonowen.com

Originally published in the United Kingdom by Welbeck
An imprint of Welbeck Non-Fiction Limited,
part of Welbeck Publishing Group
20 Mortimer Street, London W1T 3JW

Some of the material in this book was previously published in *We All Shine On*, *Working Class Hero*, and *John Lennon*.

ISBN 978-1-68188-586-5

Printed and bound in Dubai

10 9 8 7 6 5 4 3 2 1

Merry Christmas
To Kathleen
My beauty ...
you always have appreciated
all of the Music, I hope you like the
Book.
Love
Mom
12/25/20

THE COMPLETE

JOHN LENNON SONGS

ALL THE SONGS. ALL THE STORIES. ALL THE LYRICS.

PAUL DU NOYER

CONTENTS

IMA

GINE

FOREWORD

There is really only one story behind John Lennon's songs—the story of his life. As a man he was not always honest, but as a songwriter he didn't know how to lie. Lennon tackled his songs like they were episodes of an autobiography. Each of them opens a window on the man's inner self.

There are plenty of books about John Lennon's life and the Beatles' music. What's often overlooked, though, is the extraordinary solo work that he produced in his final decade. Even the worthier biographies are light on the details of that music, which is a gap this book attempts to fill. Between the end of the Beatles in 1970 and his murder in 1980, Lennon kept on weaving dreams. To the raging debates of his day, he added the power of his immense celebrity and the force of his sincerity. Now that he has joined posterity's favorite pop stars, he's remembered as a guru, a leader, a preacher. But John was more complex than such pious summaries allow. In his songs, he turned that turbulent life into poetry.

Once he was free of the Beatles, Lennon's work became unashamedly confessional, and the most enjoyable way to understand his story is through the music. With luck, this book might help you enjoy it even more.

The music has been my primary source, but there's much to be learned from the big interviews John gave in the last days of his life, promoting his album *Double Fantasy*: Andy Peebles' conversations for BBC radio, Dave Sholin's for RKO, the interviews by David Sheff in *Playboy* and Barbara Graustark in *Newsweek*. Lennon himself wrote an acerbic memoir, *The Ballad of John and Yoko*, compiled in a book of his essays, *Skywriting by Word of Mouth*.

Among the best-known biographies, Albert Goldman's attempted demolition, *The Lives of John Lennon* is, if nothing else, horribly readable. The best so far, though, is Philip Norman's *John Lennon: The Life*, for its depth, elegance and insight. Other books I've found useful include Jan Wenner's *Rolling Stone* interviews, published as *Lennon Remembers*; Peter Doggett's *The Art and Music of John Lennon*; Keith Badman's *The Beatles after the Break-Up*; May Pang's *John Lennon: The Lost Weekend*, and *Come Together: John Lennon in His Time* by Jon Wiener.

I've also drawn on my interviews with people who knew John Lennon personally. My thanks go in particular to Yoko Ono for sharing so many of her memories with me, to Paul McCartney, who has always spoken willingly about his old partner, to Sean Lennon, Cynthia Lennon, Ringo Starr, Klaus Voormann, Alan White, Bob Gruen, Neil Aspinall, Kieron "Spud" Murphy, Tony Bramwell, Bill Harry, Billy Preston, Derek Taylor, George Martin, Denis O'Dell, Andrew Loog Oldham, Pete Best, David Bowie, Tony Barrow, Mike McCartney and Larry Parnes.

Many friends and colleagues have helped me since the first edition of this book was written in 1997. I thank Steve Turner (whose Beatle book, *A Hard Day's Write*, was the template for this one), Murray Chalmers, Barry Miles, Mark Ellen, Colin Hall at Mendips, Ronnie Hughes, Robert Sandall, Spencer Leigh, Colin Shearman, Geoff Baker, Mark Lewisohn, Ian MacDonald, Mat Snow, Jon Savage, Charles Shaar Murray, Ian Cranna, David Buckley, Guy Hayden at EMI, Roland Hall at Welbeck, my agent Ros Edwards, and my wife Una. To adapt a line from John Lennon's masterpiece of democratic mysticism, may you all shine on.

Paul Du Noyer, 2020

Opposite: Lennon, loud and clear. Freed from the Beatles' collective identity, he became both deeply confessional and socially outspoken.

Overleaf: John on television in England in 1970.

BEAC
LIVE SHOWS AT THE BEA
BROA PREMIER
PER
LON CLU

Chapter One

SHINING ON

His name became an emblem of the yearning for peace, but John Lennon was born—and died—in violence. He came into the world on October 9th, 1940, when Liverpool was being bombed to rubble by Hitler's air force. The Oxford Street Maternity Hospital stood on a hill above the city center; below it were the docks that had made the seaport great, but were now earning it a terrible punishment. Night after night, the River Mersey resembled Pearl Harbor in those war years, and thousands perished in terrace slums or makeshift shelters. But Julia Lennon's war baby survived, and she took him home unharmed. All around them was the din of sirens and explosions.

The Lennons' house was small, in a working-class street off Penny Lane; John's father, Freddie, was away at sea. Liverpool was where generations of new Americans took their leave of Europe, and its maritime links with New York stayed strong. Freddie Lennon was like many Liverpudlian men, who knew the bars of Brooklyn better than the palaces of London. Seamen and GIs became a source of United States records that made Liverpool a rock 'n' roll town. Black American music found a ready market in this port, which had grown rich by selling the slaves of Africa to the masters of the New World. In a park near John's home stood a statue of Christopher Columbus, inscribed: "The discoverer of America was the maker of Liverpool."

Above: John's early home, Mendips, in the Liverpool suburbs. He favored its front porch, lower left, for teenage rehearsals with Paul McCartney.

But the Irish, especially, had dominated Liverpool since the mass migrations of the famine years a century before. These Celtic incomers, alongside the Welsh, gave the Lancashire town a hybrid accent all of its own, which John never lost. (He was, indeed, one of their descendants.) And Celtic stereotypes were soon attached to the Liverpool population: fiery and sentimental, lovers of music and words, witty and subversive. Far from breaking the mold, Lennon was that stereotype made flesh.

His upbringing, however, was conventionally British. The respectable Aunt Mimi looked after John from the age of five. With her husband George Smith she raised the boy in a neat, semi-detached house in Menlove Avenue on Liverpool's outskirts. Postwar Britain was still subject to scarcity and rationing ("G is for orange," went John's poem "Alphabet", "which we love to eat

Above: The Liverpool that Lennon knew in boyhood was scarred by bomb damage from the War, and by the social deprivation that prompted much slum clearance.

Opposite: Aunt Mimi sits by a portrait of her newly-famous nephew in the front room at Menlove Avenue.

when we can get them"), but his circumstances were comfortable. He had a loving home, and was educated at Quarry Bank, one of the city's best schools. His background was not as deprived as he sometimes implied.

Yet he could not forget that his natural parents had deserted him. Freddie left Julia, and Julia did not want her infant John. It was not until his teens that John would see his mother regularly, whereupon she was killed in a road accident. The tragedy seems to have compounded John's sense of isolation.

As a child, he claims, he used to enter deep trance-like states. He liked to paint and draw, and loved the surrealistic "nonsense" styles of Lewis Carroll, Edward Lear, and Spike Milligan. But his quick mind made him a rebel rather than an academic achiever. To Liverpool suburbanites of Mimi's generation, the city accent meant a lack of breeding, while shaggy hair and scruffy clothes, far from seeming bohemian, merely awoke prewar memories of the Depression. John made it his business to embrace all those things.

Rock 'n' roll was his salvation, arriving like a cultural H-bomb in mid-Fifties Britain when John was fifteen. But his musical education began earlier. As Yoko wrote in the sleeve notes to *Menlove Ave.*, a compilation featuring some of John's Fifties favorites, "John's American rock roots, Elvis, Fats Domino and Phil Spector are evident in these tracks. But what I hear in John's voice are the other roots of the boy who grew up in Liverpool, listening to 'Greensleeves', BBC Radio and Tessie O'Shea." As well as the light classics and novelty songs of that pre-television era, John learned many of the folk songs still sung in Liverpool ("Maggie May" among them) and the hymns he was taught in

"YOKO ENCOURAGED THE FREAK IN ME. SHE CAME IN THROUGH THE BATHROOM WINDOW."

—John Lennon

Sunday school. Like his near neighbor Paul McCartney, Lennon's subconscious understanding of melody and harmony, if not of rhythm, was already being formed many years before his road-to-Damascus encounters with Bill Haley's "Rock Around The Clock" and Elvis Presley's "Heartbreak Hotel".

By the dawn of the 1960s, when John's old skiffle band the Quarry Men had evolved into Liverpool's top beat group the Beatles, he'd absorbed rock 'n' roll into his bloodstream. The town's cognoscenti were by this time devouring the sounds of Brill Building pop or rare imports of Motown soul. When Lennon and McCartney made their first, hesitant efforts to write songs instead of copying American originals, their imaginations were a mixture of influences. Country and Western was the city's most popular live music, which is why the Beatles' George Harrison became a guitar picker instead of a blues wailer like Surrey boy Eric Clapton. Then there was anything from Broadway shows to football chants, to family memories of long-demolished music halls.

More than all of these, there was Lennon and McCartney's innate creative talent. They inspired each other, at first as friends and then as rivals. Their band, the Beatles, was simultaneously toughened and sensitized by countless shows in Hamburg, the Cavern and elsewhere. And in London they met George Martin, who was surely the most intuitive producer they could ever have worked with. Finally on their way, the Beatles were world-conquering and unstoppable.

All this was not enough for Lennon. Millions adored "Please Please Me", "She Loves You" and "I Want to Hold Your Hand", but John soon tired of any formula, however magical. Hearing the songs of Bob Dylan, he was stung into competing as a poet. Turning inwards to his own state of turmoil, he yearned to test his powers of self-expression. He began lacing the Beatles' repertoire with songs of dark portent, such as "I'm a Loser" and "You've Got to Hide Your Love Away". Attempting his most naked statement so far, he wrote a song that he simply called "Help!"—but the conventions of Top 20 pop music ensured that nobody guessed he really meant it.

Opposite: Lennon perfects the rocker rebel look, just before the 1961 "mop-top" makeover that transformed the Beatles' image.

As the Beatles gradually began to disappear behind moustaches and a sweet-scented, smoky veil, Lennon's lyrics moved towards more complex and original imagery. And yet, paradoxically, there was greater self-revelation. "Norwegian Wood", "Tomorrow Never Knows", "Strawberry Fields Forever"—while these songs were often suffused with gnomic mystery, the emotional presence of their creator remained unmistakable. He disdained the everyday, anecdotal songs that had become Paul's hallmark. "I like to write about me," he told *Playboy* magazine in 1980, "because I know me. I don't know anything about secretaries and postmen and meter maids."

His unthinking honesty almost killed him in 1966. A casual comment to a London newspaper—that the Beatles were more popular than Jesus—was shrugged off in Britain but summoned forth a torrent of death threats from America. "It put the fear of God into him," remembers Paul McCartney. "Boy, if there was one point in John's life when he was nervous. Try having the whole Bible Belt against you; it's not so funny." Coming through that, and having resolved the Beatles would not tour any more, John was ready for something else to happen in his life.

What happened was a woman named Yoko Ono. A Japanese artist, she arrived as if from nowhere and revolutionized John Lennon's life. "She came in through the bathroom window," he joked in 1969. "She encouraged the freak in me." John divorced his wife Cynthia, the girl he'd dated when they were Liverpool art students, and married the partner he described as "me in drag". Yoko was, in fact, the twice-married daughter of a wealthy Tokyo family, and a seasoned performer in her own right. The art that John understood involved writing words and music, but the key to Yoko's art was its "concept". In her world the idea was more important than the artifact, which could be anything—from a film of a smile to an evening spent onstage in a bag.

"JOHN WOULD ALWAYS WANT TO JUMP OVER THE CLIFF. THAT WAS THE DIFFERENCE IN OUR PERSONALITIES."

—Paul McCartney

In 1968 the couple made an album called Two Virgins, more renowned for their nude photo on the cover than for its contents, which were a mosaic of sound effects, conversational snippets, and random noise. Around the same time, Lennon used a similar technique for the track "Revolution 9" on the album *The Beatles* (the "White Album"). "John was turned on by it all," says McCartney, who'd introduced his partner to the work of avant-garde composers and shown him some sonic tricks. "Being John, he'd make the record of it. He'd get so excited. 'I've got to do it!' Whereas, being me, I'd experiment but just bring it to our mainstream records.

"John would always want to jump over the cliff," Paul reflects. "He may have said that to me: 'If you're faced with a cliff, have you ever thought of jumpin'?' I said, 'Fuck off. You jump, and tell me how it is.' That was basically the difference in our personalities... Once he met Yoko, he was, 'Ah, we can do it now.' Yoko gave him the freedom to do it. In fact, she wanted more. 'Do it double, be more daring, take all your clothes off.' She always pushed him. Which he liked—nobody had ever pushed him before."

Yoko and John were married in March 1969, just a week after Paul and Linda McCartney. The timing symbolized an accomplished fact: The two men had ended the central partnership of their youth as they commenced the key relationships of their maturity. Neither woman had an easy ride from press and public thereafter, but Yoko's was the harder. At one extreme there was anti-Japanese abuse; but there was also skepticism about her talent, and disapproval of her influence on John. But in spite of what many felt, she did not break up the Beatles—they were disintegrating of their own accord.

To his credit, John defended her at every turn. In the face of ridicule and hostility, they even made more records together. In May 1969 there was *Unfinished Music No. 2: Life With The Lions*, featuring distorted guitar and unearthly vocals; its second side carried a faltering heartbeat in honor of the child they lost in a miscarriage. Their *Wedding Album* was released in November—another baffling collage of sounds. They never lost an opportunity to proclaim their love for one another, although, as John confessed that same year, "Even with two people who are as lucky as us and have somebody that can be close on all levels, there's still great depths of misery to be found. That's the human condition and there isn't any answer for that."

It was a common assumption in Britain that Yoko had "stolen" John for his money and fame. But the years that followed seemed to bear out an observation by the Beatles' last manager, Allen Klein, that John needed Yoko more than she needed him. In truth, as outsiders we can only really speculate. His ready wit and common touch were always a curious contrast to her stiff, esoteric image. But he chose her, could not operate for very long without her, and produced as many great songs after he met her as he had done before.

The experimental records he made with Yoko were revealing—as everything John produced was revealing—but we can date his formal career outside the Beatles to 1969, when "Give Peace a Chance" was credited to the Plastic Ono Band. The group existed only in theory, named after a Yoko project involving plastic models of musicians, wired up to perform on stage. In the end the Lennons only ever made the models in miniature, but the Plastic Ono Band did materialize as an ad hoc pool of players, sometimes even including George and Ringo, with John and Yoko at its nucleus. His first non-Beatle records overlapped with the Beatles' final releases, but by 1970 he was out there on his own.

There was a scattering of public appearances, whether bed-ins, bag-ins or orthodox concerts. The most important of these took place at a rock 'n' roll revival show in Canada, which spawned the album *Live Peace in Toronto 1969*, with John and Yoko being joined by Eric Clapton, Klaus Voormann—the Beatles' old comrade from their Hamburg days—and drummer Alan White. Strung out on heroin, John rehearsed his instant band on the plane going over,

Opposite: John and Yoko at the time of their marriage in Gibraltar, March 1969.

BAGISM

"I HAVE DECIDED TO BE OR NOT TO BE FOR A COUPLE'A YEARS... I AIN'T IN A HURRY TO SIGN WITH ANYONE."

—John Lennon

and they played a ramshackle set of Fifties cover versions, some of Yoko's elongated improvisations and gave the first performance of "Cold Turkey". Nothing preoccupied him more, though, than his campaign for world peace, for which he and his wife were more than willing to play "the world's clowns" and be "the court jesters of the youth movement".

It was John's Imagine album, in 1971, that finally won him credibility as a rock star outside the Beatles, but it was the last record he made in England. Never a great lover of London, he found his ultimate home in New York City, where Yoko recalls him gazing nostalgically at the docks and piers and the Atlantic liners, and declaring it was "like a Liverpool that has got its act together". A few more years of bustle and upheaval preceded his virtual retirement in 1975, a turning point marked by the birth of his son Sean. He wrote to his friend Derek Taylor, "I meself have decided to be or not to be for a coupla years… I ain't in a hurry to sign with anyone or do anything. Am enjoying my pregnancy… thinking time… what's it all about time too."

A lurid picture of John's last years was painted by the author Albert Goldman in *The Lives of John Lennon*. But Goldman was, perhaps, unduly taken with his previous, masterly description of Elvis Presley's decline. His book sacrificed warmth and sympathetic understanding in an effort to show John's seventh-floor Dakota apartment as a decadent Graceland-in-the-sky. Our final sightings of John Lennon were really not of a ravaged man. He was thinner and older—but then, he had never looked especially young—while his manner was gentle and contented, as if he'd found the equilibrium which had eluded him all his life.

Unlike most Sixties stars, John showed in his final songs that his powers were not failing him in middle age. He was gunned down in 1980, and it's still a bitter thought that his development was arrested by such a freakish act of hatred. In an age when fame is thought to be all-important, no matter how it is earned, his assassin Mark Chapman must count as some kind of abominable success story.

Ever since that moment, Lennon's impact has been endlessly debated. The impulse of some fans to see him as a martyr, and to shroud him in piety, is surely misguided. It has incited others to react against this saintly aura and to discard his gifts to posterity. Fortunately, we still have his music, which was always a reliable guide to John's true nature, in all its human fallibility and occasional moral heroism.

Lennon was maddeningly inconsistent. He turned ideological cartwheels in a casual way that made his allies despair. His personality underwent transformations worthy of a B-movie werewolf. He could be the most abject prisoner of self-pity, and at other moments a husband and father uplifted by familial love. And there is Lennon music to illuminate every step of that journey.

Sometimes, John did not so much hold ideas as wear them, like Kings Road clothes. The finery that delighted him in summer would bore him by the fall. Perhaps that was his job—not necessarily to be consistent, but to sift suggestively through the thoughts and dreams that swirled about the world in his time. He was so receptive that he often seemed gullible. But he was fearless, too. He was a radar who picked up anything in the air and then, like the holy fool he was, rushed to put it into practice. He lived and breathed the ideas of his times—and brought them dramatically to life in song.

Believer and cynic, alternately muddle-headed and clear-sighted, brash and vulgar, vulnerable and compassionate—Lennon cannot be simplified or denied. Yoko Ono commented, aptly, "They say that a blind man has an honest face," because he has never learned to use his expressions to tell a lie. In this way she liked to explain the helpless candor shining through John's songs. Whatever he felt or experienced could not remain concealed, because there was always music to be made and John would bare his soul to the world.

In no other music of Lennon's life is that soul-baring as raw and sustained as on the first post-Beatle album he made. It went under the stark title *John Lennon/Plastic Ono Band.*

Opposite: Announcing "Bagism" at a Vienna press conference in March 1969, another event charted in the Beatles single 'The Ballad Of John And Yoko'.

Chapter 2

JOHN LENNON

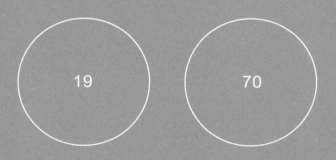

19 70

PLASTIC ONO BAND

"Mother"
"Hold On"
"I Found Out"
"Working Class Hero"
"Isolation"
"Remember"
"Love"
"Well Well Well"
"Look at Me"
"God"
"My Mummy's Dead"

Singles (not on the album)
"Give Peace a Chance"; "Cold Turkey"; "Instant Karma! (We All Shine On)"

Recorded
September/October 1970 at Ascot Sound Studios, Berkshire; Abbey Road Studios, London. "Give Peace a Chance" June 1969 at Queen Elizabeth Hotel, Montreal. "Cold Turkey" September 1969 at EMI Studios, London. "Instant Karma! (We All Shine On)" February 1970 at Abbey Road Studios, London.

Produced by
John Lennon, Yoko Ono, Phil Spector. "Give Peace a Chance" and "Cold Turkey" credited to John Lennon and Yoko Ono.

Musicians
John Lennon (vocals, acoustic and electric guitars, piano, keyboards), Klaus Voormann (bass), Ringo Starr (drums), Billy Preston (piano), Phil Spector (piano), Yoko Ono ("wind"), Mal Evans ("tea and sympathy")."Give Peace A Chance" featured numerous celebrity friends on vocals, including Timothy Leary, Allen Ginsberg, Petula Clark, Murray the K. Comedian Tommy Smothers also played acoustic guitar. "Cold Turkey" featured Eric Clapton (guitar) and Alan White (drums). "Instant Karma! (We All Shine On)" featured George Harrison (guitar).

In a British TV program at the end of 1969, John Lennon found himself nominated as Man of the Decade, though he had to share this distinction with John F. Kennedy and the North Vietnamese leader Ho Chi Minh. As the new decade opened, the Beatles were virtually finished as a recording entity and their split would soon be made public, culminating in a messy tangle of lawsuits. Yet John's personal fame and notoriety seemed to be at an all-time high.

A series of well-publicized events served to keep him in the news alongside his inseparable partner Yoko Ono. Chief among these was the second of his "bed-in" protests, held in a hotel suite in Montreal, at which he performed a new song, "Give Peace a Chance", and began to emerge as a recording artist in his own right. This single became the most memorable mass-anthem of its era, but in artistic terms it was only the prelude to an exceptional series of releases that established him as a solo star.

Behind the hullabaloo of his media career, and despite the profound attachment he had formed to his new wife, John Lennon, the inner man, was as troubled as he had ever been. His second single, "Cold Turkey", spoke openly of his heroin addiction. Its lyrics laid bare his private torment, with a frankness he could seldom express while writing under the Beatles' umbrella.

If the third Lennon single "Instant Karma!" opened the 1970s on a magnificent note of optimism, then his new album, *John Lennon/Plastic Ono Band*, was undeniably bleak. Its cycle of ravaged laments dwelt obsessively in a realm of psychic pain. For many fans it stands as John's masterpiece, although it is probably an album more admired than enjoyed. Tracks explore Lennon's ambivalent attitude to stardom, the mental scars of his childhood, the traumas of the Beatles' breakup and his lifelong struggles to find spiritual meaning and a real sense of himself.

After he issued "Cold Turkey", whose imploring words and grimly discordant sounds amount to a cry of anguish, he was sent *The Primal Scream*, a book by the psychiatrist Dr. Arthur Janov. It's no wonder that Janov's work struck Lennon to the core of his being. It was *The Primal Scream*'s contention that an adult carries the scars of his earliest upbringing, and that only by uncovering and confronting those scars can we progress to an existence free from neurosis.

These were ideas that John had been groping blindly towards for many years. He started a course under Janov's instruction, but was obliged to leave the US when his visa expired. To that extent his treatment remained incomplete, but the experience inspired him to write an album's worth of self-revelatory material in the attempt to drive out his demons. The "Instant Karma!" single had inaugurated his partnership with legendary American producer Phil Spector, with whom he now made an album of unrelenting starkness, quite unlike the lavish extravaganzas for which Spector was renowned.

On September 26th, 1970, at EMI's London studios in Abbey Road—the cradle for almost all of the Beatles' music—John and Yoko began work on two parallel solo albums. Yoko's was a relatively unstructured affair, but John's new songs were some of the most sharply focused he would ever create. Using a stripped-down team consisting of Ringo Starr on drums and Klaus Voormann—his old friend from the Beatles' Hamburg days—on bass, along with some piano embellishments from Billy Preston and Spector himself, John completed his record in a little over four weeks of intensive effort. Released just before Christmas 1970, the record's back sleeve carried a grainy snapshot of John as a small boy as if to acknowledge that old proverb: The child is father to the man.

"Of all the things I've ever played on," says Klaus Voormann, "the *Plastic Ono Band* album is my favorite, because of the freshness and the under-production. There was no messing about, no going back to put a lot of violins on top. I think those songs were still very fresh to him. Of course there's a lot in there that he didn't agree with a few months later! But it doesn't matter. It was John's statement of what he felt at the time."

Ringo, too, has good memories of playing on the album: "It was great, just the three of us in the studio, Klaus, him and me. He had the songs so we just did them. It was a lot of fun in many ways to be in a trio; a trio is a much harder job to play in. It was just 'John's making a record and I'm on it.' It was like nothing's changed really. It was just, 'Where are the other two?'"

For Yoko, also, whose own *Plastic Ono Band* LP appeared in a near-identical cover to John's and shared the same house band, the sessions remain a positive memory: "On that particular album, Phil Spector came in much later; actually, we made most of it by ourselves. If he had done it from the beginning, I am sure it would have been a totally different album, walls of sound and lush, you know. So yes, that is stripped down, especially when John is singing 'My Mummy's Dead'. Oh! And he just did it on a little cassette, you know. He showed me his avant-garde side... I thought that *John Lennon/Plastic Ono Band* was superb."

Opposite: It's 1970, and Lennon meets the new decade with a radical new look.

PEOPLE
FOR
PEACE

GIVE PEACE A CHANCE

Locked out of the United States—he was refused a visa on account of his 1968 drug conviction—John chose Montreal, Canada, as a base to bring his peace campaign to North America. Denied his first choice of the Plaza Hotel in New York City, on May 26th, 1969, he and Yoko installed themselves in a suite of the Queen Elizabeth Hotel for a seven-day "bed-in", attended by the world's media, show business celebrities and sundry hangers-on.

This bed-in was their second such event, following the one staged at the Amsterdam Hilton after their wedding two months earlier. Its origins lie in Yoko's days as a performance artist, and the notion that spectacular public action can be an art form in itself. John, too, was shrewdly aware of how the "bed-in" concept might titillate the press and TV crews with its implicit (though ultimately unfulfilled) promise of sexual exhibitionism.

"Just give peace a chance," he kept telling reporters, and began to work the refrain into a song. By June 1st, John felt he had a powerful peace anthem on his hands, and ordered up a tape machine. Still in bed with Yoko, with a placard behind them proclaiming "Hair Peace", he invited all his varied guests (including the LSD guru Timothy Leary, comedian Tommy Smothers on guitar, singer Petula Clark, a local rabbi, and several members of the Montreal Radha Krishna Temple) to sing along to his new composition. "Give Peace a Chance" was a chugging, repetitive mantra, interspersed with John's impromptu rapping, a babbled litany of random name-checks (ranging from the novelist Norman Mailer to the English comedian Tommy Cooper), and impatient

Opposite: Two months after their wedding, John and Yoko welcome the world's media to the inaugural "bed-in", at the Amsterdam Hilton in the last week of March, 1969.

Below: Police seize allegedly obscene lithographs from John's exhibition at the London Arts Gallery on January 16th, 1970.

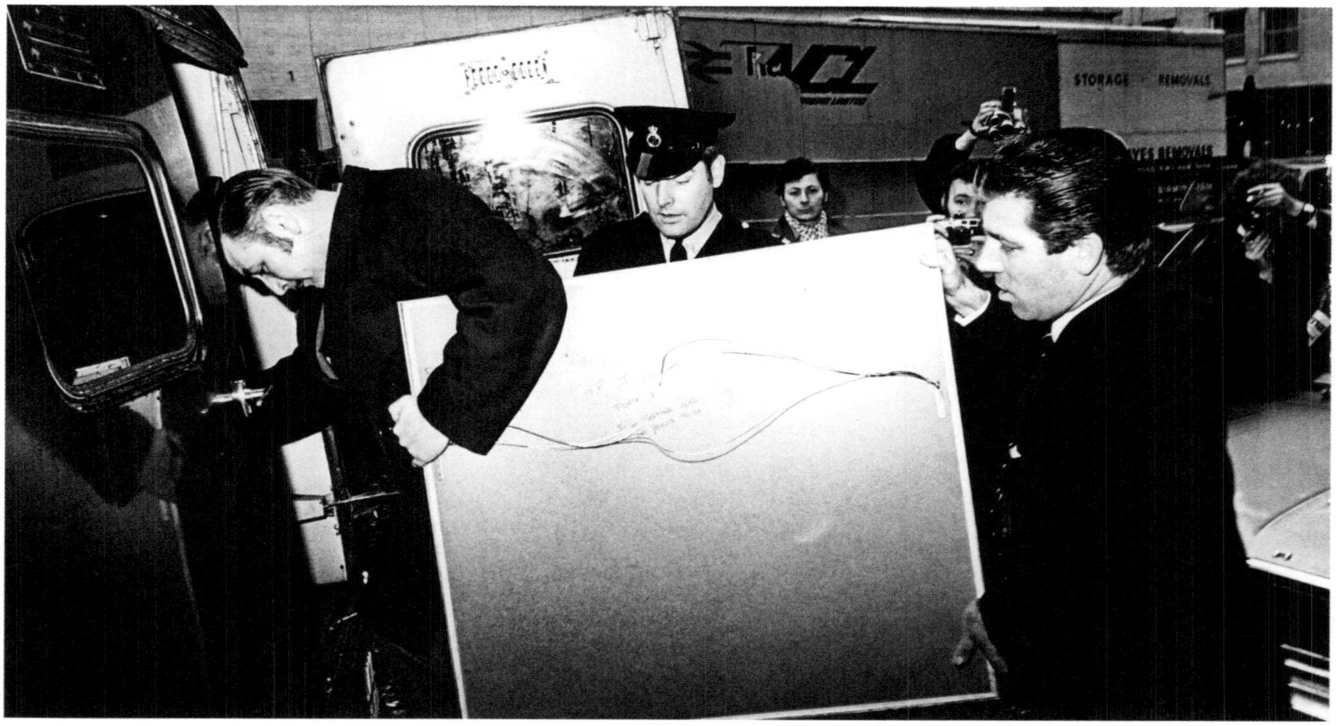

HAIR PEACE.
BED PEACE.

"IN MY SECRET HEART I WANTED TO WRITE SOMETHING THAT WOULD TAKE OVER "WE SHALL OVERCOME"."

—John Lennon

dismissals of "this-ism, that-ism". The rapping was a decade ahead of its time. But it was not of primary importance, for this was another of John's "headline" songs (presaged by "All You Need Is Love" and followed by "Power to the People") whose deliberately simplistic chorus mattered far more.

Released under the banner of the *Plastic Ono Band* on July 7th, "Give Peace a Chance" was John's first single outside the Beatles. Yet at first it carried the composer credit "Lennon & McCartney" in accordance with the partners' longstanding pact. John confessed later that he was not ready to sever links with Paul, and also felt a degree of guilt because he was the first to issue a major record away from the group. Explaining its muffled double drumbeat, he said, "My rhythm sense has always been a bit wild, and halfway through I got on the onbeat instead of the backbeat, and it was hard because of all the non-musicians playing with us. So I had to put a lot of tape echo to keep a steady beat right through the record."

Years later he revealed: "In my secret heart I wanted to write something that would take over "We Shall Overcome"." And in "Give Peace a Chance", he achieved just that. By October of 1969 the song was a universal chant at anti-Vietnam War demonstrations. On November 15th, nearly half a million people sang it outside the Nixon White House in Washington. Such a coup was storing up trouble for John in subsequent dealings with the US administration. But back in Britain when he turned on his TV and watched the protestors singing, he considered it "one of the biggest moments of my life". Towards the end of the year, he told interviewer Barry Miles, "There's a mass of propaganda gone out from those two bed-ins... Every garden party this summer in Britain, every small village everywhere, the winning couple was the kids doing John and Yoko in bed with the posters around... Instead of everybody singing, "Yeah Yeah Yeah" they're just singing "Peace" instead. And I believe in the power of the mantra."

"Give Peace a Chance" indeed entered the world's consciousness just as John had hoped. Eleven years later, as mourners gathered outside the Dakota Building on the night of his murder, this was the song that they instinctively chose to express their grief and commemorate his life.

Below: The Plastic Ono Band perform at London's Lyceum on December 15th, 1969, John and Yoko's guests including George Harrison, Eric Clapton and The Who's drummer Keith Moon.

GIVE PEACE A CHANCE

Two, one-two-three-four!
Ev'rybody's talking 'bout
Bagism, Shagism, Dragism,
Madism, Ragism, Tagism
This-ism, that-ism, is-m, is-m, is-m

All we are saying is give peace a chance
All we are saying is give peace a chance

Hit it
C'mon, ev'rybody's talking about
Ministers, sinisters, banisters and canisters
Bishops and Fishops and Rabbis and Popeyes
and bye-bye, bye-byes

All we are saying is give peace a chance
All we are saying is give peace a chance

Let me tell you now
Ev'rybody's talking 'bout
Revolution, evolution, masturbation,
flagellation, regulation, integrations
Meditations, United Nations, congratulations

All we are saying is give peace a chance
All we are saying is give peace a chance

Ev'rybody's talking 'bout
John and Yoko, Timmy Leary, Rosemary,
Tommy Smothers, Bobby Dylan, Tommy
Cooper
Derek Taylor, Norman Mailer, Alan Ginsberg,
Hare Krishna, Hare, Hare Krishna

All we are saying is give peace a chance
All we are saying is give peace a chance

All we are saying is give peace a chance
All we are saying is give peace a chance

All we are saying is give peace a chance
All we are saying is give peace a chance

All we are saying is give peace a chance
All we are saying is give peace a chance

All we are saying is give peace a chance
All we are saying is give peace a chance

All we are saying is give peace a chance
All we are saying is give peace a chance

All we are saying is give peace a chance
All we are saying is give peace a chance

COLD TURKEY

Drugs are a given in the lives of many rock musicians, yet the subject is seldom treated realistically in songs. Typically, John was one of the first to break that taboo, and he did so in a song that is still extraordinarily vivid in its raw depiction of suffering. After the LSD which fuelled the psychedelic dreamtime of the *Sgt. Pepper* album in 1967, Lennon's experiments with drugs led him on to heroin.

He was to wrestle with its potentially fatal attraction for years to come. In August 1969, driven by his desire to father a healthy child, John made another determined effort to quit the drug, and wrote "Cold Turkey" as a document of the process. He did not glamorize his self-abasement.

In the latter half of 1968, when John had finally abandoned his wife Cynthia and the family home at Kenwood, he and Yoko took up temporary residence at Ringo's old flat in Montagu Square. According to an interview she gave to former personal assistant Peter Brown, Yoko admitted to having dabbled with heroin while John was away in India with the Maharishi earlier that year. It seems almost inevitable that John would have become curious to try it for himself too.

There was a certain innocence surrounding all forms of drug-taking in the 1960s, when few people were aware of its dangers, or thought themselves immune in any case. And John was drawn by heroin's reputation as an "artistic" indulgence. His attachment grew throughout 1969 when the couple moved into their grand white mansion, Tittenhurst Park in Ascot, and there is little doubt that it contributed to estranging him further from the Beatles.

Like other inexperienced users, John was dismayed to find how difficult it was to stop taking heroin. Reluctant to use a hospital for fear of the attendant publicity, he tried at first to break his addiction by opting for sudden and complete abstinence—the method called "cold turkey". The physical effects resemble a feverish illness—two of the most common symptoms are clammy skin and goosebumps, hence the name. They are graphically described in John's verses.

The song was at first considered for recording by the Beatles, who were then completing the *Abbey Road* album. Not surprisingly it was rejected, its content so harrowing and so personal that it could only be a Lennon solo project. John premiered the number at the Toronto show on September 13th, backed by the hurriedly formed band that included Eric Clapton on guitar. Throughout, John cribbed from a lyric sheet held up by Yoko at his side. It was the only new song of John's that they attempted that night, and the crowd's reaction was muted, prompting him to snap at them, "Come on, wake up!" Clapton was duly called to EMI's studio in Abbey Road a few weeks later to help with the single. Playing to a pattern that John had devised, and recalling the monstrous, violently distorted style of the previous year's "Revolution", Eric contributes the searing guitar riff which is among this record's most compelling and brutal characteristics. It's ironic to note that Clapton would, within a year, be in the grip of a prolonged heroin habit himself.

But the most startling element of all is John's vocal performance, probably his most extreme since "Twist and Shout" six years before. He claimed the howling style came from Yoko, and it certainly predates his discovery of the "primal scream" therapy explored on his subsequent solo album, whose themes are also anticipated in his whimpering wish to be a baby again.

Unhappily John's self-prescribed treatment was not a success. On his birthday, October 9th, the pregnant Yoko was admitted to hospital and suffered a miscarriage three days later. After that, he relapsed into heroin use.

"Cold Turkey" was released in the middle of October, credited to the Plastic Ono Band. Its subject matter and sheer harshness guaranteed that radio play would be limited, and the record was not a big hit. Hence the jokey payoff in John's letter to the Queen when he returned his MBE (Member of the British Empire, a royal honor bestowed upon all four Beatles in 1965) on November 25th: "Your Majesty, I am returning this MBE in protest against Britain's involvement in this Nigeria-Biafra thing [a civil war then raging in West Africa], against our support of America in Vietnam and against "Cold Turkey" slipping down the charts. With love, John Lennon of Bag."

In the United Kingdom at least, this gesture generated even more controversy than "Cold Turkey" itself. Still, the single played its part in dismantling the Beatles' public image. Given the trouble John was already in with the authorities over drugs, he might have been wise to avoid the subject in song. But as a writer—if not always as a man—honesty was John Lennon's greatest addiction of all.

COLD TURKEY

Temperature's rising
Fever is high
Can't see no future
Can't see no sky
My feet are so heavy
So is my head
I wish I was a baby
I wish I was dead

Cold turkey has got me on the run

My body is aching
Goose-pimple bone
Can't see no body
Leave me alone
My eyes are wide open
Can't get to sleep
One thing I'm sure of
I'm in at the deep freeze

Cold turkey has got me on the run

Cold turkey has got me on the run

Thirty-six hours
Rolling in pain
Praying to someone
Free me again
Oh, I'll be a good boy
Please make me well
I promise you anything
Get me out of this hell

Cold turkey has got me on the run

Oh, oh, oh, oh

INSTANT KARMA! (WE ALL SHINE ON)

Famously impatient, John once longed "to write a song on Monday, cut it Tuesday, have it pressed Wednesday and in the shops by Friday". He nearly realized that ambition with 'Instant Karma!' A pure example of John's fast, reactive method of songwriting, it may also stand as the most uplifting rock song of his solo career. Yoko and John spent the New Year of 1970 in Denmark, visiting her daughter Kyoko and the child's father Tony Cox.

While there, the couple took the unexpected step of cutting off their long hair, and now faced the world sporting unisex crops. It seemed as if they had decided to usher in the new decade by abandoning a look whose symbolic power had dwindled. (The locks were later auctioned for one of the couple's pet causes.) Meanwhile, in John's absence, the other three Beatles convened at Abbey Road on January 4th to complete Paul's song "Let It Be". It proved to be the group's final recording session.

Back in London by late January, John wrote "Instant Karma!" in a single morning, building it around a simple riff with a passing resemblance to "Three Blind Mice". The title phrase was something he had picked up in conversation with Tony Cox's new wife, Melinde Kendall, in Denmark. Hippies of the 1960s had absorbed the Hindu doctrine of "karma" in line with their general receptivity to oriental ideas and music—encouraged largely by the Beatles themselves and George in particular. In time, Western usage tended to trivialize karma, until it meant roughly the same as "just deserts", either good or bad. But in its original context the word referred to a man's deeds across a cycle of lifetimes, and to their consequences for his ultimate spiritual fate.

"Instant" karma, then, is a contradiction in terms. But how typical of John to want the concept compressed into something more immediate. The slow-turning wheel of existence was just not running at his speed. What excited him was that karma could refer not only to past actions affecting us now, but also to our present actions shaping the future, and faster than we think. Fascinated by the language of advertising, he loved the idea of selling "Instant Karma!" in the same way as instant coffee. Parallel with this message—take responsibility for the fate of the world, and do it now—went the song's central theme, that stardom is a quality we all possess, famous or not. The only real stars are up in the heavens, but the potential for spiritual brilliance comes with being human. It is not the gift of an élite. "We all shine on."

These are majestic sentiments and, though its tune is unambitious, the finished song does ample justice to them. For this we can thank Phil Spector. 'Instant Karma!' was John's first collaboration with rock 'n' roll's most legendary producer, and it is a sonic triumph. Contacting Spector was the final coup in a productive day that had seen John write his song and round up a studio band comprising George Harrison, Klaus Voormann, and Alan White. It happened that Spector was visiting London to discuss involvement in the Beatle tapes that would become their *Let It Be* album.

The record that Lennon and Spector cut at Abbey Road that evening would mark the start of an historic two-year partnership. With its commanding, echoed vocals and the almighty wallop of White's drumbeats, "Instant Karma!" was the definitive sound of post-Beatles Lennon; he would deliberately evoke it ten years later, in "(Just Like) Starting Over".

"I'd already been experimenting with drum breaks," Alan White recalls, "that weren't in the same metre as the rest of the song. So that's what you hear. They got the backing track down and John needed a big chorus of people singing 'We all shine on'. So Mal Evans, who was the roadie for the Beatles, went down to the Revolution Club. And he spread the word around the crowd that John Lennon wanted a bunch of people to sing a backing track, so half the club came back to Abbey Road that night, and he was conducting them at the front!"

Harnessing this additional (if somewhat tipsy) lung power, "Instant Karma!" was built up in layers, in the classic Spector tradition, until it reached monumental stature. His "Wall of Sound" technique, evolved in the making of landmark Sixties hits such as "Be My Baby", "Da Doo Ron Ron" and "River Deep Mountain High", required the same instrumental parts to be played many times, with the results allowed to reverberate around the studio. A typical Spector record gave the impression of cavernous space, as if created in some vast cathedral of pop. John was content to tell Spector he wanted "a 1950s feel" and left the rest in his producer's hands. Like Lennon, Spector preferred to think of records in terms of total sound, not as collections of component details. Heretically, he even disdained the advent of stereo, coining his own slogan "Back to Mono".

"ALL WE'RE TRYING TO SAY TO THE WORLD IS: YOU'RE GONNA BE GREAT!"

—John Lennon

"Instant Karma!" was released in Britain on February 6th, barely two weeks after it was written, and on February 20th in the States. (In the US it received its sub-title "We All Shine On", which has since become the normal rendering.) British fans received another treat on February 12th when John appeared on the nation's TV weekly institution *Top of The Pops*, the first Beatle to do so since 1966. While he hammered the piano, with an armband on his denim jacket saying "People for Peace", Yoko was perched behind him, blindfolded, holding up cards with simple inscriptions such as Peace, Love, Smile and Hope. Not unusually in the career of John Lennon, much of the population decided he had gone mad, but the song's almighty, thudding drumbeat and its soaring, inspirational chorus were sufficient to give him a Top 5 hit.

Strangely perhaps, John Lennon never became blasé about chart positions, and he was gratified by the success of the single. But "Instant Karma!", like "Give Peace a Chance", had a wider purpose. He wanted to change people's minds. "The government can do it with propaganda," he reasoned. "Coca-Cola can do it with propaganda; the businessmen do it with propaganda. Why can't we? We are the hip generation." The essence of "Instant Karma!" he once insisted, was to breathe belief into people. "All we're trying to say to the world is, 'You're gonna be great.'"

Above: John leads the band through "Instant Karma!" on British TV's *Top of the Pops*, February 11th, 1970.

INSTANT KARMA!

Instant Karma's going to get you
Going to knock you right
on the head
You better get yourself together
Pretty soon you're going to be dead

What in the world you thinking of
Laughing in the face of love?
What on earth you tryin' to do?
It's up to you, yeah you!

Instant Karma's gonna get you
Going to look you right in the face
You better get yourself together,
darling
Join the human race

How in the world you gonna see
Laughing at fools like me?
Who on earth d'you think you are?
A superstar? Well right you are!

Well we all shine on
Like the moon and the stars
and the sun
Well we all shine on
Every one, come on

Instant Karma's going to get you
Going to knock you off your feet
Better recognize your brothers
Every one you meet

Why in the world are we here?
Surely not to live in pain and fear?
Why on earth are you there when
you're everywhere?
Come and get your share!

Well we all shine on
Like the moon and the
stars and the sun
Well we all shine on
Every one, come on

Yeah yeah, alright, ah haa, aaaahh
Well we all shine on
Like the moon and the stars
and the sun
And we all shine on
On and on and on on and on

Well we all shine on
Like the moon and the stars
and the sun
Yeah we all shine on

Well we all shine on
Like the moon and the stars
and the sun
Well we all shine on
Like the moon and the stars
and the sun
Well we all shine on
Like the moon and the stars
and the sun
Yeah we all shine on
Like the moon and the stars
and the sun

MOTHER

A horror movie on TV provided John with the idea for the funereal bell whose ominous toll—even gloomier when slowed down by Phil Spector—is the curtain-raiser to *John Lennon/Plastic Ono Band* and its opening track "Mother". Looking for pure gut-feeling, Lennon interrupted the session to play a recording of Jerry Lee Lewis's manic stomper "Whole Lotta Shakin' Goin' On".

It was clear that "Mother" was going to be a very emotional song for John. He traced much of his unhappiness back to a sense of rejection by his parents. And now, to free himself from that baleful legacy, he first had to say "goodbye" to them. Yet, by the song's wracked finale, he is screaming at Mummy not to go, and begging Daddy to return.

The real-life events which left John so bereft are well documented. His mother, Julia, felt ill-equipped to raise him. Almost as soon as he was born, she disowned his father, Freddie Lennon, who was in any case absent from home for long periods, serving as a merchant seaman. On his return, Freddie made a bid to take the infant John away with him. Amid all of the turmoil at home, the child spent several spells in the care of relatives. At the age of four, he was finally placed with Julia's elder sister, Mimi, and her husband, George Smith. He saw little of his real mother until his teenage years, when Julia's own rebellious nature and playful spirit drew her son closer. In adolescence he certainly found her more of a soulmate than the deeply suburban, ultra-respectable Mimi. He began spending more of his time with Julia, while she encouraged his musical ambitions by allowing him his first cheap guitar.

But when John was sixteen, their gradual reconciliation was cruelly and abruptly terminated. Following a visit to Mimi's house, Julia was knocked down and killed by a car driven by an off-duty policeman. As John reflected later, "I lost her twice."

Freddie, meanwhile, disappeared from the boy's life entirely. He got back in touch after John won fame as a Beatle, by which time Freddie was hard up and working in a series of dead-end jobs. At one point he even tried to launch himself as a recording star: his single, "That's My Life", was the self-celebrating tale of a Liverpool seafarer. But their relationship was uneasy and marked, on John's part at least, by a desire for recrimination, even though he did make financial provision for his father. Freddie fell seriously ill in the Seventies after John had moved to New York, but father and son apparently had a series of affectionate phone conversations in the days before the old man's death on April 1st, 1976.

Given John's unsettled background, it is often suggested that he sought a father figure in later life, with his managers Brian Epstein and Allen Klein, and even the Maharishi, as obvious potential substitutes. In a 1972 interview with *Record Mirror*, John appeared to endorse that theory: "Three years ago I would have been looking for a guru or looking for the answer in Karl Marx, but not any more. I was looking for a father figure, but I do not want that any more, thanks to Dr. Janov. He gave me a kind of structure and I do not need him any more. He helped me to accept myself."

It's striking, too, that he always called Yoko "Mother", albeit in a semi-mocking tone. "I've got the security of Yoko," he told Barry Miles in 1969. "And it's like having a mother. I was never relaxed before, I was always in a state of uptightness, and therefore the cynical Lennon image came out." "Mother" was one of the few solo songs that John ever played in public. At Madison Square Garden in 1972, he was anxious to widen the lyric's scope: "People think it's just about my parents. But it's about ninety-nine percent of the parents."

Above: John, aged nine, in a family snapshot with his mother Julia. Her memory haunts the opening and closing songs of John's first solo album.

MOTHER

Mother, you had me
but I never had you
I wanted you
You didn't want me

So I
I just got to tell you
Goodbye, goodbye

Father, you left me but I
never left you
I needed you
You didn't need me

So I
I just got to tell you
Goodbye, goodbye

Children, don't do
What I have done
I couldn't walk
And I tried to run

So I
I just got to tell you
Goodbye, goodbye

Mama don't go
Daddy come home
Mama don't go
Daddy come home
Mama don't go
Daddy come home
Mama don't go
Daddy come home
Mama don't go
Daddy come home
Mama don't go
Daddy come home
Mama don't go
Daddy come home
Mama don't go
Daddy come home
Mama don't go
Daddy come home
Mama don't go
Daddy come home
Mama don't go
Daddy come home
Mama don't go
Daddy come home

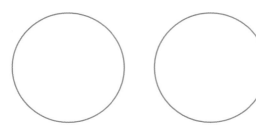

HOLD ON

The naked terror of "Mother" is genuinely disturbing, and shows the depth of John's commitment to Janov's teaching at that point. But the record is balanced by declarations of tenderness such as "Hold On". A shimmering, Japanese-influenced riff introduces this short exercise in gentle reassurance.

When John had surveyed the outer world's chaos in his 1968 song "Revolution", the best advice he could offer was, "It's gonna be all right." He repeats that message here, sustained in his faith by the nourishment of love. Speaking of Yoko in 1969, he said, "Now I can remember, even in the worst depths of misery, that we're both going through it together." With a little belief, he tells his audience, we can come through our confusion and achieve a feeling of unity, with one another and within our own personalities. It's arguable that John was singing more out of hope than experience. Nevertheless, many who knew him testify that he became a more approachable character after meeting her. And "Hold On" chimes agreeably with another Lennon aphorism from that year: "We're all frozen jellies. It just needs somebody to turn off the fridge."

Below: The Lennons present their newly-shorn heads to the world, on a visit to Denmark, January 24th, 1970.

HOLD ON

Hold on, John
John, hold on
It's gonna be alright
You're gonna win the fight

Hold on, Yoko
Yoko, hold on
It's gonna be alright
You're gonna make the
flight

When you're by yourself
And there's no-one else
You just have yourself
And you tell yourself
Just to hold on

Cookie

Hold on, world
World, hold on
It's gonna be alright
You're gonna see the light

Oh, and when you're one
Really one
Well, you get things done
Like they've never been
done
So hold on

I FOUND OUT

After the tranquil yearning of "Hold On", Lennon turned his unsentimental gaze on the forces that he believed were dangerous distractions from our quest for self-understanding. Lined up for curt condemnation are radical hippies, drugs, sex, and religion. The scornful putdowns are framed with an arrangement of effective viciousness, and John was especially proud of his truculent guitar playing on this track.

But Ringo's drumming is the most exciting feature of all, like the pounding of an agitated heart as it echoes the singer's bitter glee. Successive verses list the various snares that John has identified, now he has "found out" that liberation is something he will only attain though his own resources. First in his firing line are the "freaks on the phone," imploring John's support for their chosen causes. There is no doubt that John became a figurehead for radically minded people, whether of the hippie "counterculture" or more orthodox political activists. His phenomenal celebrity, presumed wealth, and anti-establishment sympathies made him a natural target for anyone who felt they might benefit from his attention.

Like all show business figures, he was accustomed to begging letters, usually from strangers pleading poverty, illness, or exceptional ill-fortune. The ghastliness of the Beatles' world tours had been compounded when sick children and abject invalids were presented to the group as subjects for their imaginary healing powers. The band's Apple label, initially conceived as a tax advantage, naïvely announced a philanthropic agenda, and fast became a magnet for no-hopers and hip scroungers of every description. In fact, John did make regular gestures of support—in February of 1970, for instance, he paid the fines of 100 protesters arrested in demonstrations against a UK visit by the South African rugby team. Clearly, however, he had his breaking point and constant appeals of the "brother, brother, brother" sort had eventually worn him down. In "I Found Out" it is not the money he begrudges but the claims on his time and mental energy.

He also launches a broadside against religion. For someone who had never really embraced the Church he would devote a lot of effort to repudiating it. In the 1968 song "Sexy Sadie" he had already registered his disillusionment with the Maharishi, but gurus and "pie in the sky" come in for further abuse here. His position may sound absolute, but this was a debate that John would never quite resolve in his own mind. Like so much of *John Lennon/Plastic Ono Band*, his outburst represents a temporary clearing of the mental decks more than a definitive statement.

The early loss of their mothers was a bond that had drawn John closer to Paul McCartney in the Beatles. In Lennon's case, though, there was the added element of rejection fuelling his desire for fame. The reference here to his mother and father, whose rejection "made him a star", is explained by a comment he made in 1971: "The only reason I went for that goal is that I wanted to say, 'Now, mummy-daddy, will you love me?'"

I told you before, stay away from my door
Don't give me that brother, brother, brother, brother
The freaks on the phone, won't leave me alone
So don't give me that brother, brother, brother, brother No!
I, I found out!
I, I found out!

Now that I showed you what I been through
Don't take nobody's word what you can do
There ain't no Jesus gonna come from the sky
Now that I found out I know I can cry

I, I found out!
I, I found out!
Some of you sitting there with your cock in your hand

Don't get you nowhere don't make you a man
I heard something 'bout my Ma and my Pa
They didn't want me so they made me a star

I, I found out!
I, I found out!
Old Hare Krishna got nothing on you

Just keep you crazy with nothing to do
Keep you occupied with pie in the sky
There ain't no guru who can see through your eyes

I, I found out!
I, I found out!

I seen through junkies, I been through it all
I seen religion from Jesus to Paul
Don't let them fool you with dope and cocaine
No one can harm you, feel your own pain

I, I found out!
I, I found this out!
I, I found out!

WORKING CLASS HERO

The title of "Working Class Hero" is sarcastic rather than narcissistic. Lennon writes as someone whose dreams have all come true, only for him to realize that those dreams were just illusions. The song talks of a numbness instilled by social conditioning. Encouraged by Janov's teachings, John examined his schooldays for evidence that his talents were suppressed by teachers and concluded that only conformity is rewarded.

We are all levelled down, he argues: the clever ones are hated and the stupid are despised. He goes on to borrow some ideas then current among left-wing intellectuals, chiefly that freedom and the classless society are myths designed to obscure our basic lack of power over our lives, while the media, commercialized sexuality, and drugs—legal or otherwise—likewise conspire to blunt our appetite for social change.

The minimal delivery of this song, with its threadbare acoustic strumming, induced many comparisons with Bob Dylan. While John had openly adopted Dylan as an important role model during the Beatle years, he became irritated by the frequency of these comparisons, responding that the solo acoustic style was a feature of folk music long before "Blowing in the Wind".

As a self-portrait of Lennon in his most cynical mood, "Working Class Hero" is unsurpassed. He performs it with a morbid fatigue that reeks of his own disillusionment. He has made a success of his life, he implies, but only on the narrow terms defined for us—mainly money, fame, and self-indulgence. We are easily controlled, his thesis runs, because we allow our imagination to be curtailed. But these themes are not particularly obvious, and the title "Working Class Hero" would continue to be applied to John without any shade of satire, or else be taken as a sign of his egotism. He told *Rolling Stone's* Jann Wenner that he hoped the song would become an anthem "for the workers", with the same appeal as "Give Peace a Chance". But its meaning proved much too elusive.

As soon as you're born they make you feel small
By giving you no time instead of it all
'Til the pain is so big you feel nothing at all
A working class hero is something to be
A working class hero is something to be

They hurt you at home and they hit you at school
They hate you if you're clever and they despise a fool
'Til you're so fucking crazy you can't follow their rules
A working class hero is something to be
A working class hero is something to be

When they've tortured and scared you for
twenty odd years
Then they expect you to pick a career
When you can't really function you're so full of fear
A working class hero is something to be
A working class hero is something to be

Keep you doped with religion and sex and TV
And you think you're so clever and classless and free
But you're still fucking peasants as far as I can see
A working class hero is something to be
A working class hero is something to be

There's room at the top they are telling you still
But first you must learn how to smile as you kill
If you want to be like the folks on the hill
A working class hero is something to be
A working class hero is something to be

If you want to be a hero, well, just follow me
If you want to be a hero, well, just follow me

Above left: The Beatles and friends on spiritual retreat with the Maharishi, in India, 1968. John's subsequent disillusionment would surface in songs such as "Sexy Sadie" and "I Found Out".

LOVE

Phil Spector plays the delicate piano line of this tender, uncomplicated ballad, whose sweetness anticipates the next album, *Imagine*.

In 1980, John recalled this song with some affection, no doubt because it conjured up one of the more harmonious periods in his marriage to Yoko. He was often inclined to dismiss his angrier songs as being rooted in guilt or self-hatred, or as instances of some transient discontent, whereas the romantic numbers maintained their appeal for him. In fact, he cited "Love" with "Imagine" itself as two of the compositions he considered as good as anything he'd done with the Beatles. Whether we agree with that estimate or not, "Love" is a welcome addition to this generally tortured album, and a useful reminder that Lennon's real life was never a one-dimensional affair.

Love is real, real is love
Love is feeling, feeling love
Love is wanting to be loved

Love is touch, touch is love
Love is reaching, reaching love
Love is asking to be loved

Love is you
You and me
Love is knowing
we can be

Love is free, free is love
Love is living, living love
Love is needing to be loved

WELL WELL WELL

A clenched, grunge-like guitar figure combines with some of Ringo's toughest drumming in this depiction of vignettes from John and Yoko's day-to-day existence.

Amorous interludes are described, with due account given to the tensions they felt when they addressed the world outside their own private universe, building into a bout of savage, rasping hollers. At one point, John finds his wife so beautiful he "could eat her"—certainly an improvement on his first draft, "She looked so beautiful I could wee".

Below: Between their wedding in Gibraltar and the Amsterdam bed-in, the couple explore a Parisian market in March 1969.

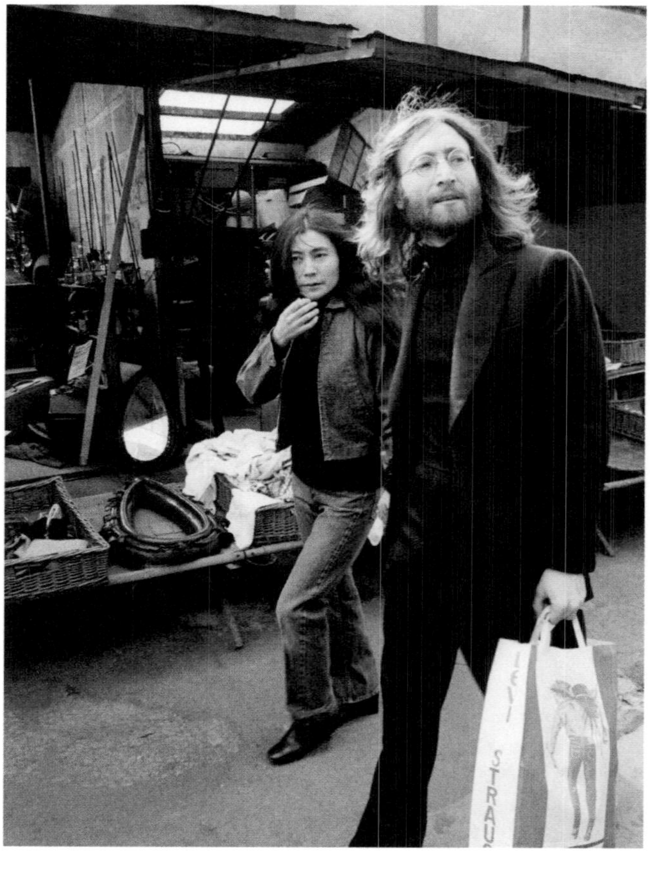

WELL WELL WELL

Well, well, well, oh well
Well, well, well, oh well
I took my loved one out to dinner
So we could get a bite to eat
And though we both had been much thinner
She looked so beautiful I could eat 'er
Well, well, well, oh well
Well, well, well, oh well
I took my loved one to the big field
So we could watch the English sky
We both were nervous feeling guilty
And neither one of us knew just why
Well, well, well, oh well
Well, well, well, oh well

Well, well, well, oh well
Well, well, well, oh well
Well, well, well, oh well
Well, well, well, oh well
Well, well, well, oh well
Well, well, well, oh well
Well, well, well, oh well
Well, well, well, oh well
Well, well, well, oh well
Well,
Well
Well
Well
Well
Well
Well
Well
Well, well
Well, well, well, oh well
Well, well, well, oh well
We sat and talked of revolution
Just like two liberals in the sun
We talked of woman's liberation
And how the hell we could get things done
Well, well, well, oh well
Well, well, well, oh well
I took my loved one to a big field
So we could catch the English sky
We both were nervous feeling guilty
And neither one of us knew just why
Well, well, well, oh well
Well, well, well, oh well
Well, well, well, oh well
Well, well, well, oh well
Well, well, well, oh well
Well, well, well, well
Well, well, well, well
Well, well!

LOOK AT ME

The piano was John's chief songwriting instrument for his early solo albums, but "Look at Me" is based around acoustic guitar picking.

This betrays its origins in 1968, when it was among the batch of songs he wrote with the Beatles' "White Album" in mind; others of the type include "Julia", "Dear Prudence", and "Cry Baby Cry". The truth is it dates from a time of crisis in John's love life, when his passion for Yoko was leading him to leave his wife Cynthia. Fittingly, the warmth of the song is tempered by John's confessions of deep uncertainty. Only when he had resolved this doubt and committed himself to Yoko could he begin to rebuild his sense of identity. The essence, then, of "Look at Me", is the story of a man who comes to believe that his only true existence is in his lover's eyes.

Above: John with his first wife Cynthia, in 1967. Emotionally, though, he was already becoming involved with Yoko.

[Okay?
Yes, thank you]

Look at me
Who am I supposed to be?
Who am I supposed to be?

Look at me
What am I supposed to be?
What am I supposed to be?

Look at me
Oh, my love
Oh, my love

Here I am
What am I supposed to do?
What am I supposed to do?

Here I am
What can I do for you?
What can I do for you?

Here I am
Oh, my love
Oh, my love

Look at me
Oh, please look at me, my love
Here I am, oh, my love
Who am I?

Nobody knows but me
Nobody knows but me
Who am I?

Nobody else can see
Just you and me
Who are we?

Oh, my love
Oh, my love, oh

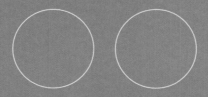

ISOLATION

Between the grand announcements and the dramatic peaks of *John Lennon/Plastic Ono Band* come the more modest numbers such as "Isolation", a momentary pause for John to quietly plead his own vulnerability.

However celebrated he may be, or reviled, he is an individual like any other, as tiny in relation to the universe and just as trapped within his own existence. In Lennon's case, isolation was something he both sought and regretted. He spoke of his wish to belong, but recognized a contrary impulse to stand apart. As a Beatle he came closer than anyone to global popularity, yet at times he seemed hell-bent on throwing it all away.

When he developed his campaigning platform in 1969, he saw there was a certain freedom in playing the clown. "I'm not a politician," he told *Oz* magazine, "so I don't rely on public opinion to tell me how to run my life—I refuse to. I mean, I don't even consider it. For a politician to go into a white bag in the Albert Hall he'd have to consider the effects it would have on his constituents, but I'm not a politician and I don't owe my constituents anything other than that I create something, whatever it is, and they accept or reject it on its own merits."

Above: "I'm not a politician," John declared. "So I don't rely on public opinion to tell me how to run my life."

While it's not among his better songs, "Isolation" transcends the well-worn "lonely at the top" trap because it is sufficiently general in describing a feeling which is apt to settle on most people at one time or another.

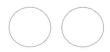

People say we got it made.
Don't they know we're so afraid?
Isolation.

We're afraid to be alone,
everybody got to have a home.
Isolation.

Just a boy and a little girl,
trying to change the whole wide world.
Isolation.

The world is just a little town,
everybody trying to put us down.
Isolation.

I don't expect you to understand,
after you've caused so much pain.
But then again, you're not to blame.
You're just a human, a victim of the insane.

We're afraid of everyone,
Afraid of the sun.
Isolation

The sun will never disappear,
but the world may not have many years.
Isolation.

REMEMBER

The jogging piano rhythm of "Remember" is reminiscent of Paul McCartney's contribution to John's song "A Day in the Life"; here it confers some urgency on what is otherwise a song of no great purpose.

If the point of primal therapy was to scrape away the archaeological layers of his memory, "Remember" settles on a series of disconnected flashbacks, coupled with a formulaic call to harbor no regrets. Much as Lennon felt compelled to escape the psychic burden of bygone times, he was actually nostalgic to an unusual degree. "Strawberry Fields Forever", named for a place where he played as a child, is the most famous instance. In "She Said, She Said" he mourns his boyhood, when "everything was right"; in "Help!" he draws a similar contrast between the untroubled past and his anxious present, while "In My Life" leafs wistfully through Lennon's back pages. It's interesting that he numbered each of these backward-looking songs as being among his best works.

The final line, a seemingly climactic call to "remember the fifth of November" was a mere afterthought. It quotes the rhyme traditionally sung by British children on that date, Guy Fawkes Night, when fireworks and bonfires celebrate the foiling of a 17th-century plot to blow up the government. John probably relished the allusion, hence the huge explosion dubbed on to the song's ending, but its appearance here owes more to chronic nostalgia than revolutionary fervor.

"WE'RE ALL FROZEN JELLIES. IT JUST NEEDS SOMEBODY TO TURN OFF THE FRIDGE."

—John Lennon

John Lennon/Plastic Ono Band

REMEMBER

Do you remember when you were young?
How the hero was never hung
Always got away

Remember how the man
Used to leave you empty handed
Always, always let you down
If you ever change your mind
About leaving it all behind
Remember, remember today

Don't feel sorry
'Bout the way it's gone
Don't you worry
'Bout what you've done

Just remember
When you were small
How people seemed so tall
Always had their way
Do you remember your ma and pa
Just wishing for movie stardom
Always, always playing a part
If you ever feel sad
And the whole world is driving you mad
Remember, remember today

Don't feel sorry
'Bout the way it's gone
Don't you worry
'Bout what you've done

No No remember, remember
The fifth of November

GOD

Both "Mother" and "Working Class Hero" belong among the outstanding tracks on *John Lennon/Plastic Ono Band*, but "God" can justly be called the album's centerpiece.

The rippling piano introduction (played by Billy Preston) interweaves with stately chords that seem to be announcing that a Grand Statement is on the way. And so it is, for in "God" we get John Lennon's most explicit statement about how he was feeling in the summer of 1970, just two months on from the official breakup of the Beatles which had been confirmed by Paul's walkout on April 10th.

Consciously or not, there is an echo in here of Ketty Lester's 1962 pop hit "Love Letters", an old Cavern favorite of John's, and a bittersweet taste of less complicated days.

The lyric begins with the central tenet of John's religious thinking, namely that God is an abstraction who actually resides within human beings themselves. It is an assertion he repeats for good measure. Having disposed of the biggest, he then proceeds to list each lesser concept in which he is no longer prepared to invest his faith. Magic, the occult, and mysticism are dismissed. Jesus, Buddha, the Kennedys, monarchy, Elvis Presley, and Bob Dylan (alias "Zimmerman", his real name) are likewise dispatched, while the track lurches forward, gathering in force as it unrolls. But the most impassioned disavowal of all—and in many ways the most shocking—is reserved for last. He does not, he declares, believe in Beatles.

God is a concept
By which we measure
Our pain
I'll say it again
God is a concept
By which we measure
Our pain

I don't believe in magic
I don't believe in I-ching
I don't believe in Bible
I don't believe in tarot
I don't believe in Hitler
I don't believe in Jesus
I don't believe in Kennedy
I don't believe in Buddha
I don't believe in Mantra
I don't believe in Gita
I don't believe in Yoga
I don't believe in kings
I don't believe in Elvis
I don't believe in Zimmerman
I don't believe in Beatles
I just believe in me
Yoko and me
And that's reality

The dream is over
What can I say?
The dream is over
Yesterday
I was the Dreamweaver
But now I'm reborn
I was the Walrus
But now I'm John
And so dear friends
You'll just have to carry on
The dream is over

Like "A Day in the Life" before it, "God" is a uniquely structured song. The litany ends abruptly, to be succeeded by a dramatic pause and, then, a quiet affirmation of his one remaining certainty. John believes in himself, and in his partnership with Yoko. The final and most poignant passage delivers his stark conclusion: "The dream is over." Calmly and even coldly, he buries the Beatle myth and counsels all of us, Beatle fans and former Beatles alike, to leave him in peace.

In all, it amounts to a majestic abdication. He has formally renounced his position as leader of the band who once embodied the dreams of a decade and who were the icons of a generation. John always resented the idea that Paul had broken up the Beatles, and insisted it had been his decision. McCartney's press announcement caught him on the hop. If John could not be the first to break the news, he now wanted the distinction, at least, of issuing the official obituary. From then on, he would say, they were on their own. He later encapsulated the message of the Beatles' era as "Learn to swim"—acquire the spiritual self-sufficiency that life demands, without recourse to gurus, politicians, or pop stars.

The Beatles never did reform during John's lifetime. But he did rekindle some of the mystical interests so roundly condemned in "God", including tarot, yoga, and mantra, as well as developing some sporadic enthusiasm for social activism. In its entirety, then, "God" is best understood as what Yoko called "a declaration of independence", part of John's continuing search. In true primal scream fashion, he was cleansing his brain of anything and everything that stood between him and the core of his being. "God" illuminates the process whereby John hoped to rediscover himself as a man, not as a Beatle, in order that he might begin his life all over again.

Opposite: Bob Dylan, alias "Zimmerman"—seen here on *The Johnny Cash Show* in 1969—was among the influences that Lennon purged from his mind in 'God'.

MY MUMMY'S DEAD

The album's brief closing track is just about the simplest composition that John ever committed to record. It's also the scariest, and all the more chilling for the blankness of John's delivery, like that of a man whose grief has drained him.

It is therefore an appropriate end to the primal scream experience. Having purged himself to the point of emptiness, John stands ready to start afresh. Naturally, "My Mummy's Dead" serves to "bookend" the record, referring back to the first song "Mother". Julia's death is recalled here as an event so awful that John could never display his hurt.

He often ascribed his youthful anger to the repressed emotions he felt at his mother's killing. Eerily the song resembles a ghostly transmission from the distant past—played as if on a toy guitar, with rudimentary chords, crudely recorded as if on a primitive tape machine in John's boyhood bedroom. The child-like lyric, he later said, was plain and short because he wanted to write his own form of *haiku*, or Japanese three-line poem. The true *haiku* is highly artificial, written to contain a precise number of syllables, but it may convey a profound observation. Although Lennon could never work to such a disciplined remit, he had a bluesman's ability to express his intimate feelings with the most basic of musical tools.

My mummy's dead
I can't get it through my head
Though it's been so many years
My mummy's dead
I can't explain, so much pain
I could never show it
My mummy's dead

Chapter 3

IMAGINE

19 71

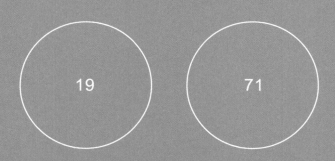

"Imagine"

"Crippled Inside"

"Jealous Guy"

"It's So Hard"

"I Don't Want to Be a Soldier"

"Gimme Some Truth"

"Oh My Love"

"How Do You Sleep?"

"How?"

"Oh Yoko!"

Single (Not on the album)

"Power to the People"

Recorded

May to July 1971 at Ascot Sound Studios, Berkshire; Record Plant, New York City.
"Power to the People" February 1971 at Ascot Sound Studios.

Produced by

John Lennon, Yoko Ono, Phil Spector

Musicians

John Lennon (vocals, guitars, piano, harmonica), Klaus Voormann (bass), Alan White (drums), Phil Spector (backing vocals), The Flux Fiddlers (strings), John Barham (keyboards, vibraphone), Steve Brendell (upright bass), King Curtis (saxophone), Andy Davis (acoustic guitar), Tom Evans (acoustic guitar), Jim Gordon (drums), George Harrison (guitars), Nicky Hopkins (keyboards), Jim Keltner (drums), Rod Linton (acoustic guitar), Joey Molland (acoustic guitar), Michael Pinder (tambourine), John Tout (acoustic guitar, piano), Ted Turner (acoustic guitar). "Power to the People" featured Bobby Keys (saxophone), and credits Rosetta Hightower "and 44 others" on backing vocals.

John completed 1970 with a trip to New York, promoting his "difficult" solo album to a doubting marketplace. He began 1971 with a first visit to Yoko's family in Japan. He had played to tougher audiences, but not many.

"THE INTERESTING THING WAS THAT JOHN LOOKED ALMOST AS IN AWE OF SPECTOR AS I WAS OF JOHN."

—Kieron Murphy

Meanwhile, in the High Court in London, lawyers picked over the mortal remains of the Beatles, as the ex-members issued ill-tempered statements that were a far cry from the balmy days of "All You Need Is Love", or even of "Give Peace a Chance". Under the growing influence of the British underground, John composed a marching song entitled "Power to the People". To raise a fighting fund for the movement's house journal, *Oz*, he also wrote a single, "God Save Us"/"Do the Oz", recorded by Bill Elliott & The Elastic Oz Band.

By June, John and Yoko were back in New York, continuing their quest for custody of Yoko's daughter Kyoko, who was still in the care of Tony Cox. While there, they met Frank Zappa and impulsively joined him on stage that very night, at the Fillmore East. Some of the gig—perhaps a little too much—would appear on a live disc with John's later album, *Some Time in New York City*. On the same visit, John fell under the spell of America's star radicals Jerry Rubin and Abbie Hoffman. He would renew this acquaintance later in the year, when he returned to America to live.

The remainder of that summer was spent at the Lennons' English country home, Tittenhurst Park, whose many gracious amenities now included a home recording studio. Here, they invited Phil Spector, and musicians including George Harrison, Klaus Voormann, and Alan White, to make the basic tracks for John's new album, *Imagine*. A young Irish photographer, Kieron Murphy, watched the cast assemble in John's kitchen: "They'd been recording all night and sleeping through the day. When I got there it was five o'clock in the afternoon and he was having breakfast. I remember being amazed at seeing him tuck into bacon and eggs... I thought people who are this famous eat more rarefied foods."

Of the legendary Spector's arrival, Murphy says, "It was almost as if he'd come up out of the floor in a puff of smoke. He had a very heavy presence. He just seemed to arrive without coming into the room. And the interesting thing was that John looked almost as in awe of Spector as I was of John. He leapt up to give him his chair, fussed around him and got him tea or coffee. Everybody else is being a bunch of boisterous lads, swapping football stories and whatever, but Spector just sat there. Then Spector says to him, very quietly, 'John, I think we should make a start.' Whereupon John leapt to his feet and literally took the cups of tea out of people's hands, frogmarching them into the studio—'Phil wants us now!' —I was amazed to see that John Lennon had to obey anybody."

When *Imagine* finally appeared, in September of 1971, the title track enchanted the world with its idealistic plea for universal altruism. Other songs continued to examine his inner doubts, and his adoration of Yoko in the face of widespread ridicule. One track, "How Do You Sleep?" simply tore into Paul McCartney. Whatever its contents, though, *Imagine* pleased the public because it was melodic, lushly arranged and kind on the ears—qualities its predecessor, *John Lennon/Plastic Ono Band*, had never been accused of.

John, of course, was less certain he had done the right thing. He often criticized the album for its softness. In 1974 he assessed its merits this way: "I prefer the "Mother'/'Working Class Hero' than *Imagine* myself... I suppose anything you do is either better or worse than something or other, I mean, that's how we seem to categorize things... 'This fish tastes as good as the fish we had in St Tropez, but not as nice as the one Arthur caught off Long Island, on the other hand, do you remember that fish and chip shop in Blackpool?'."

Opposite: The Lennons relax at Cannes, May, 1971, where the Film Festival is showing Yoko's works *Fly* and *Apotheosis*.

COME
TOGETHER

POWER TO THE PEOPLE

During the Montreal bed-in which spawned "Give Peace a Chance", John mocked the US government for considering him a political militant: "I think they might think I'm gonna hot up the revolution. But I wanna cool it down." Yet, the next eighteen months would see him drift away from smiley-badge pacifism, and closer to the hardline "agitprop" (or agitation/ propaganda) of the left wing.

Once again, he immortalized his passions of the moment in an overnight anthem. The slogan was an old one, but John's adoption of "Power to the People" would propel the phrase into everyday use. Within a few years, it would be claimed not just by socialists, but by virtually anyone from right-wing conservatives to advertising copywriters. In short, it would become meaningless.

In January 1971, John had returned from his trip to Japan with Yoko. Once more installed in the palatial setting of Tittenhurst Park, he gave an interview to the intellectual duo Tariq Ali and Robin Blackburn, representing the underground leftist magazine *Red Mole.* Ali, in particular, had been big in the 1968 student protests which provoked John's song "Revolution". Back then, John could not decide how far he supported revolutionary ideas, especially if they meant people got hurt. One version of "Revolution" appeared on the Beatles' "White Album", and John fudged his stance by singing "count me out, in". But another version, released as the B-side to "Hey Jude", has him telling the agitators they can count him "out".

By the time of his Ali/Blackburn audience, two-and-a-half years later, John is finally prepared to enlist in the movement. In the interim, conservatives had regained political power both in

"YOU CAN'T TAKE POWER WITHOUT A STRUGGLE."

—John Lennon

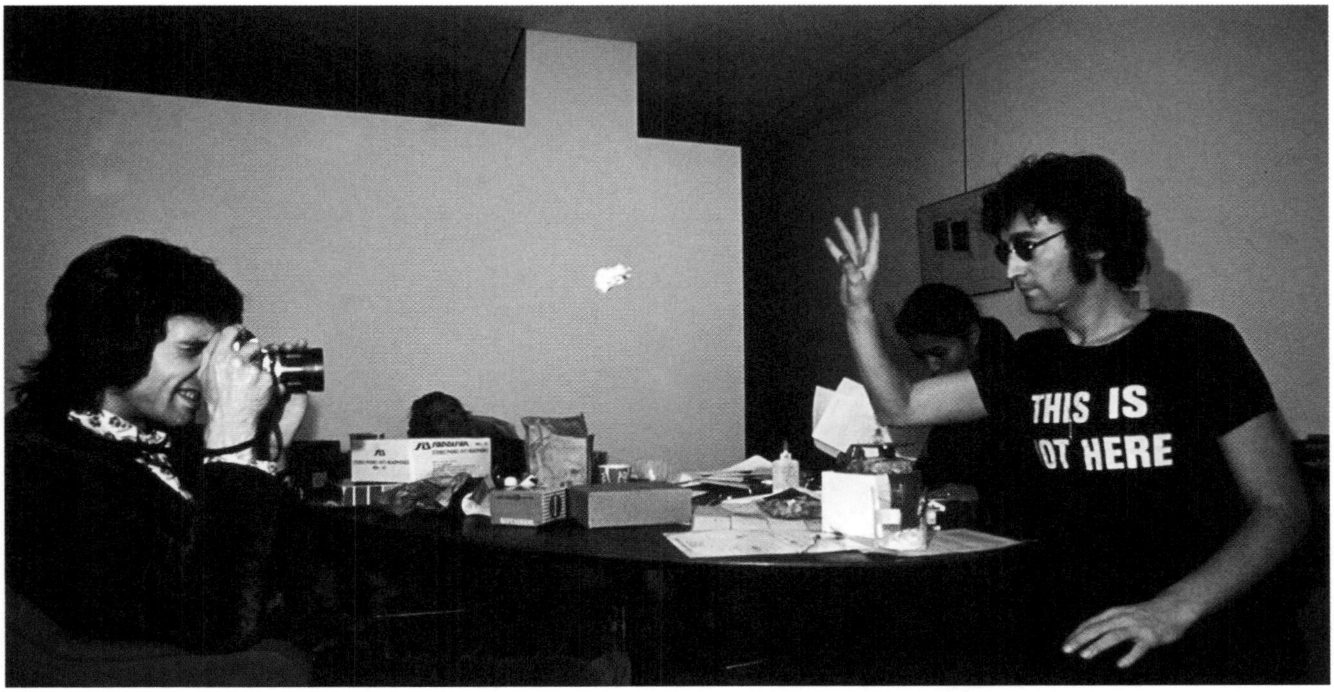

Britain and the US (Edward Heath's Tories and Richard Nixon's Republicans, respectively). Youthful opposition to government acquired a more strident tone. Lennon tells his interviewers he has always been a working-class socialist at heart. He regrets that "Revolution" did not make his allegiance clear. Yoko pleads for nonviolent revolution, but John is doubtful: "You can't take power without a struggle." He talks with pleasure of hearing Beatle songs such as "All Together Now" and "Yellow Submarine", and his own "Give Peace a Chance", being taken up by football crowds, or in pubs or on demonstrations. "That is why," he goes on, "I would like to compose songs for the revolution now."

The *Red Mole* men left Tittenhurst Park, doubtless satisfied by the superstar's submission. As good as his word, John went straight to work on a song inspired by their conversation. "Power to the People" is both battle cry and threat. Exploited workers are urged to take to the streets. Their capitalist exploiters are warned, "We got to put you down." Another verse enjoins comrades and brothers not to overlook the rights of their womenfolk. It was Yoko who introduced John to feminism; in 1971 it was far from an obligatory item on the average street fighting man's agenda.

By the next day, January 22nd, he was in the studio with his bopping manifesto, but again it was Phil Spector's efforts which made all the difference. To the swirling sax of ace sessioneer Bobby Keys, Spector added a full-blown gospel choir for righteous conviction. Next he multi-tracked the sound of the musicians' tramping feet. But then he whipped the whole number up into something that was far lighter on its feet, much more supple and funky, than the basic composition implied. It was the first ever call to mass proletarian action that you could dance to—a feat that Lenin never achieved, but Lennon did.

"Power to the People" came out in America on March 22nd. The original Yoko B-side, "Open Your Box", was replaced with another of her songs, the more romantically entitled "Touch Me".

Lennon was not proud of "Power to the People", regarding it as "a guilt song" done to appease the radicals who assailed his rich man's conscience—actually, he dismissed it as "shit". But the song's central sentiment assumed fresh relevance in 1992, when Yoko put the track to footage of the Chinese pro-democracy demonstrations in Tiananmen Square.

Above: October 1971 found John in Syracuse, New York, for the launch of Yoko's exhibition *This Is Not Here*.

Opposite: John joins Yoko in promoting her book, Grapefruit, at Selfridges store, London, on July 15th, 1971.

POWER TO THE PEOPLE

Power to the people, power to the people
Power to the people, power to the people

Power to the people, power to the people
Power to the people, power to the people, right on

Say we want a revolution
We better get on right away
Well, get then on your feet
And enter the street

Singin' power to the people, power to the people
Power to the people, power to the people, right on

A million workers workin' for nothin'
You better give 'em what they really own
We got to put you down
When we come into town

Singin' power to the people, power to the people
Power to the people, power to the people, right on

I got to ask you, comrades and brothers
How do you treat you own woman back home?
She got to be herself
So she can hear herself

Singin' power to the people, power to the people
Power to the people, power to the people, right on

Now, now, now, now

Oh well, power to the people, power to the people
Power to the people, power to the people, right on

Oh yeah, power to the people, power to the people
Power to the people, power to the people, right on

Power to the people, power to the people
Oh well, power to the people, power to the people

Oh well, power to the people, power to the people

IMAGINE

Paul McCartney's "Let It Be" and Paul Simon's "Bridge Over Troubled Water" had, almost simultaneously, struck a pseudo-religious note in the 1970 hit parade. John was openly contemptuous of "Let It Be", but he was to write the third of these definitive rock hymns himself. "Imagine" is probably the most widely revered of all John's songs, including those by the Beatles. Here, at least, he bettered Paul, whose solo work could never surpass a song like "Yesterday" in popular affections."

The restful opening notes of "Imagine" still strike a deep chord in people of all beliefs. Strangely, not even its explicitly secular message has stopped the song becoming a favorite at modern-minded religious events.

As the lyrics unfold we are asked to imagine a universe sans heaven or hell, and a world where people live for the day instead of the afterlife. Religion, like nationhood, is cited as a cause of conflict. Can we imagine ourselves without them, or material possessions, and living in global harmony? John had ended his previous album by declaring that "the dream is over". He begins this one by announcing a new dream, and inviting us to share it. There was something nearly clairvoyant too in John's critique of national boundaries. The US immigration service would become the bane of his life, and the fight for American citizenship his longest-running battle.

Below: John sings at the benefit show for activist John Sinclair in Ann Arbor, Michegan, on December 10th, 1971.

Opposite: John and Yoko at home in Tittenhurst Park, near London, in July 1971.

"IMAGINE ALL THE PEOPLE LIVING LIFE IN PEACE..."

—John Lennon

IMAGINE

Imagine there's no countries
It isn't hard to do
Nothing to kill or die for
And no religion, too
Imagine all the people
Living life in peace
You, you may say I'm a dreamer
But I'm not the only one
I hope someday you will join us
And the world will be as one
Imagine no possessions
I wonder if you can
No need for greed or hunger
A brotherhood of man
Imagine all the people
Sharing all the world
You, you may say I'm a dreamer
But I'm not the only one
I hope someday you will join us
And the world will live as one

"Imagine" has its origins in Yoko Ono's book of poems, *Grapefruit*, published in 1964. In it, Yoko begins each poem with a similar invocation. Thus, "Tunafish Sandwich Piece" starts, "Imagine one thousand suns in the sky at the same time...". "Rubber Piece" begins, "Imagine your body spreading rapidly all over the world like a thin tissue...", and "Cloud Piece" is quoted on the album sleeve itself: "Imagine the clouds dripping. Dig a hole in your garden to put them in." John would later say that he should have given Yoko a cowriter credit for the song. But, he told *Playboy*, "I wasn't man enough... I was still full of wanting my own space after being in a room with the guys all the time, having to share everything." (She finally received an official credit many years later.)

The second source of inspiration was a prayer book given to John by the American comedian Dick Gregory. Advocating "positive prayer", the book advised that to receive anything from God, we must first imagine it for ourselves. This idea impressed John greatly. Even the day before he died, he was still expounding "projection of our goals". If we wish for a positive future we should exert our mental energy and visualize one. In 1980, he observed how this idea, once considered wacko, was now being adopted by everyone from business organisations to sports stars. If we conceive of the future as something violent, like *Star Wars*, then we run the risk of creating precisely that.

Musicians present at the sessions report that Lennon could sense the song's potential. "'Imagine' itself was one that John played us before we did that whole album," remembers the drummer Alan White. "He came up to everyone that was playing, gave us a set of lyrics and said, 'This is what you're about to be saying to the whole world.' 'Imagine' was a very emotional kind of song, it had to be very delicately played."

On its release, the song struck some as hypocritical. Look at Lennon, the skeptics said, sitting in the spacious white music room of his agreeable English manor and imagining "no possessions". But his Utopian dream, with its wistful existentialism, tapped a vast reservoir of feeling in the postwar world. The song has become a standard, but John's opinion was typically perverse: He stood by *John Lennon/Plastic Ono Band*, calling it more "real" than anything else he'd done, but the softer tones of "Imagine" represented compromise—or selling out. "'Imagine' was a sincere statement," he told *NME*'s Roy Carr in 1972. "It was "Working Class Hero" with chocolate on. I was trying to think of it in terms of children." When Paul McCartney was so incautious as to praise "Imagine", Lennon quickly fired back: "So you think 'Imagine' ain't political? It's 'Working Class Hero' with sugar on for conservatives like yourself."

Below: *Imagine* was recorded in Tittenhurst's Ascot Sound Studio, and was the location for the title-track's video.

CRIPPLED INSIDE

After the claustrophobic meditations of *John Lennon/Plastic Ono Band*, the *Imagine* LP was more inclined to poke its head above the parapet and satirize the world outside.

It was certainly much brighter musically. While "Crippled Inside" is really rather dark in content, and quite as self-lacerating as its predecessors, John presents it as the jolliest of festivities. Its lyric is no more than a warning that we cannot use externals—whether they be rhetoric, religion, or nice clothes—to disguise our fundamental problems, but he deploys a battery of musical jokes to make the observation sparkle. Ragtime piano, reminiscent of American vaudeville or English pub singalongs, skips and twinkles over George's slide guitar, itself a nod to the country-funk style brought to rock's mainstream by The Band. As a song, "Crippled Inside" goes nowhere, but it gets there with considerable charm.

Above: While "*Imagine*" was far more popular, Lennon himself expressed a preference for the darker ambience of its predecessor.

You can shine your shoes and wear a suit
You can comb your hair and look quite cute
You can hide your face behind a smile
One thing you can't hide
Is when you're crippled inside

You can wear a mask and paint your face
You can call yourself the human race
You can wear a collar and a tie
One thing you can't hide
Is when you're crippled inside

Well now, you know that your cat has
nine lives, babe
Nine lives to itself
But you only got one
And a dog's life ain't fun
Mama, take a look outside

You can go to church and sing a hymn
You can judge me by the colour of my skin
You can live a lie until you die
One thing you can't hide
Is when you're crippled inside

Take it, cousin

Well now, you know that your cat has
nine lives, babe
Nine lives to itself
But you only got one
And a dog's life ain't fun
Mama, take a look outside

You can go to church and sing a hymn
Judge me by the colour of my skin
You can live a lie until you die
One thing you can't hide
Is when you're crippled inside
One thing you can't hide
Is when you're crippled inside

One thing you can't hide
Is when you're crippled inside

JEALOUS GUY

"Jealous Guy" began its life a few years earlier as "Child Of Nature", but this was never used by the Beatles. Perhaps it clashed too much with Paul's title, "Mother Nature's Son", which was unveiled at the same session and duly appeared on the group's "White Album".

In its finished form, "Jealous Guy" was a keynote song of John's maturing outlook, expressing his rejection of the macho values he had grown up with. In later interviews, he was frank about his violent tendencies, though he believed he had brought that side of his nature under control. In his youth he often got into fights. Indeed, some of his earliest press coverage arose from an incident at Paul's twenty-first birthday party in Liverpool when John attacked and hospitalized his old friend, the Cavern DJ Bob Wooler, for accusing John of a gay encounter with the Beatles' manager Brian Epstein, whom he'd just accompanied on a brief holiday to Spain.

Worse still, John confessed that he had been violent towards women. He told *Playboy*, "I was a hitter. I couldn't express myself and I hit. That is why I am always on about peace… I will have to be a lot older before I can face admitting in public how I treated women as a youngster." Jealousy was the usual reason for his outbursts, a tendency revealed in his Beatle song "Run For Your Life", in which he describes himself as a "wicked guy" with "a jealous mind", before copping a line from his hero Elvis Presley's "Baby Let's Play House", where he warns his girl he'd rather see her dead than with another man. And John admitted the truth of a line he'd given to Paul's breezy *Sgt. Pepper* song "Getting Better"—he really was cruel to his woman, to the point of beating her up.

"Jealous Guy" begins with a suggestion that John's latest transgression is a lapse back into his bad old ways, born of his insecurity. His relationship with Yoko was always stormier than the couple chose to admit—it's said that he made her list her former lovers, and resented her knowing Japanese because it removed so much of her consciousness from him. But in "Jealous Guy", one of his most persuasive melodies and Spector's airiest arrangement, the eloquence of John's repentance carries all before it.

John's first wife Cynthia saw plenty of John's volatility, especially during their early courtship in Liverpool. But she doubts that he ever changed entirely, or needed to: "He was really never a macho working-class man, John. I think his talents were above and beyond that. He was like a chrysalis. He had to be macho to cope with some of the types he came across in Liverpool. He tended to try to look like the tough guys so that the tough guys wouldn't pick on him. So what John became [in the end] was what John really was, underneath it all."

In the melancholy winter months after John's death, Roxy Music's sensitive reading of "Jealous Guy" became a worldwide hit, one of the finest musical tributes ever paid to its composer.

I was dreamin' of the past
And my heart was beating fast
I began to lose control
I began to lose control
I didn't mean to hurt you

I'm sorry that I made you cry
Oh no, I didn't want to hurt you
I'm just a jealous guy

I was feeling insecure
You might not love me anymore
I was shivering inside
I was shivering inside

Oh, I didn't mean to hurt you
I'm sorry that I made you cry
Oh no, I didn't want to hurt you
I'm just a jealous guy
I didn't mean to hurt you

I'm sorry that I made you cry
Oh no, I didn't want to hurt you
I'm just a jealous guy

I was trying to catch your eyes
Thought that you was trying to hide
I was swallowing my pain
I was swallowing my pain
I didn't mean to hurt you

I'm sorry that I made you cry
Oh no, I didn't want to hurt you

I'm just a jealous guy, watch out
I'm just a jealous guy, look out, babe
I'm just a jealous guy

IT'S SO HARD

If the fragile "Jealous Guy" depicted a wild man looking for the gentler side of his nature, then the following track, "It's So Hard", asserts that Lennon has not forgotten how to rock. A grinding blues boogie, of the sort that thick-ankled rock bands were excessively fond of back then, it has a crunch like truckwheels over gravel, and some epic Fifties saxophone.

The song is not in itself a statement of anything much, confining itself to John's stoic observations on the everyday demands of life, love, and work. Lennon was never one to make existence easier for himself—quite the contrary—but he reserved the right to complain loud and long whenever it got too much. "It's So Hard", however, is more of a boastful swagger than a self-pitying whine. And the stomping grunginess of its basic track is magically uplifted by Spector's added strings, hovering in the light, Hollywood-Oriental style that he and John became so fond of. Spector had suffered a few lean years since his heyday in the Sixties, and seemed to relish the new album's spaciousness.

The photographer Kieron Murphy remembers being invited back to Tittenhurst Park to hear the finished *Imagine* album. He found John anxious about the public's response, after the cool reception given to his previous album. But "It's So Hard", like the next track "I Don't Want to Be a Soldier", cheered him up hugely, thanks to their inclusion of the legendary sax-player King Curtis, overdubbed by Spector in New York. "He was really proud," reports Murphy. "It was 'We managed to get King Curtis!'. He didn't seem to get that people would kill their own mothers to play on one of his albums."

John, though, had every reason to be humble. As one of England's first connoisseurs of rock 'n' roll, he would have revered "King" Curtis Ousley, whose tenor sax defined The Coasters' "Yakety Yak" and dozens of Atlantic R&B classics. Just prior to the *Imagine* sessions, Curtis had played for Aretha Franklin and formed his own band featuring the Beatles' sideman Billy Preston. But only a month later, on August 15th, 1971, Curtis was stabbed to death by a vagrant on the front steps of his New York home. We may understand John's awe when we read the producer Jerry Wexler's tribute to the saxophone giant: "Six foot one, powerful, cool and radiant… Curtis was noble, ballsy, and streetwise like nobody I ever knew."

"It's So Hard", then, seems a pretty good epitaph.

Below: Formerly banished for the sake of his pop star image, John's spectacles ultimately became a trademark. The cigarettes, too, were rarely far from hand.

IT'S SO HARD

You gotta live
You gotta love
You gotta be somebody
You gotta shove
But it's so hard, it's really hard
Sometimes I feel like going down

You gotta eat
You gotta drink
You gotta feel something
You gotta worry
But it's so hard, it's really hard
Sometimes I feel like going down

But when it's good
It's really good
And when I hold you in my arms baby
Sometimes I feel like going down

You gotta run
You gotta hide
You gotta keep your woman satisfied
But it's so hard, it's really hard
Sometimes I feel like going down

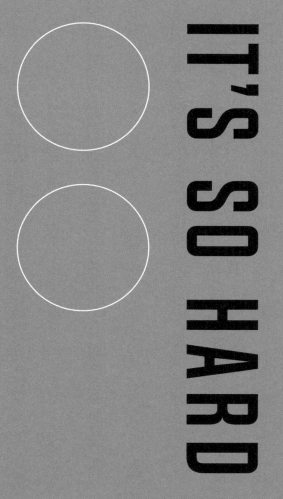

I DON'T WANT TO BE A SOLDIER

It's hard to envisage a more unlikely candidate for military discipline than John Lennon, so the sincerity of "'I Don't Want to Be a Soldier" may be taken as read.

The song had more resonance, perhaps, for young American fans, to whom Vietnam and the draft were a real issue. But, during John's childhood, Britain too had its relic of wartime conscription in National Service for young men. To John's immense relief, the scheme was abolished just before he became eligible. "I remember the news coming through," he told Barry Miles, "that it was all those born before 1940, and I was thanking God for that as I'd always had this plan about Southern Ireland (which was outside UK jurisdiction). I wasn't quite sure what I was going to do when I got to Southern Ireland, but I had no intention of fighting." In his interview with *Red Mole*, he claimed he had been brought up "to despise the army as something that takes everybody away and leaves them dead somewhere".

In fact, the closest John Lennon ever got to wearing a uniform was on the cover of *Sgt. Pepper*, or in his role as Private Gripweed in Richard Lester's movie *How I Won the War*, though he also took to affecting guerrilla fatigues during his radical phase of the early Seventies. But Lennon never forgot, or forgave, Presley's spell in the military. "Elvis died when he went into the Army" was his terse response to the King's passing in 1977.

The song's structure was loosely built around the nursery rhyme "Tinker, tailor, soldier, sailor. Rich man, poor man, beggarman, thief". Lawyer and churchman are likewise cited as careers he was keen to avoid. Echoing to the heavens, Phil Spector's production pulls out all the stops, including King Curtis's saxophone squalls and a fusillade of rock guitar. Some of the latter was contributed by Joey Molland and Tom Evans from the Beatles' Apple protégés Badfinger. This band's fate proved as sad as King Curtis'—their founder Pete Ham, and Tom Evans himself, later hanged themselves after a succession of business setbacks. Ironically, the gifted pair were responsible for writing "Without You", a massive hit for John's great friend Harry Nilsson.

Well, I don't wanna be a soldier, mama
I don't wanna die
Well, I don't wanna be a sailor, mama
I don't wanna fly
Well, I don't wanna be a failure, mama
I don't wanna cry
Well, I don't wanna be a soldier, mama
I don't wanna die
Oh, no
Oh, no
Oh, no
Oh, no

Well, I don't wanna be a rich man, mama
I don't wanna cry
Well, I don't wanna be a poor man, mama
I don't wanna fly
Well, I don't wanna be a lawyer, mama
I don't wanna lie
Well, I don't wanna be a soldier, mama
I don't wanna die
Oh, no
Oh, no
Oh, no
Oh, no
Hey

Well, I don't wanna be a soldier, mama
I don't wanna die
Well, I don't wanna be a thief now, mama
I don't wanna fly
Well, I don't wanna be a churchman, mama
I don't wanna cry
Well, I don't wanna be a soldier, mama
I don't wanna die
Oh, no
Oh, no
Oh, no
Oh, no
Oh, no
Oh, no
Hit it

Oh well, I don't wanna be a soldier, mama
I don't wanna die
Well, I don't wanna be a sailor, mama
I don't wanna fly
Well, I don't wanna be a failure, mama
I don't wanna cry, no
I don't wanna be a soldier, mama
I don't wanna die
Oh, no
Oh, no
Oh, no
Oh, no
Oh, no

GIMME SOME TRUTH

By now an avid observer of the world political scene, John Lennon took grave exception to "Tricky Dicky" Nixon, whose escalation of the Vietnam War had made him Public Enemy Number One among liberals and radicals across the globe.

John's exasperated demand for honesty prefigures the Watergate scandal, which only served to confirm his worst suspicions about the President.

The bare bones of "Gimme Some Truth", however, could be discerned as early as January 1969, when the song was attempted at the Beatles' Twickenham sessions, most of which wound up on the *Let It Be* album. It's therefore, likely that John's initial rant against deceit was born of the Beatles' internal disputes. As such, it was practically a parallel track to Paul's wistful *Abbey Road* complaint, "You Never Give Me Your Money".

It's unknown whether Nixon ever heard John's blistering tirade, but the singer's general disposition was well known to the White House, as can be seen from numerous official documents. Even if they'd missed the message, they were advised of Lennon's "subversive" proclivities by the all-American patriot Elvis Presley, who urged the administration to act against the outspoken Beatle. It's an inglorious episode in the King's career, but then as John's biographer Chris Hutchins noted wryly, "If Elvis had succeeded in having him banned from the United States, he would still be alive today."

I'm sick and tired of hearing things
From uptight, short-sighted, narrow-minded hypocritics
All I want is the truth
Just gimme some truth
I've had enough of reading things
By neurotic, psychotic, pig-headed politicians
All I want is the truth
Just gimme some truth

No short-haired, yellow-bellied, son of tricky dicky
Is gonna mother hubbard soft soap me
With just a pocketful of hope
Money for dope
Money for rope

No short-haired, yellow-bellied, son of tricky dicky
Is gonna mother hubbard soft soap me
With just a pocketful of soap
Money for dope
Money for rope

I'm sick to death of seeing things
From tight-lipped, condescending, mamas little chauvinists
All I want is the truth
Just gimme some truth now

I've had enough of watching scenes
Of schizophrenic, ego-centric, paranoiac, prima-donnas
All I want is the truth now
Just gimme some truth

No short-haired, yellow-bellied, son of tricky dicky
Is gonna mother hubbard soft soap me
With just a pocketful of soap
It's money for dope
Money for rope

Ah, I'm sick and tired of hearing things
From uptight, short-sighted, narrow-minded hypocrites
All I want is the truth now
Just gimme some truth now

I've had enough of reading things
By neurotic, psychotic, pig-headed politicians
All I want is the truth now
Just gimme some truth now

All I want is the truth now
Just gimme some truth now
All I want is the truth
Just gimme some truth
All I want is the truth
Just gimme some truth

OH MY LOVE

Jointly credited to Yoko, "Oh My Love" is another number with its origins in the batch that John prepared for the Beatles' 1968 "White Album".

A brief, gentle song of awakening tenderness, it sits demurely in between two of *Imagine*'s most enthusiastic bouts of personal abuse. One man who observed John and Yoko's blossoming romance at close hand was Paul McCartney: "In the Sixties," he reflects, "you thought, if I'm gonna go with this person for the rest of my life, like John and Yoko or me and Linda, I really ought to look them in the eye all the time. John and Yoko really did spend a lot of time [he mimes comically intense eye contact] and it got fairly mad, looking at each other going, 'It's gonna be all right, it's gonna be all right, it's gonna be all right'. After a couple of hours of that, you get fairly worn out."

Below: Paul and John see eye-to-eye at a happier point in their relationship, filming a Shakespeare skit for a TV special in April 1964.

OH MY LOVE

Oh my love for the first
time in my life
My eyes are wide open
Oh my lover for the first
time in my life
My eyes can see
I see the wind, oh I see the trees
Everything is clear in my heart
I see the clouds, oh I see the sky
Everything is clear in our world
Oh my love for the first
time in my life
My mind is wide open
Oh my lover for the first
time in my life
My mind can feel
I feel sorrow, oh I feel dreams
Everything is clear in my heart
I feel life, oh I feel love
Everything is clear in our world

HOW DO YOU SLEEP?

For all the sweetness of its "chocolate-coated" arrangements, *Imagine* has its share of sulfur, and the bitterest song of all was John's blatant assault on Paul McCartney, "How Do You Sleep?"

Amid the legal gunsmoke enveloping the defunct Beatles, relations between the old friends had sunk to an all-time low. In May, a month before the *Imagine* sessions started, Paul released his second solo album, *Ram*—replete, or so John thought, with underhand attacks on him and Yoko.

The *Ram* cover art includes a photo of a pair of beetles, arguably "screwing" one another. And the music opens with Paul apparently crooning, "Piss off, yeah." John quickly detected malice in other lines such as "We believe that we can't be wrong", and the allusion in '3 Legs' to a friend who has let him down. He was right to an extent, though as Paul comments: "It's nothing, it's so harmless really, just little digs." He points to another sleeve photo, of him and Linda wearing Halloween masks from a New York children's shop, and flatly denies they were mocking John and Yoko. At the same time, he concedes that John was correct to prick up his ears at one particular lyric, "Too many people preaching fantasies".

"I felt John and Yoko were telling everyone what to do. And I felt we didn't need to be told what to do. The whole tenor of the Beatles thing had been, like each to his own. Freedom. Suddenly it was just a bit the wagging finger; I was pissed off with it."

To most people's ears the *Ram* lyrics were probably innocuous, vague, and even throwaway. But there was to be no ambiguity about John's counter-attack. The original *Imagine* LP was even issued with a postcard of John grappling a pig, in mockery of the *Ram* cover where Paul had shown rustic aspirations by posing with a sheep. So far, so childish. But "How Do You Sleep?" really took the gloves off. Drenched in a deceptively gentle string setting, the song begins with a parody of *Sgt. Pepper*'s opening and proceeds to lambast McCartney as a baby-faced lightweight, a man who "lives with straights" who fawn on him, and a writer whose only achievement was "Yesterday". "Since you're gone," sneers John, in a reference to Paul's admittedly slight new single, "you're just 'Another Day'."

The latter line was offered to John by Allen Klein, the New Yorker brought in to oversee the Beatles' business affairs, in the teeth of opposition from Paul. On this occasion, however, Klein was not goading John to greater excesses of spite, but rather saving him from potential libel—his original couplet, according to biographer Albert Goldman, alleged Paul had probably lifted the tune of 'Yesterday' anyway. There is something almost endearing in the way that the *Imagine* album can range from the highest aspirations of global consciousness-raising to the tiny-minded bickering of the school playground. In accusing McCartney of "Muzak", John knew that he could depend on hip opinion to back him up. But in Lennon's populist heart, it always rankled with him that Paul's melodies still possessed the common touch.

Elsewhere, John jeers that the "freaks" were right to say that Paul was dead. This refers to the hoax perpetrated by an American radio station in 1969, when myriad "clues" were read into the Beatles' lyrics and album sleeves, supposedly revealing that the current McCartney was an impostor, the real Beatle having died in a 1966 car crash. This ingeniously elaborated rumour enjoyed a wide circulation. Why, for example, did Paul's *Sgt. Pepper* costume include a badge saying "O.P.D."? Surely it stood for "Officially Pronounced Dead"? And doesn't John conclude "Strawberry Fields Forever" with the words, "I buried Paul"? (Alas for conspiracy theorists, the O.P.D. badge in fact reads O.P.P.—it came from the Ontario Provincial Police—while John's actual words were "cranberry sauce".)

Photographer Kieron Murphy, who was present at the session, recalls there being no discussion of the song's lyric, but notes that Yoko sat at John's feet, writing down the words. "He was literally making the album up as he went along, and he was teaching it, playing it for them. I thought at first it was a slag-off of the fans because the first line is So Sergeant Pepper took you by surprise.' But it began to click when he sang, 'The only good thing you did was 'Yesterday' and so on."

The track aroused immediate controversy. *Rolling Stone* condemned it as "horrifying and indefensible… a song so spiteful and self-indulgent that it sanctified the victim and demeaned the accuser." McCartney refrained from any musical retaliation. In fact, his next album, *Wild Life*, seemed to carry a conciliatory song to John in "Dear Friend". But he did comment, "I think it's silly. So what if I live with straights? I like straights. I have straight babies. It doesn't affect him. He says the only thing I did was 'Yesterday'. He knows that's wrong. He knows and I know that's not true."

Paul could draw some comfort from subsequent events. Within a few years, the other three Beatles were themselves at daggers drawn with Allen Klein, and John would duly snipe at him in song. By the time John made his last album, of course, he was hymning the praises of domesticity and investing in farm animals—just two of the McCartney traits he'd so smugly satirized. By 1980, John's old grudges were, in any case, subsiding. He said that "How Do You Sleep?" had not been a personal attack. He compared the song to Dylan's vindictive "Like A Rolling Stone"—just a pouring out of all his anger, directed at himself as much as anyone else. Well, maybe. It's more likely that "How Do You Sleep?" was one more instance of John's tendency to shoot first and ask questions later.

HOW DO YOU SLEEP?

So Sgt. Pepper took
you by surprise
You better see right
through that mother's eyes
Those freaks was right
when they said you was dead
The one mistake you
made was in your head

Ah, how do you sleep?
Ah, how do you
sleep at night?

You live with straights
who tell you you was king
Jump when your
momma tell you anything

The only thing you
done was yesterday
And since you're gone
you're just another day

Ah, how do you sleep?
Ah, how do you sleep
at night?

Ah, how do you sleep?
Ah, how do you sleep
at night?
A pretty face may
last a year or two

But pretty soon they'll
see what you can do
The sound you make
is muzak to my ears
You must have learned
something in all those years

Ah, how do you sleep?
Ah, how do you sleep
at night?

HOW?

Emerging, as it did, in between the revolutionary broadsides of "Power to the People" and *Some Time in New York City*, the *Imagine* album represents a pause in John's career as counterculture spokesman.

Whenever he did speak out, he had the gift of sounding completely convinced. Yet he was prone to interludes of doubt, and "How?" describes one such hiatus. Except for its ornate orchestration, this track would sit logically inside the previous album, for its themes are old friends—lack of direction, fear of the future, emotional incapacity.

How can I go forward when I don't
know which way I'm facing?
How can I go forward when I don't
know which way to turn?
How can I go forward into something
I'm not sure of?
Oh no, oh no

How can I have feeling when I don't know if it's a feeling?
How can I feel something if I just don't know how to feel?
How can I have feelings when my feelings have always
been denied?
Oh no, oh no

You know life can be long
And you got to be so strong
And the world is so tough
Sometimes I feel I've had enough

How can I give love when I don't
know what it is I'm giving?
How can I give love when I just don't
know how to give?
How can I give love when love is
something I ain't never had?
Oh no, oh no

You know life can be long
You've got to be so strong
And the world she is tough
Sometimes I feel I've had enough

How can we go forward when we don't
know which way we're facing?
How can we go forward when we don't
know which way to turn?
How can we go forward into something
we're not sure of?
Oh no, oh no

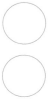

OH YOKO!

Jangling piano, wheezy harmonica and lolloping drums combine to make this the album's breeziest moment. Its chorus is a whoop of joy.

Arriving at the record's end, "Oh Yoko!" has the effect of dedicating the whole of *Imagine* to her. So it's strange, therefore, that John's earliest rehearsals of this song were slow and subdued—almost the work of a nervous man calling for reassurance. Lines like "In the middle of the night, I call your name" take on a mood of bright exuberance, but were written in a darker hour, by a man who was no stranger to fear.

Unsurprisingly, in its final state "Oh Yoko!" was a very popular track and John was advised to release it as a single. Commercially it would make a fine antidote to agitprop shanties and explorations of inner angst. But John resisted the idea. As he told *Playboy*, "I was shy and embarrassed, maybe because it didn't represent my image of myself, of the tough, hard-biting rock 'n' roller with the acid tongue."

And so a hit was missed. But worse, much worse, was to follow.

Above: The Lennons in May 1971.

Opposite: For all the couple's undoubted closeness, a song like 'How?' finds Lennon still prone to self-doubt.

In the middle of the night
In the middle of the night I call your name
Oh, Yoko
Oh, Yoko

My love will turn you on
In the middle of a bath
In the middle of a bath I call your name
Oh, Yoko
Oh, Yoko
My love will turn you on

My love
Will
Turn
You
On
In the middle of a shave

In the middle of a shave I call your name
Oh, Yoko
Oh, Yoko
My love will turn you on

In the middle of a dream
In the middle of a dream I call your name
Oh, Yoko
Oh, Yoko
My love will turn you on

My love
Will
Turn
You
On

In the middle of a cloud
In the middle of a cloud I call your name
Oh, Yoko
Oh, Yoko

My love will turn you on
Oh, Yoko
Oh, Yoko
Oh, Yoko
Oh, Yoko

Chapter 4

SOME TIME

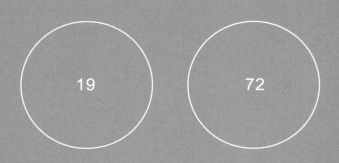

19 72

IN NEW YORK CITY

"Woman Is The Nigger Of The World"
"Attica State"
"New York City"
"Sunday Bloody Sunday"
"The Luck Of The Irish"
"John Sinclair"
"Angela"

Single (not on the album)
"Happy Xmas (War Is Over)"

Recorded
March 1972 at Record Plant, New York City.
"Happy Xmas (War Is Over)" October 1971 at Record Plant, New York City.

Produced by
John Lennon, Yoko Ono, Phil Spector.

Musicians
John Lennon (vocals, guitars), Yoko Ono (drums, vocals), Jim Keltner (drums, percussion). Elephant's Memory: Stan Bronstein (flute, saxophone), Wayne 'Tex' Gabriel (guitar), Richard Frank Jr. (drums, percussion), Adam Ippolito (keyboards, piano), Gary Van Scyoc (bass guitar), John La Bosca (piano). "Happy Xmas (War Is Over)": Harlem Community Choir (vocals), Nicky Hopkins (keyboards, chimes and glockenspiel), Hugh McCracken (guitar), Chris Osborn (guitar), Teddy Irwin (guitar), Stuart Scharf (guitar), May Pang (backing vocals).

Nobody realized, when John left England for New York City on September 3rd, 1971, that he would never see his homeland again. The US government kept trying to revoke his visa and deny him full resident status, but he stalled them long enough to get his own way. An unfortunate side-effect of the fight was that he was scared to leave the States in case he could not get back in. But the ultimate irony of Lennon's life was that he loved New York and was determined to settle there because he believed this city would leave him in peace.

There were other attractions, too. "A big Liverpool" was John's fond tag for New York City. The parallels were real enough when you got away from Manhattan's midtown glamor; they were a couple of tough old seaports, self-obsessed and self-mythologizing, where Irish-featured stevedores barked in curiously similar accents ("Youse guys over dere, shift dis."). He never stopped comparing the two cities, and both felt like home—only London, which represented the Beatle years in between, was unreal.

At first, September's trip was just another shuttle in John and Yoko's nomadic routine. Still pursuing legal custody of Kyoko, Yoko's daughter by her previous husband Tony Cox, they set up camp in a luxury suite on the seventeenth floor of the elegant St. Regis Hotel on 55th Street. A few weeks later, they rented a tiny apartment downtown in the altogether funkier district of Greenwich Village.

The immigration squabble conspired to keep John in New York, even if the Kyoko case faded from his agenda, but the situation suited him. For years in England, he'd lived nowhere but the stockbroker belt, in isolated mansions. Suddenly he found himself at the heart of things. Moreover, he felt accepted. "New York remains the center of the universe for me," he said. He fell in quickly with the radical gang, like Chicago Seven defendants Jerry Rubin and Abbie Hoffman. They were Yippies (that is, of the Youth International Party) and their playful tendencies were far more congenial to John than the heavy Marxist austerity of European thinkers such as Tariq Ali and Robin Blackburn.

John held court in Greenwich Village. White Panthers dropped by, and Black Panthers sent their regards. His peacenik Christmas single, "Happy Xmas (War Is Over)", was already out of step with John's new mood, for these years had seen the two-fingered peace sign fold inside the clenched fist salute.

He'd appear on street demonstrations and pose for photos in the sort of hard hat worn by rioting Japanese students. Instead of posting acorns for peace, he'd bawl through megaphones about the IRA (Irish Republican Army). Like a lot of New Yorkers, he rather played up his remote Irish heritage. Likewise, he'd romanticize his slim links with the Liverpool proletariat.

As we've learned in later years, John's enemies by now included Richard Nixon, J. Edgar Hoover, and Elvis Presley. But the irony is that John had the makings of a classic American patriot, because he was a fervently grateful immigrant. Where Europeans might revere their native soil for its history, most Americans honor theirs for its opportunities. "I profoundly regret that I was not born an American," he said. He could feel the awesome power of New York to absorb any kind of human being or human activity. As for Britain, its antipathy to Yoko made him even more scornful of its provincialism.

From this new sense of liberation came one rather poor album. *Some Time in New York City* tackled a range of contemporary issues (feminism, Northern Ireland, black activism) with dogged sincerity rather than artistic inspiration. Nor was it entirely John's record—Yoko contributed several tracks of her own. Although her songs ("Sisters, O Sisters", "Born in a Prison" and "We're All Water") were more orthodox affairs than previously, their appeal is still limited. John could take his pick of New York's musical expertise; instead he picked a radical bar band, Elephant's Memory, whose roughhouse energy enchanted him. More ominously, Phil Spector's role was reduced to overseer of the final mixes.

Above: The Dakota apartment building, on New York's 72nd Street and Central Park West, was the Lennons' home from 1973 and, in 1980, the scene of John's murder.

"I PROFOUNDLY REGRET THAT I WAS NOT BORN AN AMERICAN."

—John Lennon

There was a bonus disc, *Live Jam*, from two sources. First was a December 1969 gig by the "Plastic Ono Supergroup" at London's Lyceum. Billed as a "Peace for Christmas" event, the night saw John and Yoko joined by a sprawling cast that included George Harrison, Eric Clapton, and Keith Moon. They performed an efficient "Cold Turkey", with John declaiming in his best postcard-from-Hell fashion. Next came a challenging fifteen minutes' worth of "Don't Worry Kyoko", which we may listen to for the same reason people climb Mount Everest: because it's there. Amid the chaos, a horn section labors stoically. The remaining tracks are from John's surprise appearance at Frank Zappa's Fillmore East show in June 1971. Easily the best of these is "Well (Baby Please Don't Go)", a game take on the old Olympics B-side, introduced by John as "a song I used to sing when I was at the Cavern in Liverpool". Yoko wails in a strange but interesting counterpoint. Three more freeform cuts—"Jamrag", "Scumbag", and "Au"—are gruelling and aimless.

Some Time in New York City appeared in America in June 1972; the British release came three months later. Its artwork was a pastiche of the *New York Times*, indicating John's crush on "headline" songs written at journalistic speed—mistakes and all—in reaction to the day's events. Its reviews were nearly all negative and John was back on the defensive. "I tried to make my songs uncomplicated so that people could understand them," he told Roy Carr. "Now they're openly attacking me for writing simplistic lyrics. 'I Want to Hold Your Hand', that was simplistic. If I want more praise I can write more things like 'I Am the Walrus' and songs full of surrealism… There was one criticism that said, 'Please write us some images, not the way you're saying it now.' Well, all I've got to say to people like that is, get drunk or whatever it is you do… lay on a bed… make your own damn images."

But the world was still softly humming "Imagine", and had no time for *Some Time in New York City*, which sold badly and, more damningly, soon became prominent in the second-hand racks. John's "front page songs" had the immediacy that he craved, but not the durability. They soon became, to quote the Rolling Stones, "yesterday's papers". By 1975, John had admitted as much, remarking that his real job was poetry, not journalism. In his self-conscious effort to reach the masses, he had succeeded in reaching fewer people than ever before.

Above: John and Yoko host a press conference in New York, August 1972, prior to rehearsals for benefit shows at Madison Square Garden.

HAPPY XMAS (WAR IS OVER)

The Beatles used to make annual Christmas discs for their Fan Club, normally a cheerful package of jokes and jingles. But John hankered after something more substantial. He'd already penned a series of bespoke anthems: "All You Need Is Love", "Give Peace a Chance", and "Power to the People". That left one ambition unfulfilled.

He confessed, "I always wanted to write a Christmas record. Something that would last forever." In "Happy Xmas (War Is Over)", he succeeded. In his homeland, it would become a Yuletide family favorite—the last great populist singalong for which he was responsible.

He already had the perfect accomplice in Phil Spector, for this small, furtive figure was a past master at hanging tinsel around rock 'n' roll. In 1963, the producer had assembled his roster of hit acts, including the Ronettes, the Crystals, and more, conducting them through souped-up versions of "White Christmas", "Frosty The Snowman", and so forth. All performed in Spector's hyperbolic, teen-symphonic style, these cornball songs coalesced into one of pop's most wonderful albums, *A Christmas Gift For You*, otherwise known as *Phil Spector's Christmas Album*.

"Happy Xmas (War Is Over)" was the first of John's New York recordings, made in October 1971, his first full month as an American resident. He began by asking Spector to replicate the backing of "Try Some, Buy Some", a recent single by Phil's wife Ronnie Spector (of the Ronettes), written by George Harrison. Accounts differ, but Lennon remembered the session as a "beautiful" experience; Spector requisitioned children from the Harlem Community Choir to enhance the song's uplifting feel.

The chorus was not new. Back in December 1969, at the height of their peace campaign, John and Yoko paid for billboard posters in eleven world cities, declaring, "War Is Over! If You Want It. Happy Christmas from John & Yoko." Among the sites selected were Times Square, Piccadilly Circus, Sunset Strip, and the Champs-Elysées. The message was translated into the relevant local language, and followed up by a second poster, saying simply, "We Want It." These starkly arresting public statements were a type of performance art in themselves.

Yoko recalls her cowriting of the song with John as spontaneous and "a very intense moment… I was not used to creating songs with someone else, I think it was for him a bit easier because he had done that… John is so quick and I am so quick, so it was like a little storm, over in two minutes."

With the disaster in Southeast Asia dragging on, the couple felt their message had not lost its relevance. Most important was the "If You Want It" component, which echoes the "Imagine" theme of a future depending on our collective ability to visualize it. John would restate his belief in the "projection of goals" in his 1980 *Playboy* interview. Peace, he said, was our responsibility and could not be assigned to some outside agency: "We're just as responsible as the man who pushes the button… As long as people imagine that someone is doing something to them and that they have no control, then they have no control."

"Happy Xmas (War Is Over)" was released in the US on December 1st to a disappointing response. In Britain, the single was delayed for another year, held up by rumours of a publishing dispute over Yoko's credits. But when it did appear, it went into the Top 5, appealing to the home market's partiality to seasonal singles. The song would enjoy the same recurring popularity as two other stocking-stuffers of the period: Slade's "Merry Xmas Everybody", and Wizzard's "I Wish It Could Be Christmas Every Day". Rare indeed was the English pub jukebox that did not give all three hits an annual airing.

Above: One of the December 1969 posters—this example from New York City—that found their musical expression in 1971's "Happy Xmas" single.

HAPPY XMAS (WAR IS OVER)

Happy Christmas, Kyoko
Happy Christmas, Julian

So this is Christmas and what
have you done?
Another year over, a new one
just begun.

And so this is Christmas, I hope
you have fun,
The near and the dear one
The old and the young

A very merry Christmas
And a happy new year,
Let's hope it's a good one
Without any fear

And so this is Christmas
For weak and for strong,
(War is over if you want it)
For the rich and the poor ones,
The road is so long.
(War is over now)

And so happy Christmas for
black and for whites,
(War is over if you want it)
For the yellow and red ones,
Let's stop all the fight.
(War is over now)

A very merry Christmas
And a happy new year
Let's hope it's a good one
Without any fear

And so this is Christmas
And what have we done?
(War is over if you want it)
Another year over,
A new one just begun.
(War is over if you want it)

And so this is Christmas,
We hope you have fun
(War is over if you want it)
The near and the dear one,
The old and the young
(War is over now)

A very merry Christmas
And a Happy New Year,
Let's hope it's a good one
Without any fear

War is over
If you want it
War is over now

Happy Christmas!
Happy Christmas!
Happy Christmas!
(War is over if you want it)
The near and the dear one,
The old and the young
(War is over now)

A very merry Christmas
And a Happy New Year,
Let's hope it's a good one
Without any fear

War is over
If you want it
War is over now

WOMAN IS THE NIGGER OF THE WORLD

Once ensconced in New York City, John became even more susceptible to feminist thinking, for this town had been the crucible of Women's Liberation since the late Sixties. A fine 1972 drawing by John, "New York Woman" depicts a naked African-American female standing by Manhattan's skyscrapers, holding a plump, bald, cigar-smoking little man in the palm of her hand.

But of course, his foremost tutor in the subject was Yoko, coauthor of this song. "Woman Is the Nigger of the world", implying the universal nature of sexual inequality, was an aphorism of Yoko's, unveiled in a March 1969 profile of Yoko in the British women's magazine *Nova*. She later revealed that the idea was inspired by her first experiences with John. The Beatles, she considered, brought a new sensitivity to pop music, but in their private lives they remained four traditional Liverpool men. (John, for example, would always get to read the newspaper before she did.) For his part, John acknowledged that Yoko was the first woman he had ever met who demanded parity with him—all the more audacious given that he was a famous rock star. "But I'm King John of England!" was his attitude. Yoko, then, was the little boy who told the Emperor he was naked.

Recorded in March 1972, "Woman Is the Nigger of the World" was issued as a single, preceding the *Some Time in New York City* album. Spector and the Elephant's Memory band bestowed the song with a strong performance, distinguished yet again by some magisterial saxophone, this time by Stan Bronstein. But John felt that his lyrics did not match the power of Yoko's title. Like several of his political songs, the verses have a secondhand quality, with John merely relaying received opinions. They lack the tang of individual artistry of, say, "Strawberry Fields Forever". Nonetheless, they are vivid, and effective enough at introducing unfamiliar ideas into the mainstream.

Controversy was inevitable. A few feminist voices condemned the song for portraying women as weak and passive. Prior to John's debut of the song on Dick Cavett's TV show in May, the host apologized in advance for any offensce it might give to middle America—although, as he wryly noted afterwards, most of the eventual complaints objected to his apology rather than to the song itself. In fact, the media's chief difficulty with the single, as it turned out, was not the feminist content, but the use of that incendiary n-word. Consequently, most radio stations steered clear of the record altogether.

To John's relief, black Congressman Ron Dellums issued a statement of support: "If you define 'nigger' as someone whose lifestyle is defined by others, whose opportunities are defined by others, whose role in society is defined by others, the good news is you don't have to be black to be a nigger in this society. Most of the people in America are niggers." Be that as it may, the song's capacity to offend seems, if anything, even greater today than it was back in 1972.

Below: Backstage at Madison Square Garden, August 30th, 1972. John's two sets would be the last full concerts of his life.

WOMAN IS THE NIGGER OF THE WORLD

Woman is the nigger of the world
Yes she is... think about it
Woman is the nigger of the world
Think about it... do something about it

We make her paint her face and dance
If she won't be a slave, we say that she don't love us
If she's real, we say she's trying to be a man
While putting her down we pretend that she is above us
Woman is the nigger of the world... yes she is
If you don't believe me take a look to the one you're with
Woman is the slave of the slaves
Ah yeah... better scream about it
We make her bear and raise our children
And then we leave her flat for being a fat old mother hen
We tell her home is the only place she should be
Then we complain that she's too unworldly to be our friend
Woman is the nigger of the world...yes she is
If you don't believe me take a look to the one you're with
Woman is the slave to the slaves
Yeah (think about it)

We insult her every day on TV
And wonder why she has no guts or confidence
When she's young we kill her will to be free
While telling her not to be so smart we put her down for being so dumb
Woman is the nigger of the world... yes she is
If you don't believe me take a look to the one you're with
Woman is the slave to the slaves
Yes she is... if you believe me, you better scream about it

We make her paint her face and dance
We make her paint her face and dance
We make her paint her face and dance

ATTICA STATE

On October 9th, 1971, in a hotel in Syracuse, New York, John held a party to celebrate both his thirty-first birthday, and the local opening of Yoko's new exhibition, This Is Not Here.

The *Imagine* album had been released just twenty-four hours earlier. Revels that night included a six-hour jam session with guests such as Phil Spector, Ringo Starr, and the poet Allen Ginsberg. John used the occasion to work up a new song that commented on the recent bloodbath at the Attica Correctional Facility in upstate New York.

On September 13th, a riot had broken out in the prison after 1,200 inmates, mostly black, had taken fifty hostages and issued demands regarding conditions and terms for amnesty. The army and police went in shooting; thirty-two prisoners and ten guards were left dead as a result. John was among those who blamed the brutality of the authorities' response on state governor Nelson Rockefeller.

Though always at pains to stress that their sympathies lay with relatives of the guards as well, John and Yoko did make a surprise appearance at a benefit for the families of the dead prisoners, held at Harlem's Apollo Theater on December 17th. Aretha Franklin was among the other artists who lent their support to the event. Meanwhile, life returned to normal in Attica State. Among its future inmates, come December 1980, would be one Mark Chapman.

Above: The beat poet Allen Ginsberg, already a confidante of Bob Dylan, was an ally of John in his radical years.

What a waste of human power
What a waste of human lives
Shoot the prisoners in the towers
Forty-three poor widowed wives
Attica State, Attica State
We're all mates with Attica State

Media blames it on the prisoners
But the prisoners did not kill
Rockefeller pulled the trigger
That is what the people feel
Attica State, Attica State

We're all mates with Attica State
Free the prisoners, jail the judges
Free all prisoners everywhere
All they want is truth and justice
All they need is love and care
Attica State, Attica State
We're all mates with Attica State

They all live in suffocation
Let's not watch them die in sorrow
Now's the time for revolution
Give them all a chance to grow
Attica State, Attica State
We're all mates with Attica State

Come together, join the movement
Take a stand for human rights
Fear and hatred clouds our
judgement
Free us all from endless night
Attica State, Attica State

We're all mates with Attica State
Attica State, Attica State
We all live in Attica State
Attica State, Attica State
Attica, Attica, Attica State

NEW YORK CITY

In 1980, Lennon described "New York City" as "a bit of journalese". Virtually a sequel to 1969's "The Ballad of John And Yoko", it's a straightforward diary of his recent adventures, but delivered with a boisterous drive that testifies to the new lease of life that the Big Apple had given him.

He loved the feeling he could walk its streets unmolested, in a way that he had found wasn't possible in London. The song makes a passing reference to his problems with the immigration service, but in spite of that, "the Statue of Liberty said 'Come'!"

Among the episodes recounted are his Fillmore concert with Frank Zappa, the Attica benefit at the Apollo, and a visit to the New York rock club Max's Kansas City. There is also a description of his meeting with a local street musician, David Peel, whose favorite pitch was Washington Square Park. It was here, on the same day that he met Frank Zappa, that John stood in the crowd and heard Peel sing "The Pope Smokes Dope" in tribute to Lennon and his criminal past. (The busker's own album was entitled *Have a Marijuana.*) Encouraged by his Yippie friend Jerry Rubin, he met Peel again the next week, jamming with him in the East Village and—to the delight of John's romantic rebel heart—getting moved on by the police.

John went on to produce Peel's album, *The Pope Smokes Dope*, releasing it through Apple. Lennon, Peel, and Rubin announced they were "the Rock Liberation Front"; the FBI, preparing a dossier on John, actually pasted Peel's photo in their file by mistake.

A solid, rousing rocker, "New York City" is the best defense witness in the case of *Some Time in New York City*. Elsewhere, there are symptoms of John's lack of confidence in his new material, and it's likely Phil Spector was losing interest too. But Elephant's Memory, while by no means a versatile or subtle band, could storm superbly through a number such as this. John was attracted to their brassy sound because, most of all, it bore little resemblance to the Beatles.

Above: The Lennons dine out in New York City, 1972.

NEW YORK CITY

Standin' on the corner
Just me and Yoko Ono
We was waitin' for Jerry to land
Up come a man with a guitar in his hand
Singin' "Have a marijuana if you can"
His name was David Peel
We found that he was real
He sang "The Pope smokes dope every day"
Up come the policeman shoved us up the street
Singin' "Power to the people today"

New York City
New York City
New York City
Que pasa, New York?
Que pasa, New York?
Hey, hey

Well, down to Max's City
Put down the nitty gritty
With the Elephant's Memory Band
Played somethin' down
As the news spread around
About the Plastic Ono Elephant's Mem'ry Band
We made some funky boogie
And laid some tutti frutti
Singin' "Long Tall Sally's a man"
Up come the preacher man tryin' to be a teacher
Singin' "God's a red herring in drag"

New York City
New York City
New York City
Que pasa, New York?
Que pasa, New York?
Uh-huh

Woo-hoo-hoo

Hey, New York City
All right, New York City
New York City
Que pasa, New York?
Que pasa, New York?
Hey, hey

Well, we did the Staten Island Ferry
Makin' movies for the telly
Played the Fillmore and Apollo for freedom
Tried to shake our image
Just a-cyclin' through the Village
But found out that we had left it back in London
Well, nobody came to bug us
Hustle us or shove us
We decided to make it our home
The man wants to shove us out
We gonna jump and shout
Statue of Liberty said "Come"

New York City
New York City
New York City
Que pasa, New York?
Que pasa, New York?
Hey, hey

Ah, ah, boogie
Woo-oo-oo, oo, oo-oo
Hey, boogie, boogie

Hey, New York City
Back in New York City
Hey, New York City
Que pasa, New York?
Que pasa, New York?
Hey, City
Down in the City
Hey, New York City

Que pasa, New York?
Que pasa, New York?
Yeah, too awesome

Ah, boogie
Yeah
Que pasa, New York?
Que pasa, New York?

Yeah,
What a bad, bad city
Bad ass city
Bad ass city

Que pasa, New York?
Que pasa, New York?
Yeah, boogie, boogie
I want some boogie

SUNDAY BLOODY SUNDAY

On August 11th, 1971, in one of John's last acts as a British resident, he joined a street demonstration in London, urging the government to pull its troops out of Northern Ireland. Since 1969, there had been renewed violence in this province of the United Kingdom, bitterly divided between its "Nationalist" Catholic minority (who wanted union with the Irish Republic) and the "Loyalist" Protestant majority, fiercely committed to the British link.

Initially, troops were sent in to keep the warring factions apart, but the Catholics soon regarded them as an army of foreign occupation. Some Nationalists gave support to the newly revived Irish Republican Army (IRA).

Some six months later, on Sunday afternoon, January 30th, 1972, about 10,000 people marched in the Catholic Bogside district of Derry. Targets of their protest included the new policy of internment, or imprisonment without trial, for terrorist suspects. Fighting broke out and soldiers of the British Parachute Regiment opened fire, killing thirteen civilians. The massacre was instantly dubbed "Bloody Sunday", in reference to a day of similar bloodshed back in 1920.

Lennon, by now in New York, was outraged by the news. His radical sympathies, combined with awareness of his own Irish roots, had disposed him towards the Nationalist cause. Within days, he'd dashed off an angry song of response. Its title probably prompted by a 1971 John Schlesinger movie, *Sunday Bloody Sunday*, rails against "Anglo pigs and Scotties" (the English had encouraged Scottish Protestants to settle in Ireland) and "concentration camps", and prays that the Falls Road, the Catholic area of Belfast, be "free forever".

Even Paul McCartney, usually considered the less political of the pair, was moved to indignation. At almost the same time that John was composing "Sunday Bloody Sunday", Paul was in London recording "Give Ireland Back to the Irish", with an atypically strident lyric that invokes his own Irish ancestry, albeit tempered by a statement of his British patriotism. It would be interesting to know if they were aware of each other's efforts at the time.

John explained that he wrote songs like 'Sunday Bloody Sunday' because he wanted to state his views as simply as rock 'n' roll itself: "So now it's Awop bop a loobop, Get outta Ireland." He told his interviewer Roy Carr: "Here am I in New York and I hear about the thirteen people shot dead in Ireland, and I react immediately. And being what I am, I react in four-to-the-bar with a guitar break in the middle... It's all over now. It's gone. My songs are not there to be digested and pulled apart like the Mona Lisa. If people on the street think about it, that's all there is to it."

There is a defensive note to John's comment. His disgust at the murder of innocent people was real enough, but topical punditry was not the equal of lasting art. Nor were simplistic choruses, however heartfelt, always adequate in the face of complex historical problems. Over time, Lennon's "Sunday Bloody Sunday" has been all but forgotten—displaced, since 1983, by U2's more thoughtful song of the same name.

"SO NOW IT'S AWOP BOP A LOOBOP, GET OUTTA IRELAND."

—John Lennon

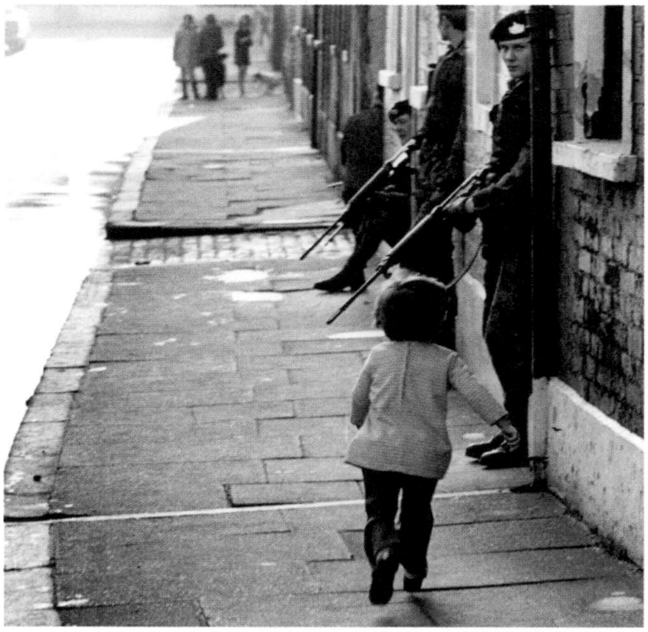

Above: A street scene from Belfast, Northern Ireland, at the height of civil unrest in 1972.

SUNDAY BLOODY SUNDAY

Well it was Sunday Bloody Sunday
When they shot the people there
The cries of thirteen martyrs
Filled the free Derry air
Is there any one among you
Dare to blame it on the kids?
Not a soldier boy was bleeding
When they nailed the coffin lids!

Sunday bloody Sunday
Bloody Sunday's the day!

You claim to be majority
Well you know that it's a lie
You're really a minority
On this sweet Emerald Isle
When Stormont bans our marchers
They've got a lot to learn
Internment is no answer
It's those mother's turn to burn!

Sunday bloody Sunday
Bloody Sunday's the day!

Sunday bloody Sunday
Bloody Sunday's the day!

You Anglo pigs and Scotties
Sent to colonize the north
You wave your bloody Union Jacks
And you know what it's worth!
How dare you hold on to ransom
A people proud and free
Keep Ireland for the Irish
Put the English back to sea!

Sunday bloody Sunday
Bloody Sunday's the day!

Sunday bloody Sunday
Bloody Sunday's the day!

Yes it's always bloody Sunday
In the concentration camps
Keep Falls and roads free forever
From the bloody English hands
Repatriate to Britain
All of you who call it home
Leave Ireland to the Irish
Not for London or for Rome!

([REPEAT] do it, do it, do it, do it)

Sunday bloody Sunday
Bloody Sunday's the day!

Sunday bloody Sunday
Bloody Sunday's the day!

Sunday bloody Sunday
Bloody Sunday's the day!

Sunday bloody Sunday
Bloody Sunday's the day!

Sunday bloody Sunday
Bloody Sunday's the day!

THE LUCK OF THE IRISH

A few days after Bloody Sunday, on February 5th, Lennon and about 5,000 others protested outside the New York offices of the now defunct British airline BOAC. John weighed in with a rendition of "The Luck of the Irish", a song he'd written the previous November.

For once, John was agreeably struck by police handling of a demo—most of those cops, he concluded, were Irish too.

In a speech to the multitudes, John stressed his own Irish heritage. Just as the song mentions Liverpool, so he explained his home town's unofficial status as "the capital of Ireland" due to the huge numbers who had emigrated there. But "the Irish question", as it was known to generations of perplexed English politicians, caused John deep misgivings. It was one thing to indulge a sentimental affinity with old-time republicanism, but quite another to endorse the new, hardline paramilitaries. In time, the Provisional IRA looked less like defenders of the ghetto and more like terrorists. Essentially a liberal pacifist, John's interest was in Civil Rights rather than armed struggle.

Alas, "The Luck of the Irish" was a poor vehicle for any viewpoint. Simplistic polemic rubs shoulders with tourist brochure clichés ("Let's walk over rainbows like leprechauns") in a lame folk song pastiche, trilled in part by Yoko, which induces more embarrassment than enlightenment.

Above: Onstage with Elephant's Memory at Madison Square Garden.

If you had the luck of the Irish
You'd be sorry and wish you were dead
You should have the luck of the Irish
And you'd wish you was English instead!

A thousand years of torture and hunger
Drove the people away from their land
A land full of beauty and wonder
Was raped by the British brigands! Goddamn!
Goddamn!

If you could keep voices like flowers
There'd be shamrock all over the world
If you could drink dreams like Irish streams
Then the world would be high as the mountain
of morn

In the 'Pool they told us the story
How the English divided the land
Of the pain, the death and the glory
And the poets of auld Eireland

If we could make chains with the morning dew
The world would be like Galway Bay
Let's walk over rainbows like leprechauns
The world would be one big Blarney stone
Why the hell are the English there anyway?

As they kill with God on their side
Blame it all on the kids the IRA
As the bastards commit genocide! Aye! Aye!
Genocide!

If you had the luck of the Irish
You'd be sorry and wish you was dead
You should have the luck of the Irish
And you'd wish you was English instead!
Yes you'd wish you was English instead!

JOHN SINCLAIR

John Sinclair was a leading light of the American Sixties counter-culture. A left-wing author and former beat poet, he was manager of the confrontational Detroit rock band MC5 and political organizer of the White Panther party, a student/hippie equivalent of the ghetto-based Black Panther movement. He liked to summarize his manifesto as "rock and roll and dope and fucking in the streets".

If the Vietnam War was a rallying point for opposition groups, then official repression of the underground lifestyle—drugs in particular—fuelled youthful dissent even further. By 1970, the worsening climate drove a section of the Woodstock generation into more committed forms of militancy. For his pains, Sinclair received a savage ten-year jail sentence for passing two marijuana joints to an undercover narcotics agent. Remembering his own marijuana conviction in England in 1968, Lennon saw John Sinclair's fate as more evidence of the establishment using the drug laws to hound its enemies.

On December 10th, 1971, John and Yoko made a guest appearance at a pro-Sinclair rally in Ann Arbor, Michigan. Among the numbers he played at the event were "The Luck Of The Irish" and, specially written for the event, "John Sinclair". To everyone's amazement, the authorities released Sinclair three days later, just twenty-seven months into his sentence. Their move was prompted by recent changes in drug legislation, but they were also aware, no doubt, that the issue was becoming a cause célèbre. Rarely, if ever, had a protest song appeared to achieve change at such dramatic speed. Free at last, Sinclair placed a call to John in New York, thanking him for his contribution.

Though it's no classic, John's song has a compelling urgency about it, and some pungent lyrics about the CIA's involvement in drug-trafficking in Asia. What the verses lack in elegance, they make up for in honest anger. The Ann Arbor concert inspired him to plan a nationwide protest tour—he hoped to get Bob Dylan on board, too—that would culminate outside the Republican Party's National Convention. It never came to pass, but the rumours did nothing to soften the administration's dislike of Lennon, and they redoubled their efforts to get him expelled.

Opposite: Radical activist John Sinclair, pictured just before his arrest in 1969. Lennon would take up his cause.

It ain't fair, John Sinclair
In the stir for breathing air
Won't you care for John Sinclair
In the stir for breathing air
Let him be
Set him free
Let him be like you and me

They gave him ten for two
What else can the judges do
You got to, got to, got to, got to, got to, got to, got to, got to, got to, got to, got to, got to, got to
Got to set him free

If he had been a soldier man
Shooting gooks in Vietnam
If he was the CIA
Selling dope and making hay
He'd be free
They'd let him be
Breathing air like you and me
Back home

They gave him ten for two
What else can the judges do
Got to, got to, got to, got to, got to,
got to, got to, got to, got to, got to,
got to, got to, got to
Got to set him free
Free

They gave him ten for two
They got Lee Otis too
They got to, got to
Got to set him free

Was he jailed for what he'd done
Representing everyone
Free John now if we can
From the clutches of the man
Let him be
Lift the lid
Bring him to his wife and kids

They gave him ten for two
What more can the bastards do
Got to, got to, got to, got to, got to, got to,
got to, got to, got to, got to, got to, got to,
got to
Got to set him free

ANGELA

Ever observant of Dylan's progress, John was impressed by Bob's return to social commentary in the form of a November 1971 single, "George Jackson". In it, Dylan laments the killing of Jackson, a Black Panther being held at San Quentin Prison on a one-year-to-life sentence for robbery.

A year earlier, some Jackson supporters had taken hostages at the Marin County Courthouse in a bid to get him freed, but the attempt failed in a fatal shootout. Another Black Panther, UCLA lecturer Angela Davis, was charged with kidnapping, conspiracy, and murder for having helped the hostage-takers. After spending a year on the run, she was captured in late 1970. But Jackson himself was shot in August 1971 following an "escape bid" which some suspected was a frameup.

John was approached by friends of the imprisoned Davis and asked to contribute a song to the campaign for her release. The resulting "Angela" is largely sung by Yoko and does not rank among the couple's best collaborations. It may, indeed, be one of their worst, on a record which offers some formidable contenders for that title. It was also completely upstaged by Mick Jagger's own Davis tribute, "Sweet Black Angel", on the Rolling Stones' epochal *Exile On Main Street* album.

The comparison is telling, because rock music was no longer led by Beatles or by ex-Beatles. It was left to their Sixties contemporaries, the Stones, to make the definitive rock album of the early Seventies. Simultaneously, the American heartland was falling for a younger British band, Led Zeppelin. Britain had found its "new Beatles" in T. Rex, while another newcomer, David Bowie, was recording his groundbreaking *The Rise and Fall of Ziggy Stardust and the Spiders from Mars.* One way or another, while John was making *Some Time in New York City*, the future was being made without him. His overtly political music had brought him very little reward, either creatively or commercially. In search of fresh inspiration, he would have to turn inward once more.

The trouble was, however, at first sight there seemed to be nothing much left in there.

Below: Angela Davis, of the Black Panther movement, whose imprisonment became the subject of another Lennon protest.

ANGELA

Angela, they put you in prison
Angela, they shot down your man
Angela, you're one of the
Millions of political prisoners in the world

Sister, there's the wind that never dies
Sister, we're breathing together
Sister, our loves and hopes forever keep
On moving oh so slowly
In the world

They gave you sunshine
They gave you sea
They gave you everything but
The jailhouse key
They gave you coffee
They gave you tea
They gave you everything
But equality

Angela, can you hear the earth is turning?
Angela, the world watches you
Angela, you soon will be
Returning to your sisters and
Brothers of the world

Sister, you're still a people teacher
Sister, your word reaches far
Sister, there's a million
Different races but we all
Share the same future
In the world

They gave you sunshine
They gave you sea
They gave you everything but
The jailhouse key
They gave you coffee
They gave you tea
They gave you everything
But equality

Angela, they put you in prison
Angela, they shot down your man
Angela, you're one of the millions of political prisoners in the world

Chapter 5

MIND

19 73

GAMES

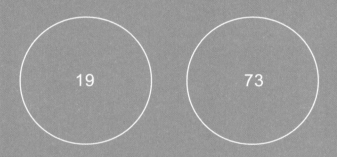

"Mind Games"
"Tight A$"
"Aisumasen (I'm Sorry)"
"One Day (at a Time)"
"Bring on the Lucie (Freda Peeple)"
"Nutopian International Anthem"
"Intuition"
"Out the Blue"
"Only People"
"I Know (I Know)"
"You Are Here"
"Meat City"

Recorded
July/August 1973 at Record Plant, New York City.

Produced by
John Lennon.

Musicians
John Lennon (vocals, guitars, clavinet, percussion), David Spinozza (guitar), Ken Ascher (piano, organ, Mellotron), Jim Keltner (drums), Rick Marotta (drums), Gordon Edwards (bass), Arthur Jenkins (percussion), Sneaky Pete Kleinow (pedal steel guitar), Michael Brecker (saxophone), Something Different Choir (backing vocals).

The story of Lennon's Seventies is, in retrospect, strewn with fateful landmarks. On August 30th, 1972, for example, when he played two shows with Elephant's Memory at Madison Square Garden, he was performing what turned out to be the last full concerts of his life.

"HIS SONGS WERE INCREDIBLE BUT HIS POSITION AS THE 'TOP POP STAR' WAS GOING DOWN THE DRAIN."

—Yoko Ono

Happily they were good ones, raising funds for the handicapped children's charity One To One. Such a public-spirited gesture may have been John's way of improving his image in the eyes of officialdom. At the same time, however, the paramilitary duds he wore on stage were a reminder that he was still a fighter of sorts, and not the beatific peacenik of former years.

Meanwhile, in his war with the US immigration service, John won testimonials from many Americans: just a few include Norman Mailer, Fred Astaire, Kurt Vonnegut, and Tony Curtis. *The New York Post* said, "He has improved this town just by showing up." The deportation hearings even got a handwritten letter from Bob Dylan: "John and Yoko add a great voice and drive to this country's so-called ART INSTITUTION. They inspire and transcend and stimulate and by doing so, only help others to see pure light and in doing that, put an end to this mild dull taste of petty commercialism which is being passed off as artist art by the overpowering mass media. Hurray for John and Yoko. Let them stay and live here and breathe."

John's own view was sardonic: "It keeps the conservatives happy that they're doing something about me, and what I represent. And it keeps the liberals happy, because I haven't actually been thrown out. So everybody's happy." His prospects were briefly improved when news arrived from England of the arrest of Scotland Yard's Sergeant Pilcher. The man responsible for John's 1968 marijuana bust was now on trial himself, charged with "conspiracy to pervert the course of justice", casting doubt on the validity of John's original conviction.

Whether it was mere expediency or some deeper shift in his thinking, Lennon now presented a more acceptable face to the authorities by suddenly dumping a lot of his radical baggage. On the advice of his lawyers, plans were abandoned for the nationwide antiwar tour. The protest songs tailed off. He grew tired of his Yippie allies; having secured a slot for them on *The Mike Douglas Show*, he was appalled that "none of them knew how to talk to the people, let alone lead them". Characters like Rubin, Hoffman, and David Peel dropped out of the picture. Peel has since talked of the Cinderella effect felt by the friends of celebrities. In their company, you are a kind of prince, made radiant by the reflected fame. But when midnight arrives, your limousine becomes a pumpkin. You're alone once more and back in your rags.

The wider climate was changing, too. By 1973, the Sixties' Woodstock Nation was a faded dream, and the "Me Decade" was beginning to kick in, alongside a global recession. Furthermore, Lennon's old nemesis Richard Nixon was on the ropes. On June 27th, John traveled to Washington to watch the Watergate hearings. On the same visit, he joined a demonstration outside the South Vietnamese embassy, but even the war would soon subside, taking with it the chief rallying point for dissenters.

There was symbolism, too, in his April 1973 move to the Dakota Building on 72nd Street. He'd forsaken funky downtown Greenwich Village for an uptown celebrity bolt-hole. The Dakota, which has been Yoko's home ever since, was a luxury apartment block, built in 1888, whose gothic gauntness made it the setting for *Rosemary's Baby*. From John's new windows, he could overlook the lushness of Central Park—modelled, as it happened, on a humbler Victorian expanse back on his native Merseyside.

Another change was in the air. There were rumours of a rift between John and Yoko. While he idled away his time, she was much busier, releasing her *Approximately Infinite Universe* album to better reviews (though inevitably even poorer sales) than *Some Time in New York City*. Perhaps they really did work better apart.

When John eventually roused himself to make another album as his contract demanded, he seemed dispirited. Early in 1973, a DJ asked him how the new music was shaping up. "It's getting to be work," came his slack response. "It's ruining the music. It's like after you leave school and you don't want to read a book. Every time I strap the guitar on, it's the same old jazz. I just feel like breathing a bit."

Sessions began in August at New York's Record Plant, with John producing. His chosen guitarist was a local session ace, David Spinozza, who had played on McCartney's hated *Ram* album two years earlier. (His co-player on that record, Hugh McCracken, would later become John's guitarist on *Double Fantasy*.)

Released in October, *Mind Games* was an often flaccid album whose chief claim to popularity was that it wasn't *Some Time in New York City*. He'd successfully shrugged off the ranting image, but his private life was unravelling and the strain of his constant fight against deportation was beginning to wear him down.

Embarrassingly for John, *Mind Games* was outpaced in the charts by Ringo's new album, released the same day. Even worse, he was thoroughly eclipsed a month later when Paul McCartney hit peak solo form with his Number 1 success *Band on the Run*. Called upon to promote his record, John could not muster much enthusiasm: "It's just an album," he shrugged. "It's rock 'n' roll at different speeds. There's no very deep message about it. The only reason I make albums is because you're supposed to."

By now it was Yoko that seemed the more focused recording artist. Far from an afterthought, her next album was actually made just before *Mind Games*, and John used much the same personnel. In June, she recalls, the pair had performed for a feminist conference in Cambridge, Massachusetts, and found it exciting. "So, in that sort of mood, John was saying, you should be able to go and do your album, without me hovering over you. I did *Feeling The Space*... But *Mind Games*, I was so disappointed that it didn't make a splash. But you see by then, after *Imagine*, and *Some Time in New York City*—oh my God!—I just felt terribly responsible about our partnership. His songs were incredible, but his position as the 'top pop star' or whatever was going down the drain in a way."

Observe the vinyl version of *Mind Games*' artwork and there is an interesting quirk. Against Bob Gruen's photo of Yoko as a mountain range, a blurred Lennon steps across the plain. On the reverse he is larger and closer. According to John's new friend May Pang, he described this as himself "walking away from Yoko". By the time of the record's release, he and his wife were living on opposite coasts of the United States.

Below: At work on *Mind Games* in New York's Record Plant: "It's rock 'n' roll at different speeds."

MIND GAMES

The older John became, the more he turned to books for the information that his hungry mind required. Janov's *The Primal Scream*, indeed, had sparked off the enthusiasm that produced an entire album of material.

The *Mind Games* title track was itself named after a book, this time a psychological tract by Robert Masters and Jean Houston that tapped into the post-hippie theme of consciousness raising. After the relative harshness of the *Some Time in New York City* songs, "Mind Games" reflected a more meditative Lennon, guitars overdubbed into a quasi-orchestral lushness that marked a partial return to *Imagine* territory. We're back on familiar ground as John prescribes a global projection of the power of love.

While "Mind Games" proved to be one of the more popular late-Lennon compositions, it's arguable that the song would have been even greater had John stuck to his first idea and called it "Make Love, Not War". This was its original chorus, and there is a tantalising remnant at the song's fade, where John sings, "I want you to make love, not war", in place of the "Mind games forever" refrain. He'd abandoned the plan, feeling that by 1973 the slogan's hour had passed, and that people would now regard it as a cliché ("I know you've heard it before," he adds at the very end). But, cliché or not, "make love not war" might have had more lasting impact. It certainly carries more emotive weight than the dated psycho-jargon of its replacement.

"Mind Games", then, is the anthem that never was. Still, it contains some enjoyable imagery, notably the "druid dudes" and "mind guerrillas" exercising their cosmic powers in mankind's quest for enlightenment. The song's chief significance lies in its mystical atmosphere—an abrupt signal of John's loss of interest in orthodox political agendas.

He liked to say that its middle-eight section ("Love is the answer...") was reggae-derived, though neither he nor his musicians were used to the style at that time.

"I WANT YOU TO MAKE LOVE, NOT WAR. I KNOW YOU'VE HEARD IT BEFORE."

—John Lennon

Above: In 1973, John was showing signs of fatigue in both his creative and personal life.

MIND GAMES

We're playing those mind games together
Pushing the barriers planting seeds
Playing the mind guerrilla
Chanting the Mantra peace on earth

We all been playing those mind games forever
Some kinda druid dudes lifting the veil
Doing the mind guerrilla
Some call it magic the search for the grail

Love is the answer and you know that for sure
Love is a flower
You got to let it, you gotta let it grow

So keep on playing those mind games together
Faith in the future out of the now
You just can't beat on those mind guerrillas

Absolute elsewhere in the stones of your mind
Yeah we're playing those mind games forever
Projecting our images in space and in time
Yes is the answer and you know that for sure
Yes is surrender
You got to let it, you gotta let it go

So keep on playing those mind games together
Doing the ritual dance in the sun
Millions of mind guerrillas
Putting their soul power to the karmic wheel

Keep on playing those mind games forever
Raising the spirit of peace and love
Love

I want you to make love, not war
I know you've heard it before

TIGHT A$

The second song was worrying evidence that everything John had left to say—and it was little enough—he'd already said on the opening track.

All the musicianly talent assembled could not disguise the slightness of "Tight A$", although "Sneaky" Pete Kleinow, of Gram Parsons' Flying Burrito Brothers, contributes some scintillating pedal-steel guitar. Essentially, the song was John's tribute to New York's hard-living, hard-playing ethos, but the city's energy is hardly captured here. The fact was that John's inner exhaustion was beginning to tell. He was falling back on his old facility for puns, and knocking off songs to fulfill the album's quota rather than for their own sake.

Above: Pedal steel guitarist Sneaky Pete Kleinov adds some of *Mind Games*' best instrumental moments.

Just as tight a$ you can make it
Hard and slow ain't hard enough
Just as tight a$ you can shake it girl
Git it on and do your stuff
Tight a$ you can get it
Tight a$ got it made
Uptight's alright but if ya can't stand the heat
You better get back in the shade

Well, just as tight a$ an Indian rope trick
Long and tough ain't hard enough
Just as tight a$ a dope fiend's fix my friend
Git it up and do your stuff

Tight a$ you can boogie
Tight a$ got it made
Uptight's alright but if ya can't stand the heat
you better get back in the shade
Well, alright

Alright, hooo, oohoo
Well, tight a$ you can make it
Hard and slow ain't hard enough
Just as tight a$ you can shake it girl
Git it on and do your stuff
Tight a$ you can get it
Tight a$ got it made
Uptight's alright but if ya can't stand the heat
You better get back in the shade

Well, tight a$ an Indian rope trick
Hard along ain't hard enough
Just as tight a$ a dope fiend's fix my friend
Git it up and do your stuff

Tight a$ you can boogie
Tight a$ got it made
Uptight's alright but if ya can't stand the heat
you better get back in the shade
Well

Well, tight a$ got me cornered
Tight a$ got me laid
Tight a$ strut your stuff so tough, girl
Just a sittin'in the midnight shade
Tight a$ she can do it
Tight a$ she got laid

Uptight's alright but if ya can't stand the heat
you better get back in the shade
Uptight's alright but if ya can't stand the heat
Well you better get back in the shade
Oh, woo, oh yeah..

AISUMASEN (I'M SORRY)

John had been toying with this tune since 1971, when its working title was "Call My Name". In its finished form, however, it is John who is calling Yoko's name, thus inverting his role from comforter to supplicant.

This meekly submissive tone would soon become a staple feature of his songwriting, with numerous examples to follow. It's extremely revealing that one of the few fragments of Japanese that John had so far mastered was "Aisumasen"—"I'm sorry". It's unknown whether he was apologizing for any specific incident, but a favorite candidate must be the US election night of November 7th, 1972, when John, Yoko, and a group of their radical friends watched the TV in dismay as Richard Nixon chalked up a landslide victory over his Democratic opponent George McGovern. Political disillusionment hit John hard that evening; hopes of an end to his visa problems took a knock as well. Worst of all, however, it was rumoured that John had humiliated Yoko by openly seducing another woman at the party.

Whatever the exact origins of "Aisumasen", its weak tone compares unfavorably with "Jealous Guy", and did much to cement the image of Yoko as John's domineering dragon lady in the public mind.

When I'm down, really yin
And I don't know what I'm doing
Aisumasen, aisumasen Yoko
All I had to do was call your name
All I had to do was call your name

And when I hurt you and cause you pain
Darling I promise I won't do it again
Aisumasen, aisumasen Yoko
It's hard enough I know just to feel your own pain
It's hard enough I know to feel, feel your own pain

All that I know is just what you tell me
All that I know is just what you show me

When I'm down real sanpaku
And I don't know what to do
Aisumasen, aisumasen Yoko san
All I had to do was call your name
Yes, all I had to do was call your name

ONE DAY (AT A TIME)

In the vacuum caused by John's loss of political faith, the nature of his partnership with Yoko assumes center stage in *Mind Games*.

The duality of their relationship is captured at the outset of this song when John describes her as being both his weakness and his strength.

Unfortunately, perhaps, it is the element of weakness which seems to predominate here. The very title, borrowed from the language of recovering alcoholics, betrays an unhealthy streak of dependency on Lennon's part, with little indication that the condition might be mutual. "Mrs Lennon" was tired of her passive public role. On the next album, *Walls and Bridges*, the full extent of John's predicament would be made apparent.

The arrangement, too, with its echoes of old-fashioned Tin Pan Alley hackery, reminds us that John was not above the facile, lightweight style that he used to scorn in Paul McCartney's songs. The track captures Lennon in a rare period of aimlessness.

You are my weakness, you are my strength
Nothing I have in the world makes better sense
Cause I'm the fish and you're the sea
When we're together or when we're apart
There's never a space in between the beat of our hearts
Cause I'm the apple and you're the tree

One day at a time is all we do
One day at a time is good for you
You, yeah, you, yeah, you, yeah, ooh

You are my woman, I am your man
Nothing else matters at all, now I understand
That I'm the door and you're the key
And every morning I wake in your smile
Feeling your breath on my face and the love in your eyes
Cause you're the honey and I'm the bee

One day at a time is all we do-be-doo-be-doo
One day at a time is good for
You
Us two
You too
Oh-oh
Do do do do
Do do do do
Do do do do do do
Do do do do
'Cause I'm the fish and you're the sea
'Cause I'm the apple and you're the tree
'Cause I'm the door and you're the key
'Cause I'm a honey and you're the bee

BRING ON THE LUCIE (FREDA PEEPLE)

John recovered some of his rock 'n' roll bite, as well as radical indignation, on this stomping condemnation of the Nixon administration, who stand accused of warmongering abroad and corruption at home.

Only a passing jibe that the enemy's name is "666"—the Biblical code for the Antichrist, and Lennon's nickname for Nixon—marks it as a *Mind Games* song instead of one from its predecessor. As John put it later, "It was Bell, Book, and Candle against Mr 666 Nixon. We used magic, prayer, and children to fight the good fight." There is more punning in the song title, and a reassuring flash of Lennon wit in the track's intro, when he urges his band "over the hill", in the manner of a war-movie sergeant to his platoon. Once again, though, thanks are due to "Sneaky" Pete's keening pedal steel, and to Jim Keltner's galumphing drums, for hauling John's track above the mediocre.

[SPOKEN] Alright, boys, this is it, over the hill!

We don't care what flag you're waving,
We don't even want to know your name.
We don't care where you're from or where you're going,
All we know it that you came.
You're making all our decisions,
We have just one request of you,
That while you're thinking things over,
Here's something you just better do.

Free the people now, (do it, do it, do it, do it)
Do it, do it, do it, do it, do it now.
(Do it, do it, do it, do it)
Free the people now, (do it, do it, do it, do it)
Do it, do it, do it, do it, do it now.

Well, we were caught with our hands in the air,
Don't despair, paranoia's ev'rywhere.
We can shake it with love when we're scared,
So let's shout it aloud like a prayer.

Free the people now, (do it, do it, do it, do it)
Do it, do it, do it, do it, do it now.
(Do it, do it, do it, do it)
Free the people now, (do it, do it, do it, do it)
Do it, do it, do it, do it, do it now.

We understand your paranoia,
But we don't wanna play your game.
You think you're cool and know what you're doing,
666 is your name.

So while you jerking off each other,
You better bear this in mind;
Your time is up, you better know it,
But maybe you don't read the signs.
Free the people now, (do it, do it, do it, do it)
Do it, do it, do it, do it, do it (do it) now.
(Do it, do it, do it, do it)
Free the people now, (do it, do it, do it, do it)
Do it, do it, do it, do it, do it now.

Well, you were caught with your hands in the kill,
And you still gotta swallow your pill,
As you slip and you slide down the hill
On the blood of the people you killed.

Stop the killing!
(Free the people now) (do it, do it)
Do! (do it, do it, do it, do it, do it now)
(Do it, do it, do it)
Stop the killing!
(Free the people now) (do it, do it, do it, do it)
Do it, do it, do it, do it, do it now.
(Do it, do it, do it, do it)

Stop the killing!
(Free the people now) (do it, do it, do it, do it)
(Do it, do it, do it, do it, do it now)
(Do it, do it, do it, do it)
Stop the killing!
(Free the people now) (do it, do it, do it, do it)
(Do it, do it) do it, do it, do it.
Bring on the lucie!
(Free the people now) (do it, do it, do it)

NUTOPIAN INTERNATIONAL ANTHEM

On April 1st, 1973—April Fools' Day—John and Yoko called a press conference at which they were expected to discuss their deportation fight. To widespread bemusement, however, they chose the occasion to unveil nothing less than a new nation.

This "Declaration of Nutopia" appears on the *Mind Games* album sleeve: "We announce the birth of a conceptual country, NUTOPIA. Citizenship of the country can be obtained by declaration of your awareness of NUTOPIA. NUTOPIA has no land, no boundaries, no passports, only people. NUTOPIA has no laws other than cosmic. All people of NUTOPIA are ambassadors of the country. As two ambassadors of NUTOPIA, we ask for diplomatic immunity and recognition in the United Nations of our country and its people."

The original *Utopia* was a book published in 1516 by Sir Thomas More, an English chancellor beheaded by King Henry VIII for remaining loyal to the Pope. Just as More attacked inequitable social and economic conditions, and described an imaginary, ideal commonwealth based on reason, so John Lennon's "new Utopia" represented a fantasy world, like that of "Imagine", where our freedoms are not confined by national divisions. Given his immigration problems, John's satirical intentions were obvious. Nevertheless, his lawyers felt it best to carry on contesting the case through the courts.

It really comes as no surprise that John's "Nutopian International Anthem" turns out to be a few seconds of complete silence. The name of Sir Thomas More's imaginary happy land came from ancient Greek, meaning "Nowhere". In asserting his Nutopian citizenship, therefore, John at last became "a real Nowhere Man".

Having failed to seize the public imagination to even the smallest degree, "Nutopia" was never heard of again, while Lennon himself was forced to continue wondering where he would be living in a few months' time. The uncertainty was just one more destabilizing factor at work in his life.

Above: John and Yoko announce the birth of "Nutopia" on April Fools' Day, 1973.

INTUITION

In a figure less likeable than Lennon, "Intuition" would indeed be a very annoying song. Set to a cloying, bouncy melody, it's a number that catches John on a good day, celebrating his supposed talent for making the best of life and—just a little smugly—implying we could all do worse than to follow his example.

John may well have been right to trust his instincts—they may not be rational, he implies, but they have a wisdom of their own—but his better songs acknowledged the darkness and the turbulence of his inner life, as this disposable ditty so lamentably fails to do. As a skip-along lilt, it's poor. As a recipe for psychic sunshine, it's a case of "the blind leading the blind".

Hey, hey, hey, alright
Hey, hey, hey, alright

My intentions are good
I use my intuition, it takes me for a ride
But I never understood
Other people's superstitions
It seemed like suicide

As I play the game of life
I try to make it better each and every day
And when I struggle in the night
The magic of the music seems to light the way

Intuition takes me there
Intuition takes me everywhere

Well, my instincts are fine
I had to learn to use them in order to survive
And time after time confirmed an old suspicion
It's good to be alive

And when I'm deep down and out
And lose communication
With nothing left to say
It's then I realize it's only a condition
Of seeing things that way

Intuition takes me there
Intuition takes me anywhere
It takes me anywhere, alright

Intuition takes me there
Intuition takes me there
Intuition takes me there
Intuition takes me there
Intuition takes me there
Intuition takes me there

OUT THE BLUE

One of John's many songs of devotion to Yoko, "Out the Blue" boasts a heavenly choir in the background, but otherwise confines itself to a modest statement of gratitude.

John expresses a sense of wonder at Yoko's unforeseen arrival in his life, "out [of] the blue". Years later, he described his recurrent yearning for a fantasy soulmate: "Someone that I had already known, but somehow had lost." At first he pictured this ideal woman as dark-haired, with high cheekbones, a "free-spirited artist" in the style of French actress Juliette Greco. In time, his allegiance switched to Brigitte Bardot (he even persuaded his first wife Cynthia to imitate the blonde goddess's look). But in Yoko, John felt he'd finally found the embodiment of his original vision. For all her virtues, Cynthia was a conventional choice of wife for John, whereas her successor—an assertive, avant-garde Japanese artist—was the partner that people least expected. She came, in all her strangeness, "like a UFO". Out of the blue.

Above: The French star Juliette Greco had represented a feminine ideal for the young John Lennon.

Out the blue you came to me
And blew away life's misery
Out the blue life's energy
Out the blue you came to me

Every day I thank the Lord and Lady
For the way that you came to me
Anyway it had to be two minds
One destiny

Out the blue you came to me
And blew away life's misery
Out the blue life's energy
Out the blue you came to me

All my life's been a long slow knife
I was born just to get to you
Anyway I survived long enough
To make you my wife

Out the blue you came to me
And blew away life's misery
Out the blue life's energy
Out the blue you came to me

Like a U.F.O. you came to me
And blew away life's misery
Out the blue life's energy
Out the blue you came to me

ONLY PEOPLE

The germ of this jolly, inconsequential rocker lies in Yoko Ono's pronouncement, quoted on the album sleeve, that "Only people can change the world."

Lennon couples it with a less portentous aphorism of his own: "Madness is the first sign of dandruff." One wonders if the latter line might have made a better song. As it stands, "Only People" revisits the general thought behind "Instant Karma!"—namely our collective potential for shaping the future—but without that song's joyful confidence. It's questionable whether John was repeating his theme because he believed in mantra-like repetition, or because he was running out of fresh ideas. Various forces were at work, in that summer of 1973, to hasten Nixon's downfall—he finally resigned one year later—but a crowd in New York's Record Plant, chanting, "We don't want no pig brother scene!" was probably not among them.

Let's go

Only people know just how to talk to people

Only people know just how to change the world
Only people realize the power of people
Well, a million heads are better than one
So come on, get it on

Well I know how we tried, the millions of tears that we cried
Now we are hipper we been through the trip
And we can't be denied with woman and man side by side

Make no mistake it's our future we're making
Bake the cake and eat it too
We don't want no big brother scene

Only people know just how to talk to people
Only people know just how to change the world
Only people realize the power of people
Well, a million heads are better than one
So come on, get it on

We'll it's long overdue, there ain't nothing better to do
Now we are hipper we been through the trip
We can fly right on through, there's nothing on earth
we can't do

We'll it's long overdue, there ain't nothing better to do
Now we are hipper we been through the trip
We can fly right on through, there's nothing on earth
we can't do

Fish or cut bait it's our future we're making
All together now pull the chain
We don't want no big brother scene

Only people know just how to talk to people
Only people know just how to change the world
Only people know just how to talk to people
Only people know just how to change the world

Only people know just how to talk to people
Only people know just how to change the world
Only people know just how to talk to people
Only people know just how to change the world

I KNOW (I KNOW)

With a finger-picked guitar pattern reminiscent of the Beatles, 'I Know (I Know)' is one of John's stronger ballads in this set, although its lyric plows what was rapidly becoming a familiar furrow.

Once more, then, he professes his loyalty to Yoko, while also pausing to apologize for his unworthiness. But the evidence is that his wife remained unmoved. Before the record had even appeared in the shops, John was already living apart from Yoko—apparently at her request.

Above: John and May Pang attend the Los Angeles premiere of *The Rocky Horror Show* in March 1974.

The years have passed so quickly
One thing I've understood
I am only learning
To tell the trees from wood

I know what's coming down
And I know where it's coming from
And I know and I'm sorry (yes I am)
But I never could speak my mind

And I know just how you feel
And I know now what I have done
And I know and I'm guilty
But I never could speak my mind

I know what I was missing
But now my eyes can see
I put myself in your place
As you did for me

Today I love you more than yesterday
Right now I love you more right now

Now I know what's coming down
I can feel where it's coming from
And I know it's getting better all the time
As we share in each other's minds

Today, I love you more than yesterday
Right now, I love you more right now

Ooo, no more crying
Ooo, no more crying
Ooo, no more crying
Ooo, no more crying

YOU ARE HERE

John presents his romance with Yoko in a global light, portraying their relationship as the union of Liverpool and Tokyo, or a symbolic marriage of the hemispheres. In the final verse, he contradicts a quotation from the English poet Rudyard Kipling, "East is East and West is West and never the twain shall meet."

Prejudice against foreigners such as Yoko helped to turn John against his homeland, and to seek sanctuary in the more cosmopolitan world of New York City. "It was humiliating and painful for both of us," he recalled. "I was ashamed of Britain."

The title for "You Are Here" came from a "conceptual" exhibition that John staged in London in 1968. The centerpiece of *You Are Here* was a circular white screen, on which he'd written those three words for anyone who cared to inspect them. He then released 365 helium balloons from the event, with reply cards attached, to be found by random members of the British public. Of more than a hunded cards returned, John was dismayed to find that many expressed contempt for his recent eccentricities and his new Japanese girlfriend. He took a morbid fascination in the racist hate-mail he received, and even considered getting it published. He also thought of asking advice from London musicians Johnny Dankworth and Cleo Laine, who were themselves a mixed-race couple. Residual anti-Japanese feeling was an unfortunate feature of postwar Britain, and remarkable in that it exceeded any lingering hostility towards the Germans.

The issue of interracial marriage was clearly important to John, but his strong feelings did not inspire a vivid song in "You Are Here". Its imagery is hackneyed ("Three thousand light years from the land of the rising sun"), while the musical exotica is trite—it would be a few more years until John began listening seriously to Japanese music, and he never got the chance to make meaningful use of it in his own work. Strangely, the track begins with John grunting "Nine". The number was of peculiar significance to him, as we shall see.

"I WANT TO TAKE A ROCK BAND TO CHINA. THEY HAVE YET TO SEE THAT."

—John Lennon

From Liverpool to Tokyo
What a way to go
From distant lands one
woman one man
Let the four winds blow

Three thousand miles
over the ocean
Three thousand light years
from the land of the rising
sun

Love has opened up my eyes
Love has blown right through
Wherever you are, you
are here
Wherever you are, you
are here

Three thousand miles
over the ocean
Three thousand light years
from the land of
the surprising sun

Well now east is east and
west is west
The twain shall meet
East is west and west is east
Let it be complete

Three thousand miles over
the ocean
Three thousand light years
from the land of the
morning star, ooh-ho

MEAT CITY

Much as he railed against its politicians, John was deeply excited by America—after all, it was the birthplace of his beloved rock 'n' roll—and "Meat City" captures that excitement wonderfully. The song began to take shape almost as soon as he arrived to live in New York City.

At first it was a boogie called "Shoeshine", but this grew from a simple celebration of the music into a powerful account of his pilgrimage: "I been to the mountain to see for myself." He may be appalled or bewildered by some of the sights that greet him in the madness of the city, but he exults in its vitality. In John's mind, his early infatuation with Elvis Presley and Chuck Berry was a prelude to his life. America was where he should have been born, and the land where he was destined to live.

Then he turns his thoughts to China, a land as far away and otherworldly as America itself had once seemed. John saw China as the next frontier. "I shall go there," he declared in 1972. "I will take the opportunity to try to see Mao. If he is ill or dead or refuses to see me, too bad. But if I go there I want to meet people who are doing something important. I want to take a rock band to China. That is really what I want to do. To play rock in China. They have yet to see that." In the low-key travels of his final years, John did get to visit Hong Kong—but China's communist mainland remained off-limits to the average rock 'n' roll tour.

The title of the song may have come to John from a popular cartoon poster of the time, showing a mother pig and her offspring, chatting complacently while they're trucked towards their fatal destination—"Meat City". The porcine theme is underscored by shouts of "Pig meat city" and, reportedly, by a backwards message: the inverted vocal interlude has been deciphered as "Fuck a pig".

The last track on the *Mind Games* album, "Meat City" presents a satisfying counterpoint to the opening number—earthy and physical where the title track is ethereal and contemplative. These two extremes would continue doing battle inside John Lennon's life and work. But, for the next few years, it would be his "Meat City" side that emerged on top—with almost catastrophic consequences.

Well Hell
I been Meat City to see for myself
Well, I been Meat City to see for myself
Been Meat City, been Meat
Just gotta give me some rock 'n roll

People were dancin' like there's no
tomorrow, Meat City
Finger lickin', chicken pickin' Meat
City, Shookdown U.S.A.

Well, I been the mountain to see for myself
Well, I been the mountain to see for myself
Been the mountain, been the
Just gotta give me some rock 'n roll

Snake doctors shakin' like there's no
tomorrow, Freak City
Chicken suckin', mother truckin'
Meat City, Shookdown U.S.A.
(Pig Meat City)

Well, I'm gonna China to see for myself
Well, I'm gonna China to see for myself
Gonna China gonna
Just gotta give me some rock 'n' roll
(Whoa)

People were jumpin' like there's no
tomorrow, Meat City
Finger lickin', chicken pickin'
Meat City, Shookdown U.S.A.
(Pig Meat City)

Well, I'm gonna China
Yes, I'm gonna China
Well, I'm gonna China
Well, I'm gonna China, come one
Whoa, whoa-whoa-whoa
Yeah, yeah, come on
I'm gonna China, go, go, go
Well, I'm gonna China
Alright
Hold it, yes
Who is that? Who is that?
Who is that?
And why are they doin' those strange (What?) things?

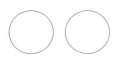

Above left: China's communist leader, Mao Tse-Tung, in 1967. John's plan to meet him never materialized.

Chapter 6

WALLS

19 74

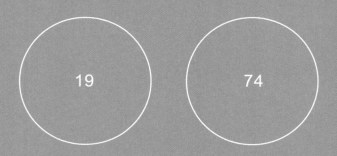

AND BRIDGES

"Going Down on Love"
"Whatever Gets You Thru the Night"
"Old Dirt Road"
"What You Got"
"Bless You"
"Scared"
"#9 Dream"
"Surprise Surprise (Sweet Bird of Paradox)"
"Steel and Glass"
"Beef Jerky"
"Nobody Loves You (When You're Down and Out)"

Recorded
July/August 1974 at Record Plant, New York City.

Produced by
John Lennon.

Musicians
John Lennon (vocals, guitar, piano, whistling and percussion), Jesse Ed Davis (guitar), Jim Keltner (drums), Ken Ascher (electric piano, clavinet, Mellotron), Arthur Jenkins (percussion), Klaus Voormann (bass), Nicky Hopkins (piano), Bobby Keys (saxophone), Eddie Mottau (acoustic guitar); strings and brass musicians from the New York Philharmonic Orchestra; Little Big Horns: Bobby Keys, Steve Madaio, Howard Johnson, Ron Apra, Frank Vicari (brass). Special guests Julian Lennon (drums on "Ya Ya"); Elton John (piano and harmony vocals on "Whatever Gets You Thru The Night" and Hammond organ and background vocals on "Surprise, Surprise (Sweet Bird of Paradox)"; Harry Nilsson (backing vocals on "Old Dirt Road"); Joey Dambra, Lori Burton and May Pang (backing vocals).

In 1973, John went haywire. As he later put it to BBC interviewer Andy Peebles, "The feminist side of me died slightly." May Pang was a New York-Chinese girl who had worked for the Lennons and their manager Allen Klein since 1969. When John and Yoko moved into the Dakota Building, May became their in-house assistant and, at Yoko's instigation (according to May Pang's account), began an affair with him.

So commenced the most bizarre interlude in Lennon's extraordinary life, the legendary "lost weekend".

Yoko promotes the view that she banished John from the Dakota in order to confront his demons, to return only when she deemed him ready. "She don't suffer fools gladly," said John in 1980, "even if she's married to him." Tiring of him, and of her role as "Mrs. Lennon", Yoko was ready to assert herself. For his own part, John seemed keen to escape. He quickly fell for May, and the pair soon hit Los Angeles like eloping runaways, staying at a variety of addresses.

Whatever its cause, this lost weekend was an almighty bender, a fifteen-month rampage. Suddenly off the leash, John was a born-again Rock Pig, running free across LA on a binge of drink and general boorishness. In later years, reunited with Yoko, he was careful not to call it a period of liberation. In fact, his 1980 view was, "I was like an elephant in a zoo, aware that it's trapped but not able to get out." Though in exile, he would still make or receive up to twenty calls a day to and from Yoko at the Dakota.

May Pang was undoubtedly a comfort to him, but he also needed a new sort of stability—something to restore his artistic focus and give him direction. Instead, what he got was Phil Spector and a gang of good ol' boys that starred Keith Moon, Harry Nilsson, and Ringo Starr. It was Brandy Alexanders all round.

Spector and Lennon concocted a plan for an album of rock 'n' roll cover versions, which would reinvigorate John with a blast of back-to-basics Fifties fundamentalism. Spector would once again be his savior. Furthermore, the project had a second advantage. John had just been accused of plagiarism by an opportunist music publisher called Morris Levy—a veteran Tin Pan Alley hustler who had once attempted to copyright the term "rock 'n' roll" itself. Levy owned Chuck Berry's song "You Can't Catch Me", briefly pastiched on "Come Together" from the Beatles' *Abbey Road.* To forestall a lawsuit, John promised to record three other Levy copyrights on his next LP.

But the October *Rock 'n' Roll* sessions at A&M's LA studios were an all-star nightmare of drunken disorganisation, punctuated by the odd gunshot. Deafened by his pistol-toting producer's pranks, John said, "Phil, if you're going to kill me, kill me. But don't fuck with my ears. I need 'em." Spector was gifted at orchestrating sonic excess, but these recordings were a mess. Scores of eminent players such as Leon Russell, Dr. John, and Charlie Watts were hired, playing their parts over and over. But the chaotic self-indulgence and chronic indecision proved too much. Evicted from A&M, the team decamped to Record Plant West with scarcely improved results. Then Spector disappeared with the tapes, and the whole unhappy project was shelved. To compound John's misery, *Mind Games* went on sale soon after to universal apathy.

In Yoko's opinion, the LA tapes suggested "a lot of fun, and a lot of commotion! He and Phil Spector did not always get along

Above: Allen Klein, the presumed object of John's acrimonious "Steel And Glass".

Opposite: May Pang and John at the opening of a *Sgt. Pepper*-inspired musical in New York, November 1974.

"IT WAS REALLY SAD, BECAUSE I MISSED HIM AND HE MISSED ME."

—Yoko Ono

about it. He wasn't feeling too happy, obviously. So, I was called by somebody in LA, a music industry person: 'Come and pick him up, please!' No, *you* just take care of him… When I was with him, everyone thought I was being extremely possessive. And now that I have released him, so they want me to quickly pick him up!! [*Laughs*]. It was really sad, because I missed him and he missed me, but we couldn't really hack it. I mean, *we* could hack it, but the world didn't let us, you know."

Meanwhile John himself was going off the rails. The night he arrived at Ann Peebles' Troubadour show, sporting a sanitary towel on his head, is merely the most notorious in a string of sordid incidents. In 1974, he claimed the stories of depravity were "mostly fiction, with a grain of alcohol", but as he admitted at the time, "I've never drunk so much in my life." Identifying the source of his desolation, he admitted, "I get my daily Yoko out of a bottle these days." In March 1974, he was back at the Troubadour, brawling with anyone who stopped him, and heckling that night's act, The Smothers Brothers—a bitter moment for Tommy Smothers, who'd strummed guitar at John's side during "Give Peace A Chance". When he hit a waitress, she remarked, "It's not the pain that hurts, it's finding out that one of your idols is a real asshole."

With *Rock 'n' Roll* on hold, John agreed to produce Harry Nilsson's new album *Pussy Cats*. Sessions began in LA, until John decided it would be better for everyone's health and sanity if they switched to New York. With May Pang, he found a penthouse apartment on East 52nd Street, a little way up from the United Nations building. Once the Nilsson project was completed, John began his own climb back from artistic decrepitude by starting an all-new album, *Walls and Bridges*. There was a further distraction in July, when the government issued a new ultimatum, giving him sixty days to leave the country. He commented at the time, "I can't leave here or they'd do a Charlie Chaplin on me and I don't want an award at sixty telling me how wonderful I used to be, but not quite wonderful enough to be allowed to live here now."

Of the *Walls and Bridges* title, John seems to have heard the phrase on TV, "[it was] sent from above in the guise of a public service

Left: Phil Spector, the producer of many pop classics including some of John's best work.

announcement," but it chimes nicely with the music's constant theme of barriers between him and Yoko. Whatever pain he was in, it inspired a great album. Released on October 4th, 1974, the record also gave him a precious Number 1 hit in "Whatever Gets You Thru the Night". The *Walls and Bridges* sleeve was adorned by artwork he'd produced as a child in 1952. The images include, as Yoko points out, "a crayon drawing of two people on horseback. When you look in the corner it says 'February 18th'. February 18th is my birthday. And then when you look at the two people on horseback, you see that one is not white, one is like Indian or Asian or something, and is definitely a woman. So he was predicting, without knowing, he already knew that he was going to meet me. Isn't it amazing?"

There was also this cryptic message: "On the 23rd Aug. 1974 at 9 o'clock I saw a U.F.O." The number nine held mystic significance for him, but of the sighting itself he said, "I went to the window, just dreaming around in my usual poetic frame of mind… hovering over the building, no more than a hundred feet away was this thing with ordinary electric light bulbs flashing on and off round the bottom, one non-blinking red light on top… What the Nixon is that?"

But John was not a fan of *Walls and Bridges*. "The only thing about it is it's new" was the best he could say on its behalf. By 1980, he was ready to disown it entirely, calling it the work of "a semi-sick craftsman… There's no inspiration and there's misery. It gives off an aura of misery."

Yoko's verdict is somewhat kinder: "*Walls and Bridges* was beautiful, one of the best albums that he made." And yet she cannot detach the music from the unhappiness of its making: "Whenever I hear it, it's very painful for me because the pain of being separated created that work. He created that album out of sadness. He would come to the Dakota and let me listen to one or two tracks. And I really felt that it was fantastic."

Could the album, then, even have played a part in their reunion?

"Well," she considers, "it was very hard for me, but I had to remember how difficult it was for us together. As you know, the whole world hated me. And as a result, they hated John as well for being with me. It was not a very easy situation, so I was trying to not get back to that."

Had the separation been her idea?

"Yes. Because I really thought that we were being totally destructive about ourselves. It was not helping John. And it was not helping me. And we were artists who should have the space and the freedom to express ourselves without being hated."

As recording began, the tapes of his abortive LA *Rock 'n' Roll* sessions suddenly arrived from Phil Spector. Once *Walls and Bridges* was completed, John returned to them and used his New York musicians to complete the project. From such unpromising origins, he fashioned a very respectable album. He nicknamed it "Old Hat", but *Rock 'n' Roll* turned out to be a sophisticated take on the music of his adolescence. Both affectionate and distanced, he closed the record with a mock show business voiceover, signing off from Record Plant East. He later guessed he'd meant the farewell with unconscious seriousness because he did not record again for another five years.

As to the "lost weekend", which ended in his return to Yoko and the Dakota, May Pang disputes that it was "lost" at all. In that time, he made some of the finest music of his whole career.

"*WALLS AND BRIDGES*? THE ONLY THING ABOUT IT IS IT'S NEW."

—John Lennon

GOING DOWN ON LOVE

In a restrained but deeply felt performance, John raises the curtain on *Walls And Bridges* with a song that could practically be sub-titled "The Ballad of the Lost Weekend".

He mourns the loss of love, laments his own descent into aimless pleasure-seeking, and cries out for help. As an album, *Walls and Bridges* never deviates from the path indicated by "Going Down on Love". The record amounts to Lennon's *De profundis*—a long, piteous call for Yoko to haul him out of this abyss. It's a melancholy note to open on: "Nothing doin' nowhere…" The irony is that in creative terms, there is more happening on *Walls and Bridges* than on records John made before and after, when he was in a happier frame of mind.

Above: John attends a Hollywood tribute evening for the actor James Cagney, in March 1974.

Got to get down, down on my knees
Got to get down, down on my knees
Doo-doo-doo-doo, doo-doo-doo-doo
Going down on love
Going down on love
Going down, going down, going down

When the real thing goes wrong
And you can't get it on
And your love, she has gone
And you got to carry on
And you shoot out the light
Ain't coming home for the night
You know you got to, got to, got to pay the price

Somebody please, please help me
You know I'm drowning in the sea of hatred

Got to get down, down on my knees
Got to get down, down on my knees
Doo-doo-doo-doo, doo-doo-doo-doo
Going down on love
Going down on love
Going down, going down, going down

Something precious and rare
Disappears in thin air
And it seems so unfair
Nothing doing nowhere
Well, you burn all your boats
And you sow your wild oats
Well, you know, you know, you know the price is right

Got to get down, down on my knees
Got to get down, down on my knees
Got to get down, down on my knees
Got to get down, down on my knees

WHATEVER GETS YOU THRU THE NIGHT

During his separation from Yoko, John's new habit of socializing with fellow musicians had some dire consequences. One of the more fruitful friendships, however, was with Elton John, by now the most successful English pop star of the day.

Lennon played Elton a tape of his new songs, inviting him to supply piano and backing vocals on any track he liked. Rather to John's disappointment, his guest plumped for Lennon's "least favorite" number, feeling it gave him the most space to contribute something extra. "Whatever Gets You Thru the Night" turned out to be a lyrically slight but sonically storming rocker that would give John his first solo Number 1 hit.

John had his doubts about the song, a vague ode to self-preservation that echoed his own insecurity and loss of direction. (He took the title from a line he'd heard on a TV program about alcoholism.) But Elton John's commercial instincts were keener than John Lennon's at that time, and he reckoned the track was a surefire success. If it reached the top of the charts, he challenged, then John should repay the favor by appearing at one of Elton's live shows. "Whatever Gets You Thru the Night", helped in large measure by Bobby Keys' gusting tenor sax, duly became the US Number 1 on November 16th, 1974, and John was honor-bound to show up at Elton John's concert at Madison Square Garden on Thanksgiving Day, the 28th of that month.

The gig was to have a double significance in John's life. At the after-show party in New York's Pierre Hotel, he began his reconciliation with Yoko. Less happily, it was also John's last-ever appearance on a public stage. He joined Elton for versions of "Whatever Gets You Thru The Night", "Lucy in the Sky with Diamonds" and—poignantly, for his final song before a live audience—the McCartney number which had kicked off the first Beatles LP eleven years earlier, "I Saw Her Standing There". John dedicated it to "an old estranged fiancé of mine called Paul".

Pleased as he was with the popularity of "Whatever Gets You Thru the Night"—the song virtually revived his career—John never cared much for it. "We didn't get a good take on the musicians," he reflected in 1980. He even went so far as to remark, half-seriously, that it should have gone to Number 39, not Number 1.

Whatever gets you through the night
It's all right, it's all right
It's your money or your life
It's all right, it's all right
Don't need a sword to cut thru flowers
Oh no, oh no

Whatever gets you through your life
It's all right, it's all right
Do it wrong or do it right
It's all right, it's all right
Don't need a watch to waste your time
Oh no, oh no

Hold me, darlin', come on, listen to me
I won't do you no harm
Trust me, darlin', come on, listen to me
Come on, listen to me, come on, listen, listen

Whatever gets you to the light
It's all right, it's all right
Out the blue or out of sight
It's all right, it's all right
Don't need a gun to blow you mind
Oh no, oh no

Hold me, darlin', come on, listen to me
I won't do you no harm
Trust me, darlin', come on, listen to me
Come on, listen to me, come on, listen, listen

"GET ONE BEATLE DRUNK AND SEE WHAT HAPPENS!"

—Harry Nilsson

OLD DIRT ROAD

Laced with a high and lonesome guitar wail by Jesse Ed Davis, "Old Dirt Road" carries backing vocals by Harry Nilsson, who co-wrote the song with John during their sessions for the *Pussy Cats* album. Foremost among his "lost weekend" partners in crime, Nilsson was a singer and songwriter so admired by John's old band that they used to call him "the Beatle across the water".

By 1980, Lennon was inclined to belittle his work from this period, and dismissed the number as a product of his and Nilsson's drunken sojourn. "It's just a song, you know," he told *Playboy*. "Well, seeing we're stuck in this bottle of vodka, we might as well try and do something." But it deserves higher praise than that. A possible descendant of the old Charlie Patton blues song 'Ain't Goin' Down That Dirt Road', which was resurrected by Howlin' Wolf in his 1970 London sessions with Eric Clapton, this Lennon/Nilsson collaboration has a drifting sadness that is truly affecting.

John's murder was to hit his old drinking buddy harder than most. In the decade up to his own death in January 1994, Harry Nilsson played an active role in America's Coalition to Stop Gun Violence. By that time, Nilsson had lived to rue his involvement in John's wild holiday. He felt that blame for incidents such as the Troubadour scuffles was often laid at his door. "That incident ruined my reputation for ten years," he said. "Get one Beatle drunk and see what happens!" John himself had protested, "So I was drunk. When it's Errol Flynn, the showbiz writers say, 'Those were the days, when men were men.' When I do it, I'm a bum."

Ain't no people on the old dirt road
No more weather on the old dirt road
It's better than a mudslide mamma when the dry spell come, yeah
Yeah, oh, oh, oh, oh, old dirt road

Ain't no difference on the old dirt road
Tarred and feathered on the old dirt road
Trying to shovel smoke with a pitchfork in the wind, yeah, yeah, yeah

Breezing through the deadwood on a hot summer day
I saw a human being lazy boning out in the hay
I said uh, "Hey Mr. Human can you rainmaker too?"
He said I guess it's O.K. you know the only thing we need is water
Cool, clear water, water
Water, water

Ain't no people on the old dirt road
No more weather on the old dirt road
It's better than a mudslide mamma when the morning comes
Yeah, oh, oh, oh, oh, old dirt road

Keep on keeping on [x6]
So long, so long
So long, so long
Bye bye
Bye bye
Keep on keeping on
Keep on, keep on, keep on, keep on, keep on, keep on, keep on
Keep on, keep on, keep on, keep on, keep on, keep on, keep on

WHAT YOU GOT

There is a forceful current of emotion running through *Walls and Bridges* that sometimes outstrips John's powers of invention. In cursing his separation from Yoko, he cannot offer much more here than the stock phrase "You don't know what you got, until you lose it."

He quotes the Little Richard rocker, "Rip It Up" (reprised at the NY *Rock 'n' Roll* sessions a few months later), when he declares that "it's Saturday night"; but this time he is not celebrating the fact so much as, perhaps, charting all the weeks that he's squandered in drinking to forget. Still, he screams the words at full throttle, while the band attempt a tough, rubbery take on Seventies funk. "What You Got" is admittedly short on poetry, but it's satisfyingly stuffed with drama.

One
Hey, hey!
Don't want to be a drag
Everybody got to bag
I know you know
About the emperor's clothes

You don't know what you got until you lose it
You don't know what you got until you lose it
You don't know what you got until you lose it
Oh, baby, baby, baby, give me one more chance

Ow, alright, hey

Well, it's Saturday night and I just got to rip it up
Sunday morning, I just got to give it up
Come Monday, momma, and I just got to run away
You know it's such a drag to face another day

You don't know what you got until you lose it
You don't know what you got until you lose it
You don't know what you got until you lose it
Oh, baby, baby, baby, give me one more chance
Hey, alright, ow

You know the more it change
The more it stays the same
You got to hang on in
You got to cut the string

You don't know what you got until you lose it
You don't know what you got until you lose it
You don't know, you don't know what you got until
you lose it
Oh, baby, baby, baby, give me one more chance
Come on, girl, hey, alright
Hey, alright

Above: A low-point of the "Lost Weekend" came on March 12th, 1974: John is ejected from the Smothers Brothers' show at the Troubadour club, Los Angeles.

BLESS YOU

Being absent from its making, Yoko becomes more present on *Walls and Bridges* than any Lennon album she actually participated in.

With its vaguely oriental shimmer, "Bless You" invokes her most romantically. A ballad as fine as any he ever wrote, its lyric has John relaying his tenderest good wishes to the departed partner and whatever new lover she may have found. As such, it stands in total contrast to the "Jealous Guy" school of Lennon songs—there is no suggestion here that he would rather see her dead than with another man. And yet, if he has found the strength and maturity to accept her independence, he does not relinquish his love. The final message of "Bless You" is that he and Yoko remain spiritually connected. Their love transcends their physical separation.

In fact, Yoko was not alone during John's "lost weekend". During sessions for the previous album *Mind Games*, she had grown fond of their star guitarist David Spinozza, around the same time that John was beginning his affair with May Pang. If John felt any misgivings about his wife's affection for Spinozza, he'd at least acquired sufficient maturity to compose a song as noble as "Bless You". Had the track appeared on, say, *Imagine*, it would be better recognized today. But, since all Lennon's best work was drawn from the well of his own experiences, "Bless You" had to wait until he hit the emotional wastelands of 1974.

Though it's a little-known Lennon number, there is evidence that the song found favor with its intended target, an audience of one. It's not surprising that "Bless You" was one of the compositions that Yoko chose to include on the *Menlove Avenue* album, a 1986 compilation of John's demo tracks and unreleased recordings from the mid-Seventies. When he first played "Bless You" to May Pang, she reassured him that Yoko would receive the tribute in the right spirit. "It's a beautiful song," she told him. "She's going to love it."

"John came to the Dakota and played 'Bless You' to me," Yoko confirms. "I was crying and he was crying and we were just holding each other. And, I thought, 'God, it is very dangerous that we might come back together because it would not be right.' And I said, 'John, you have to go now.' And it was difficult for me to say that."

Bless you, wherever you are
Windswept child on a shooting star
Restless Spirits depart
Still we're deep in each other's hearts

Some people say it's over
Now that we spread our wings
But we know better, darling
The hollow ring is only last year's echo

Bless you, whoever you are
Holding her now
Be warm and kind-hearted
And remember though love is strange
Now and forever our love will remain

SCARED

In a significant touch, the brooding "Scared" opens with the howl of a lone wolf. On the one hand, John is a timid traveler in the moonlit wilderness. On the other, he's a sort of werewolf himself, possessed by urges he cannot quite control.

The song is manacled to an ominous marching beat, tramping forward like a prisoner to the gallows. In all, it seethes with underlying tension and dread inevitability.

John described "Scared" as a summary of his feelings when away from Yoko as the gloom descended and he was mired by an awful helplessness. In this predicament, he sings, "no bell, book, or candle" can help him. This medieval phrase was a favorite of his, whether taken from Shakespeare's *King John* or the 1958 movie starring Kim Novak. Homeless and uprooted, he next borrows Bob Dylan's line and describes himself as being "like a rolling stone". Coincidentally, Lennon later wondered if Mick Jagger had been listening to "Scared" when he wrote the Rolling Stones' disco-flavored 1978 hit "Some Girls". True, there are some parallels in the lyrics' theme of arid isolation, but the influence is far from obvious.

John himself saw "Scared" as a confession of his private terror in the same tradition as "Help!". He confirmed the link when he first played his new song to a subdued May Pang. Of the old Beatle hits, he remarked that "Help!" was his favorite, and one day he would like to record it in the style of "Scared". After the gentle resolution of "Bless You", jealousy is once more gnawing at his heart. He feels hatred, too, and casts a cold eye over himself, the man who will "sing out about love and peace" when his own emotions are a morass of negativity.

To Yoko, "Scared" "is like a classic song that could have come from, I don't know, German *Lieder* or something."

Brilliant and chilling it may be, but there is a certain theatricality about "Scared", and only the sincerity of John's delivery prevents it from tipping over into melodrama. A less assured, and therefore even bleaker, version of it can be found on *Menlove Avenue*. Of all the zany pseudonyms that John adopts in the credits to *Walls and Bridges* (Dwarf McDougal, Rev Fred Ghurkin, Dr. Winston O'Reggae, etc.), his name-check on "Scared" is the most apt—punning on the name of American crooner Mel Tormé, John becomes Mel Torment.

Opposite: John performs a guest spot for Elton John at Madison Square Garden on November 28th, 1974.

I'm scared, I'm scared, I'm scared
I'm scared, so scared
I'm scared, I'm scared, I'm scared
As the years roll away
And the price that I paid
And the straws slip away

You don't have to suffer
It is what it is
No bell, book or candle
Can get you out of this, oh no!

I'm scarred, I'm scarred, I'm scarred
I'm scarred, uh huh
I'm scarred, I'm scarred, I'm scarred
Every day of my life
I just manage to survive
I just want to stay alive

You don't have to worry
In heaven or hell
Just dance to the music
You do it so well, well, well!
Hatred and jealousy, gonna be the death of me

I guess I knew it right from the start
Sing out about love and peace
Don't want to see the red raw meat
The green eyed goddamn straight from your heart

I'm tired, I'm tired, I'm tired
Of being so alone
No place to call my own
Like a rollin' stone

Spare me, babe!
Yeah, whoa
Ahh, hey
Ow!

#9 DREAM

Speaking to the famous media theorist Marshall McLuhan in 1969, John offered an astute view of the artistic impulse. To write a song, he said, "is just like trying to describe a dream… Because we don't have telepathy, we try and describe the dream to each other, to verify to each other what we know, what we believe to be inside each other." In the classic '#9 Dream', he applied this approach quite literally.

It's a mesmeric song that floats enchantingly in the space between peaceful sleep and fearful awakening.

"Yesterday" had come to Paul McCartney in a dream (or, at least, the melody did: he used the title "Scrambled Eggs" until something better occurred to him) and some of John's song had a similar origin. He already had the basis of a melody, simply recycling his string arrangement for Harry Nilsson's version of "Many Rivers To Cross" on *Pussy Cats*. (This song, by reggae star Jimmy Cliff, is itself a perfect expression of John's anguish at the time: "And this loneliness won't leave me alone.") He awoke one day and told May Pang that he'd dreamt about two women echoing his name, and also heard the strange refrain "Ah, böwakawa poussé, poussé." There was no translation for the words, but the female spirits were readily identifiable as May and Yoko.

When it came to recording the song, which was initially known as "So Long" after John's opening line, May Pang was duly invited to whisper "John" at the relevant point. There is also a faintly murmured "Hare Krishna, George," by way of a greeting to John's old Beatle comrade, with whom he'd just had one of his periodic arguments. It's likely, too, that Jesse Ed Davis's celestial guitar was a conscious tribute to Harrison's style. Once again, though, John was less than generous to this music in 1980. In a BBC interview, he referred to it as "craftsmanship writing"—which, in his terms, was not a compliment.

Why, though, was it finally called "#9 Dream"? Numerology—the occult study of numbers and their hidden significance—was among the fringe interests that John had cultivated since the mid-Sixties. He fastened upon the number nine as being especially important in his life. He was born on October 9th (as was his second son, Sean) and lived at 9 Newcastle Road in Liverpool. Among his earliest song-writing efforts was "One after 909". He named his most adventurous Beatle track "Revolution 9". Even the Dakota Building was on 72nd Street (seven plus two making nine), and he once predicted that he would die on the ninth day of the month. In the event, he was shot on 72nd Street, and declared dead at 11:07 p.m. (the numerals again add up to nine) at the Roosevelt Hospital on Ninth Avenue. The date in New York, of course, was December. 8th. But his native time zone is five hours ahead: In Liverpool, it was already morning—the morning of the ninth.

Below: With May Pang and drinking buddy Harry Nilsson at the Troubadour.

#9 DREAM

So long ago
Was it in a dream, was it just a dream?
I know, yes I know
Seemed so very real, it seemed so real to me

Took a walk down the street
Through the heat whispered trees
I thought I could hear, hear
Hear, hear

Somebody call out my name (John)
As it started to rain (John)
Two spirits dancing so strange

Ah, bowakawa pousse, pousse
Ah, bowakawa pousse, pousse
Ah, bowakawa pousse, pousse

Dream, dream away
Magic in the air, was magic in the air?
I believe, yes I believe
More I cannot say, what more can I say?

On a river of sound
Through the mirror go around, around
I thought I could feel, feel
Feel, feel

Music touching my soul (nhoJ)
Something warm, sudden cold (nhoJ)
The spirit dance was unfolding

Ah, bowakawa pousse, pousse
Ah, bowakawa pousse, pousse
Ah, bowakawa pousse, pousse
Ah, bowakawa pousse, pousse
Ah, bowakawa pousse, pousse
Ah, bowakawa pousse, pousse
Ah, bowakawa pousse, pousse
Ah, bowakawa pousse, pousse
Ah, bowakawa pousse, pousse
Ah, bowakawa pousse, pousse
Ah, bowakawa pousse, pousse
Ah, bowakawa pousse, pousse
Ah, bowakawa pousse, pousse

SURPRISE SURPRISE (SWEET BIRD OF PARADOX)

Amid so many messages to Yoko, it seems only right that May Pang should have one song explicitly devoted to her, the girl who gets John "through this God-awful loneliness."

May reports that John wrote this frankly sensual tribute to his "bird of paradise" at the outset of their affair in New York. She cried with emotion when he first played it to her. From the playful punning of its title to the "tweet-tweet, tweet-tweet" sounds at its fade (a jokey echo of the "beep beep" ending of the Beatles' "Drive My Car"), "Surprise Surprise" brings a welcome upbeat to the album. In writing it, John had begun with yet another golden oldie on his mind—in this case, the Diamonds' 1957 hit "Little Darlin'", though almost nothing of it survives in the finished article. Elton John attempted to add a backing vocal, but apparently found Lennon's phrasing very difficult to match.

Above: Julian Lennon with John and May at Palm Beach, Florida, on a trip that took in a visit to Disneyland.

Hey!

Sweet as the smell of success
Her body's warm and wet
She gets me through this god awful loneliness
A natural high, butterfly
Oh I need, need, need her

Just like a willow tree
A breath of spring you see
And oh boy you don't know what she do to me
She makes me sweat and forget who I am
Oh, I, I need, need, need, need, need her

Well, I was wondering how long this could go on, on and on
Well, I thought I could never be surprised
But could it be that I bit my own tongue?
Oh yeah, it's so hard to swallow when you're wrong

A bird of paradise
The sunrise in her eyes
God only knows such a sweet surprise
I was blind, she blew my mind, think that I
I love, love, love, love, love her
I love her, I love her, I love her, I love her

Sweet sweet, sweet sweet love
Sweet sweet, sweet sweet love
Sweet sweet, sweet sweet love
Sweet sweet, sweet sweet love
Sweet sweet, sweet sweet love
Ah yeah
Ah yeah

STEEL AND GLASS

The most avidly discussed number on *Walls and Bridges* was this cold-hearted masterpiece of invective. Soaked in those familiar, quasi-oriental strings, "Steel and Glass" revisits the symphonic spite of *Imagine*'s anti-Paul epistle "How Do You Sleep?".

It is ironic, given his involvement in the prototype, that the presumed target of this equally nasty sequel should be Allen Klein.

John, however, was atypically coy about the victim's identity, and rather enjoyed the tease. Chuckling throatily over the song's mock-cowboy intro, he calls it a tale of "your friend and mine", while urgent whispers enquire, "Who is it? Who is it?" In a piece he wrote for Andy Warhol's *Interview* magazine, he taunts, "Next you'll be asking who 'Steel and Glass' is about. I can tell you who it isn't about, for instance: it's not about Jackie Kennedy, Mort Sahl, Sammy Davis, Bette Midler… Eartha Kitt, it's not about her either." Nor, he goes on to confirm, is it about Paul McCartney. Of his rift with Allen Klein, he merely says, "He was unfaithful."

For all their legendary fame, the Beatles did not earn huge amounts of money until Allen Klein took charge of their affairs. He was successful on their behalf to an extent that even Paul, who had been opposed to his appointment, had to acknowledge. But the manager's brash New York style was always out of place at Apple's HQ in Savile Row—where the last bastion of traditional English gentlemen met the new generation of Aquarian flower children. Klein, it goes without saying, was patently neither.

By 1974, he was back in Manhattan, where it is easier to picture him, at the desk of his top-floor office in the forty-one-story "steel and glass" tower at 1700 Broadway. A year earlier, he had fallen from favor with the other three Beatles when his Apple contract lapsed. Soon, he and John were deep in litigation, issuing claim and counter-claim. The song paints the most unflattering portrait of an aggressive wheeler-dealer who is now losing his grip. An especially unfeeling touch is John's reference to the mother who "left you when you were small": Klein's own mother had died of cancer when he was a baby.

In spite of it all, these two bruisers maintained a sneaking regard for one another. It's entirely possible that, despite their outward differences, they were kindred spirits. John actually stayed as Klein's house guest in 1974, even while litigation continued, and mere weeks before John wrote "Steel and Glass". The case was eventually settled in 1977.

According to photographer Bob Gruen, who had observed their peculiar friendship at close hand: "John told me that the contract for Allen to be their manager was one or two paragraphs on one sheet of paper. The contract to break up their original agreement was eighty-seven pages… They liked Allen Klein before and they liked him after; it was just during the negotiations [that they didn't]."

Lennon could be strangely unaware of how cruel he sometimes sounded. Perhaps he felt penitence later when he described "Steel and Glass" as "a son of 'How Do You Sleep?'" and denied that either song was about any one person. He even claimed that "Steel and Glass" was a dig at himself, just like "Nowhere Man". But this was unconvincing. Lesser writers often have their songs misinterpreted, but John used words with deadly precision. He might have regretted it afterward, but his original meaning was usually unmistakable.

This is a story about your friend and mine
Who is it, who is it, who is it?

There you stand with your L.A. tan
And your New York walk and your New York talk
Your mother left you when you were small
But you're going to wish you wasn't born at all

Steel and glass
Steel and glass
Steel and glass
Steel and glass

Your phone don't ring, no one answers your call
How does it feel to be off the wall

Well, your mouthpiece squawks as he spreads your lies
But you can't pull strings if your hands are tied
Well, your teeth are clean but your mind is capped
You leave your smell like an alley cat

Steel and glass
Steel and glass
Steel and glass
Steel and glass

BEEF JERKY

Instrumental tracks are almost nonexistent in Lennon's catalogue. It seems his love of music always came second to his passion for words. He could not see what performing was for, unless it was to say something.

Nevertheless, a useful aspect of the "lost weekend" was John's new fondness for the fellowship of the recording studio. (Bear in mind that Yoko had been at his shoulder ever since the Beatles' "White Album" in 1968, which did little to improve the atmosphere at Abbey Road.) While "Beef Jerky" is nothing special—just an efficiently funky, bustling rocker—it's a welcome interlude in *Walls and Bridges,* whose most tortured track was still to come. The relative jolliness of "Beef Jerky" is underlined by John's sleeve credit, rearranging soul band Booker T & the MG's into his best gag so far, Booker Table & the Maitre D's.

Beef Jerky, beef jerky, beef jerky, beef jerky
Beef, beef, beef, beef

Below: With Mick Jagger at the all-star James Cagney evening. Its host was Frank Sinatra.

Opposite: Another night at the Troubadour, with Canadian singer Anne Murray, Nilsson, Alice Cooper, and Micky Dolenz of the Monkees.

NOBODY LOVES YOU (WHEN YOU'RE DOWN AND OUT)

This colossal ballad came out of a bad time in Lennon's life. Not only was he separated from the wife he loved, but his professional career was at its lowest ebb ever. A sprawling testament to John's cynicism and self-pity, "Nobody Loves You (When You're Down and Out)" sounds nothing but sincere.

He told *Playboy*: "That exactly expressed the whole period I was apart from Yoko." He always imagined the number being sung by Frank Sinatra and its low-key, late-night feel recalls the downbeat barfly of "One for My Baby" or "In The Wee Small Hours of the Morning". The title itself is a variant on Jimmie Cox's old blues standard "Nobody Knows You When You're Down And Out"—John would certainly be familiar with Eric Clapton's 1970 version on Derek & The Dominos' *Layla and Other Assorted Love Songs*.

As a grand statement of John's position in the mid-Seventies, "Nobody Loves You" stands in a trilogy with "God" (which opened the decade) and "Starting Over" (which ended it). An ode to his marriage, it is also an address to his ageing generation, and the audience which has turned its back on him. In "God", he had declared an end to the illusions of youth. In "Starting Over", he would announce a renewed sense of purpose. But right now, in between those twin moments of resolution, he is simply exhausted, defeated by life's confusion.

Probably the song's key element is John's concept of himself as one who's "been across to the other side" and returned to share the experience. This, in other words, was the "shaman" role of ancient mythologies that he sensed himself fulfilling in a modern, media-driven world where people's dreams are awakened and enacted by mass-entertainers. It was not a job he had ever particularly sought, and the demands of stardom had almost killed him. Ultimately, that is exactly what they did.

Below: John's appearance at Elton John's concert would prove to be his final live show.

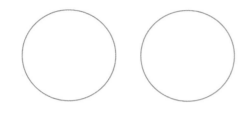

NOBODY LOVES YOU (WHEN YOU'RE DOWN AND OUT)

Nobody loves you when you're down and out
Nobody sees you when you're on cloud nine
Everybody's hustling for a buck and a dime
I'll scratch your back and you scratch mine

I've been across to the other side
I've shown you everything, I got
nothing to hide
And still you ask me, do I love you?
What it is, what it is
All I can tell you is, it's all show biz
All I can tell you is, it's all show biz

Nobody loves you when you're down and out
Nobody knows you when you're on cloud nine
Everybody's hustling for a buck and a dime
I'll scratch your back and you knife mine

I've been across the water now so many times
I've seen the one eyed witchdoctor leading
the blind
And still you ask me, do I love you?
What you say, what you say
Everytime I put my finger on it, it slips away
Everytime I put my finger on it, it slips away

Well I get up in the morning and I'm
looking in the mirror to see
Ooo wee!
Then I'm lying in the darkness and
I know I can't get to sleep
Ooo wee!

Nobody loves you when you're old and grey
Nobody needs you when you're upside down
Everybody's hollering about their own birthday
Everybody loves you when you're six foot in
the ground

THE ROCK 'N' ROLL ALBUM

The *Walls and Bridges* album actually ends with a snippet of an old Lee Dorsey song "Ya Ya", with some tentative drumming by John's young son Julian, on a visit to New York with his mother Cynthia. The point of its inclusion was that it was owned by Morris Levy, but it failed to satisfy the publisher's demand that three of his numbers be covered.

Reluctantly, John now turned his attentions to the Spector tapes, despite their painful associations with his spell in LA. "These are awful," he told May Pang. "I must have felt terrible when I did these." Nevertheless, with Levy at his heels, he agreed to revive the project, and in October he reentered the Record Plant with his *Walls and Bridges* crew. Here, he cleaned up what he could of the old sessions and recorded additional material to make a whole album. He later said of the exercise, "It was a contractual obligation to Morris Levy. It was a humiliation and I regret having to be in that position, but I did it." The Fifties idea had been so hot a year ago, especially after *American Graffiti*, and now it only seemed tedious.

But the vintage material came surprisingly easily to him. In his heart of hearts, John never forsook the raw simplicity of Fifties music. In 1974, at the height of "progressive rock", he was foreshadowing the upsurge of punk. The Beatles' old producer George Martin was as surprised as anyone at Lennon's loyalty to rock's roots. He'd believed that after *Sgt. Pepper* and *Abbey Road*, John would go on refining rock into "a mainstream of good new music. And I was disillusioned when that came to naught, because punk rock came along, the Sex Pistols and 'God Save The Queen' and everybody dropping their trousers. I thought, 'it's really not going this way after all.' There was a rebellion against it. Even John Lennon didn't like the overproduced stuff. He wanted good old rousing rock 'n' roll. So I was wrong, it didn't happen."

Yet, John handles *Rock 'n' Roll* with more nostalgia than outright passion. The rockers are low-voltage, like a work of mellow retrospection, and artfully airbrushed. With the exception of Lloyd Price's "Just Because", which he'd not heard until Spector played it to him, the tracks selected paid tribute to John's teenage idols. Little Richard is heavily represented, with "Rip It Up", "Ready Teddy" and "Slippin' and Slidin'", Chuck Berry is honored with 'Sweet Little Sixteen' and the song that started all the trouble with Levy, "You Can't Catch Me". Larry Williams was a particular favorite—to the Beatles' covers of "Dizzy Miss Lizzy", "Slow Down", and "Bad Boy", John now added "Bonfsy Moronie". Other raves from the grave included Gene Vincent's "Be-Bop-A-Lula" and Fats Domino's "Ain't That a Shame".

On the final tracklisting, only four cuts survived from Spector's troubled sessions. Upon sober reflection, Lennon said of his gifted, erratic collaborator: "I'm fond of his work a lot. His personality I'm not crazy about." But Spector never lost a sense of his own legend. Speaking in 1976, he announced, "I only went into the studio to do one thing, and you can tell this to John Lennon. They were making records, but I was making Art..."

The *Rock 'n' Roll* cover carried a beautiful archive photograph of John as a young teddy boy standing in a Hamburg doorway. Looking at the picture in 1974, he felt his life had come full cycle. "I thought, is this some kind of karmic thing? Here I am with this old picture of me in Hamburg from '61, and I'm ending as I started, singing this straight rock 'n' roll stuff."

Opposite: A current-day photograph of the street in Hamburg where the young John was photographed for the cover of his *Rock 'n' Roll* album (inset).

"I'M ENDING AS I STARTED, SINGING STRAIGHT ROCK 'N' ROLL."

—John Lennon

JOHN
LENNON

Chapter 7

DOUBLE

19 80

FANTASY

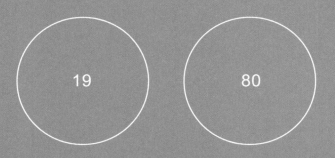

"(Just Like) Starting Over"
"Cleanup Time"
"I'm Losing You"
"Beautiful Boy (Darling Boy)"
"Watching The Wheels"
"Woman"
"Dear Yoko"

Recorded
August to September 1980, The Hit Factory, New York City.

Produced by
John Lennon, Yoko Ono, Jack Douglas.

Musicians
John Lennon (vocals, rhythm and acoustic guitars, piano and keyboards), Yoko Ono (vocals), Earl Slick (lead guitar), Hugh McCracken (lead guitar), Tony Levin (bass), George Small (keyboards), Andy Newmark (drums), Arthur Jenkins (percussion), Ed Walsh (synthesizer), Robert Greenidge (steel drum), Matthew Cunningham (hammered dulcimer), Randy Stein (concertina), Howard Johnson, Grant Hungerford, John Parran, Seldon Powell, George "Young" Opalisky, Roger Rosenberg, David Tofani, Ronald Tooley (horns), Michelle Simpson, Cassandra Wooten, Cheryl Mason Jacks, Eric Troyer, Benny Cummings Singers, The Kings Temple Choir (backing vocals).

"Our separation was a failure." With that typically Lennonesque verdict, John put the public seal on his reunion with Yoko. Consummating the process which began after Elton John's Madison Square show, John moved back into his Dakota home in early 1975. He continued to visit his mistress May Pang, sporadically at least, for some time afterwards. But, from now until the end of his days, he was officially reinstated in the "Johnandyoko" partnership.

In March 1975, recollecting the mayhem he had only narrowly survived, John told *Rolling Stone*, "This last year has been extraordinary for me... I feel like I've been on Sinbad's voyage and I've battled all those monsters and I've got back." With no little symbolism, 1975 began with the formal dissolution, in London's High Court, of the Beatles as a legal entity. And, within a month, Yoko became pregnant. The couple's only child, Sean, was conceived within days of John's return to the marital fold.

Domesticity beckoned at last. But there was still work to be done before he could relax. In February his old adversary Morris Levy released an album of John's *Rock 'n' Roll* sessions, entitled *Roots*. Lennon and his record company, EMI/Capitol, promptly sued Levy for his unauthorized release and issued the official version on February 17th. John and Yoko made their first public appearance together on March 1st, attending the Grammy Awards ceremony where they were pictured in the skeletal company of David Bowie, the rising superstar of the moment.

Just a few weeks previously, John had helped Bowie complete his *Young Americans* album in New York, playing guitar on a version of his own "Across The Universe" and a new song that the pair co-wrote with Bowie's guitarist Carlos Alomar. Improvised around a scratchy funk riff, "Fame" was a bleak meditation on the barren nature of celebrity, made as John was walking away from stardom and Bowie was rushing to embrace it. The one disillusioned, the other ambitious, they were scarcely singing from the same hymn sheet, but the match of old master and young pretender was effective. John's touch proved Midas-like, granting David Bowie a Number 1 hit and making the singer's name in America.

On April 18th, Lennon played before an audience for the final time in his life. On a TV tribute to the entertainment mogul Lew Grade, introduced by the comedian Dave Allen, John led a band in sci-fi costumes through perfunctory renditions of "Imagine" and, from the *Rock 'n' Roll* album, "Slippin' and Slidin'" and Ben E. King's "Stand by Me". The invited audience, dressed to the nines, sat at their tables and applauded politely. Broadcast two months later, it was all a million miles from the Cavern or Hamburg's Star Club, and a strangely anticlimactic end to John's career as a live performer.

Great news came on October 7th when the New York Supreme Court overturned John's deportation order and asked the Immigration Service to reconsider their case. "Lennon's four-year battle to remain in our country is a testament to his faith in that American Dream," they noted. Even more momentous was John's thirty-fifth birthday, October 9th, which also saw the birth of Sean Taro Ono Lennon. Facing the reporters John said, "I feel higher than the Empire State Building."

With the simultaneous breakthrough in his immigration fight, the stage was set for John's withdrawal from the wider world. On October 24th, as if to emphasize that another chapter was ended, he issued the *Shaved Fish* compilation of his post-Beatle hits. Like the other three Beatles, he'd been haunted by the likelihood that his entire life after thirty would be a mere appendix to the Big Book. By now, though, he could face that prospect calmly. He allowed whole weeks to pass in which he did no more than play with the baby, and potter about the apartment. He had become a "househusband".

In July 1976 he was granted US resident's status—"It's great to be legal again," he quipped, clutching the precious Green Card—and was promised full citizenship by 1981. Having acquired a mantle of respectability, in 1977 he attended the inauguration gala of President Jimmy Carter—a sign of how much the establishment and the old troublemaker had come together. Two years later, the former scourge of authority donated $1,000 to buy bulletproof vests for the New York police. While Yoko assumed the role of John's business representative, investing the family fortune in real estate and farm animals, John used his new freedom to make several trips to foreign countries, though never to Britain. In 1979, the other three Beatles played together at Eric Clapton's wedding party in England; John claimed that he would have attended but did not find out in time.

Yoko encouraged John to travel, hoping to bolster her man's fragile sense of independence. His routes were seemingly dictated by her readings of the Tarot cards and ancient Japanese beliefs concerning the magical validity of directions, but his 1980 journey to Bermuda was the most important, being the prelude to his long-awaited comeback. During his stay on the island he wrote or refined most of the songs he would record later that year. Strolling in June through the Botanical Gardens he came across a flower, the "Double Fantasy" freesia whose name encapsulated the idea behind the couple's next project. It would be a jointly credited album in the form of a "Heart Play", or a dialogue between John's songs and Yoko's.

Like John, Yoko had spent the recent years in seeming retreat from music, following her run of post-*Plastic Ono Band* albums in the early part of the decade. *Fly* (1971), *Approximately Infinite Universe*, and *Feeling The Space* (both 1973) were diverse and accomplished records. They were much closer to the commercial mainstream, though still distinctively Yoko-esque: it's ironic that her most exposed tracks (on the *Toronto* and *New York City* live discs, and her B-sides for some of John's big hit singles) had been the least

Right: Lennon's last ever public performance: April 18th, 1975, at the Salute to Lew Grade, New York Hilton Hotel, NYC.

accessible pieces she ever produced. By 1980, though, the prospect of her sharing half an album with John was not the drastic mismatch that might have been expected.

What took them so long to create it? According to Yoko, "John said, 'We're not gonna record anything! I'm gonna take care of Sean and you're gonna take care of the business!' He wanted me to promise that. It was difficult because I'd get some ideas for a song and write them down, and he was doing it too. At one point I realized that he had two very good songs, and I had two songs, so I said, 'Okay, why don't we make an EP?' He said, 'You mean we're going to record again?' The minute I said that, he started to create so many songs. And finally we said, 'Okay, this is an LP.' And he was so happy about that.

"When we thought of this idea he said, 'Oh let's do this right away! I don't want someone else to do it, some other couple might do it.' So we were in a hurry. But nobody did it. It was a unique idea but also very difficult because it involved two people... of a certain arrogance, shall we say? [Laughs] But it couldn't be done in any other way: if the woman was a bit weaker or the man was bit weaker. We were lucky that the combination was just right."

In an August press release the couple announced that *Double Fantasy* would be an "exploration of sexual fantasies between men and women". It would be a concept album of sorts, and John joked that they could have called themselves "Ziggy" and "Tommy", after the famous rock fictions of Bowie and The Who, but they wanted something true to their actual lives. The underlying reason for his return to music? He simply said: "You breathe in, you breathe out."

First, he needed a new record company. Every label was interested in John Lennon, but the serious contenders were dismayed to learn he planned a joint effort with Yoko. One man with faith, however, was the young executive David Geffen. A high-flyer who retired prematurely when diagnosed with cancer, he'd returned in 1980 with a clean bill of health and his very own Geffen label. Among his first signings was Elton John (later clients would include Guns N' Roses and Nirvana) and, on September 22nd, John and Yoko duly came aboard.

"I think David was extremely wise," smiles Yoko. "Can you imagine, all the other presidents of record companies could not *stand* that they had to talk to me. So John was saying, 'Forget them. They all know that you're doing the business. And if they cannot understand that, we're not gonna go with them.' Then one day David Geffen sent me a telegram. That's very clever. I don't think David, at that point, wanted to talk to me but he figured that was how he would get it.

"After the five-year hiatus, for John to come out and do his album, the whole of the music industry was totally, totally excited and was not very happy that I was there. So, while we were creating, while we were recording, John was really protecting me, he had to protect me."

Sessions began on August 4th at New York's Hit Factory, supervised by John's old engineer Jack Douglas. Despite approaches from other former colleagues, Jesse Ed Davis and Elephant's Memory included, Lennon chose a new team featuring guitarists Hugh McCracken and Bowie sideman Earl Slick. With a sleeve dedication to everyone who'd helped them stay in the US, John and Yoko's *Double Fantasy* appeared on November 17th, to a generally lukewarm response from the critics. Still, the initial sales were fair and would, of course, receive a gruesome boost in the weeks to follow.

John was reinvigorated by his comeback. He now gave a series of lengthy, entertaining interviews, and soon turned his attention towards producing a new Yoko track, "Walking on Thin Ice". Yoko herself would later recall: "John and I were gloriously happy in the first week of December. *Double Fantasy* was in the Top 10. It was just a matter of time for it to go up to Number 1, since we still had two weeks to Christmas and it was selling well. We kept saying, 'We did it, we did it,' and hugged each other."

In conversation John hinted at a world tour in 1981. He'd see Britain, too, but there was no need to rush. "What do you think," he teased one interviewer, "that it's going to vanish?". He confessed, too, that he didn't understand the new decimal currency. On December 7th, he was seen to grow emotional as he leafed through a book about Liverpool. On December 8th, he and Yoko went to the studio to work on "Thin Ice". Meanwhile, in all the renewed activity, growing numbers of fans were braving the New York winter. Clutching album covers and autograph books, they gathered around the doors of the Dakota.

(JUST LIKE) STARTING OVER

Back in 1970, John Lennon's first solo album began with a tolling bell. Now, in a deliberate echo, he opened the final album of his life with another bell. This time it was no slowed-down harbinger of doom, but the benevolent tinkling of a traditional Japanese "wishing bell", and the track it introduced, "(Just Like) Starting Over", was in every sense a message of renewal. If the mournful 1970 album proclaimed the purging of his past, John's new song faced the future with a heart full of hope.

Building on a 1979 Dakota demo called "My Life", John developed the track during his 1980 summer holiday in Bermuda, while Sean played in the sun and Yoko looked after business back in New York. His central theme is of a long-standing couple whose love is strong, but who need time out to recapture the spirit of their early romance. John mentioned in a BBC interview that he took the title from a country song. This would presumably have been "Starting Over Again"—actually written by the disco star Donna Summer—which became a Number 1 country hit for Dolly Parton in late May of 1980, at the time John was assembling songs for his album. Ironically, though, Dolly's ballad tells the story of a middle-aged couple who cap their thirty years of marriage by deciding to divorce.

At one point, John considered ditching the line "It's time to spread our wings" in case people assumed a reference to Paul

Below: Roy Orbison's lingering influence on John is heard in "(Just Like) Starting Over".

(JUST LIKE) STARTING OVER

Our life together is so precious together
We have grown, we have grown
Although our love is still special
Let's take a chance and fly away somewhere alone
It's been too long since we took the time
No-one's to blame, I know time flies so quickly
But when I see you darling
It's like we both are falling in love again
It'll be just like starting over, starting over
Everyday we used to make it love
Why can't we be making love nice and easy
It's time to spread our wings and fly
Don't let another day go by my love
It'll be just like starting over, starting over
Why don't we take off alone
Take a trip somewhere far, far away
We'll be together all alone again
Like we used to in the early days
Well, well, well darling
It's been too long since we took the time
No-one's to blame, I know time flies so quickly
But when I see you darling
It's like we both are falling in love again
It'll be just like starting over, starting over
Our life together is so precious together
We have grown, we have grown
Although our love is still special
Let's take a chance and fly away somewhere
Starting over
Starting over
Over and over

McCartney's band of the Seventies. In reality the career that is charted by "(Just Like) Starting Over" is John's. Its spacious echoes and thudding drums were a subliminal reminder of the old solo Lennon of "Instant Karma!" And, since he was making a fresh start, why not go even further back, to the pre-Beatles music he had loved in his youth? Dubbing himself "Elvis Orbison", he camped up his recording with old-fashioned touches, lovingly borrowed from Roy Orbison's "Only The Lonely" and Elvis Presley's "I Want You, I Need You, I Love You".

Thus the "tough, unsentimental" Beatle once more revealed his weakness for nostalgia. He would stress that "(Just Like) Starting Over" was addressed to his own generation. "All we are saying," he told *Playboy*, "is this is what's happening to us." Yoko elaborated, explaining that the Sixties gave people a taste for freedom, but the Seventies had seen men and women in conflict, destroying their relationships and damaging family life. In the Eighties, she and John were voicing the hope that people would begin to find one another again.

In the event, these were ideas that Lennon never had the chance to investigate more deeply. Though it hints at what might have become important strands in his thinking—the value of family, the need for social cohesion, the role of responsibilities as distinct from rights—the song's delivery was perhaps too whimsical to stake any claim to greatness. At the time of its release, on October 27th, 1980, much of its appeal was simply the delight of hearing his voice once more.

Opposite: One of the last known photographs of John, taken shortly before his death in December 1980.

Below: The Lennons seen out together in that final year, pictured in New York City.

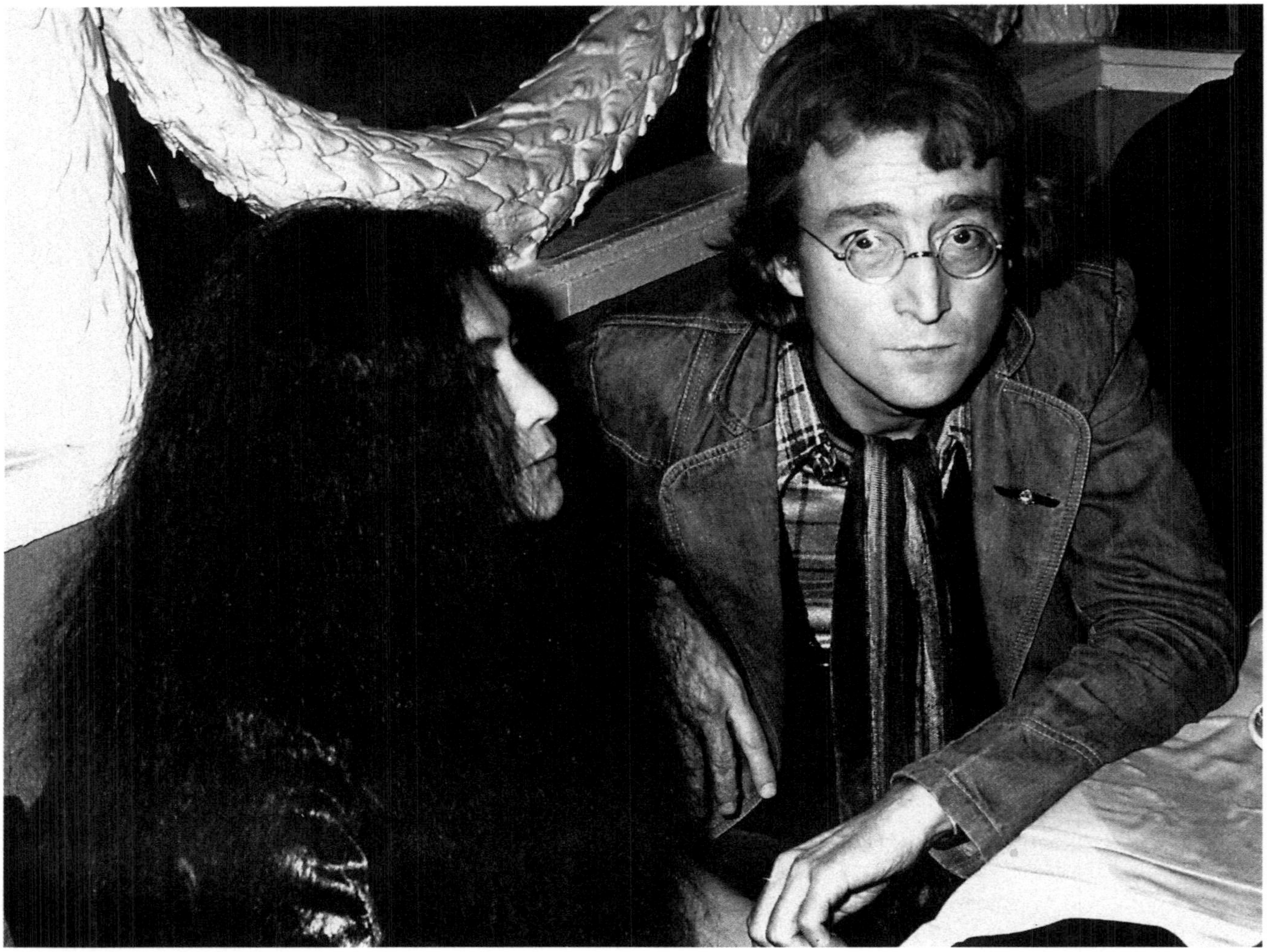

"WHEN WE THOUGHT OF THIS IDEA HE SAID, 'OH, LET'S DO THIS RIGHT AWAY!'"

—Yoko Ono

CLEANUP TIME

On the phone from Bermuda to his producer Jack Douglas in New York, John discussed a seeming trend for people to give up the drink and drug excesses of the Seventies. Said Douglas: "Well, it's cleanup time, right?"

Taken by the phrase, John replied, "It sure is." With that he ended the conversation, went straight to his piano and "just started boogieing". Now that he had a tune and a title, he needed a story. Turning his thoughts to home, he hit upon a description of his and Yoko's life at the Dakota, in their "Palace of Versailles", based on the king and queen of the old nursery rhyme "Sing A Song Of Sixpence". ("The King was in the counting house, counting out his money/The Queen was in the parlour, eating bread and honey.")

This was a scenario he had visited before in the Beatles' "Cry Baby Cry". But here was a twist in the tale. Yoko and John had undergone a role reversal in their marriage—man and wife had become businesswoman and househusband. She was in the counting house seeing to their finances, while John was in the kitchen making bread of the other sort… or so they liked to say. It's known that Yoko did become a formidable negotiator, but there is less hard evidence that John turned into the apron-wearing homemaker and childminder that he liked to pretend he was. In truth, Yoko had never been terribly domestic and John was incapable of concentrating on business.

A question mark remains, however, over whose "Cleanup Time" it actually was. By John's account, he was making a general observation, but the song is clearly set at home. The Lennons always professed to having been free of drugs from the year of Sean's birth, 1975. Even so, a 1988 *Rolling Stone* article that helped to demolish some of Albert Goldman's wilder theories about the couple could be interpreted as an admission by Yoko of a brief relapse in late 1979. "It was not a good thing to do," she conceded. "But at the same time, I'm proud that I conquered it."

Moonlight on the water
Sunlight on my face
You and me together
We are in our place

The Gods are in the heavens
Angels treat us well
Oracle has spoken
We cast the perfect spell

The queen is in the counting house
Counting out the money
The king is in the kitchen
Making bread and honey
No friends and yet no enemies
Absolutely free
No rats aboard the magic ship
Of perfect harmony

Now it begins, let it begin
Cleanup time, hey, cleanup time
Cleanup time, well, well, well

However far we travel
Wherever we may roam
The center of the circle
Will always be our home, yeah, yeah

Yeah, cleanup time
Cleanup time, cleanup time
Cleanup time, cleanup time
Cleanup time, cleanup time

Opposite: John signs autographs after a *Double Fantasy* session at the Hit Factory, August 1980.

I'M LOSING YOU

This was a number that John first tried in 1978 as "Stranger's Room". As such, it has the air of some adulterous escapade. But John preferred to claim his song had its beginnings in Bermuda after he'd tried to phone Yoko in New York. Yoko visited John only briefly during the trip, returning to her office at the Dakota where John found it frustratingly difficult to contact her.

Failing to connect, he said later, "I was just mad as hell, feeling lost and separate." He likened this state of isolation to his mid-Seventies "lost weekend", or even to the loss of his mother.

Still, "I'm Losing You" is primarily a song about the experience of domestic conflict. The Lennons were often accused of using *Double Fantasy* and its attendant interviews to paint a falsely benign portrait of their marriage. But, as ever, their songs make no attempt to varnish the truth. Whenever John and Yoko attained harmony, they always celebrated the fact, but if they failed occasionally, their failure was never disguised. The unflinching realism of "I'm Losing You" is firmly reinforced by the angry song it segues into, Yoko's sneering goodbye "I'm Moving On". Linked by a harsh sequence of electronic bleeps and sharing Earl Slick's jagged, nagging guitar lick, the two tracks represent a full-on confrontation. It's an instance where the "Heart Play" dialogue idea works well. "It's not happy-go-lucky," Yoko agrees. "Even now when I hear that, I get choked up."

Small wonder that "I'm Losing You" took John back to his dark night of the soul in 1973—the year that Yoko wrote "I'm Moving On" and promptly kicked him out. We cannot know if history was about to repeat itself, but "I'm Losing You" is proof, at least, that *Double Fantasy* is a work of greater emotional complexity than many of its critics have been prepared to admit.

Opposite: Lennon at the Hit Factory, New York in November, 1980.

Here in some stranger's room
Late in the afternoon
What am I doing here at all?
Ain't no doubt about it

I'm losing you
I'm losing you

Somehow the wires have crossed
Communication's lost
Can't even get you on the telephone
Just got to shout about it

I'm losing you
I'm losing you

Well, here in the valley of indecision
I don't know what to do
I feel you slipping away
I feel you slipping away

I'm losing you
I'm losing you
You say you're not getting enough
But I remind you of all that bad, bad, bad stuff
So what the hell am I supposed to do?
Just put a band-aid on it?
And stop the bleeding now
Stop the bleeding now

I'm losing you
I'm losing you

Well, well, well

I know I hurt you then
But that was way back when
And well, do you still have to carry that cross? (drop it)
Don't want to hear about it

I'm losing you
I'm losing you
Don't wanna lose you now
Well
No, no, no, no

BEAUTIFUL BOY (DARLING BOY)

For John, the central event of 1975 had been his wife's pregnancy. It came, of course, after years of miscarriages, and in spite of John's belief that his own system was too weakened ever to sire a child again. His first son, Julian, had been unplanned—a fact he tactlessly referred to by remarking, "Ninety percent of the people on this planet were born out of a bottle of whisky on a Saturday night."

However, Sean was the child that he and Yoko had longed for, and they lavished care upon her pregnancy. Guided by the same Chinese doctor who John claimed had weaned him off drugs, they put their faith in clean living, macrobiotic diets, and acupuncture.

In Sean, they saw the word made flesh. Their union, the union of East and West, had been made incarnate in a way that, previously, they could only sing about. After the baby's birth, John's artistic output slackened considerably, but he welcomed the paternal responsibilities he'd never faced up to for Julian. A genuinely touching lullaby, gracefully embellished by some Caribbean steel drumming, the words and music of "Beautiful Boy" came to John more or less simultaneously, a sign of its easy sincerity. He took pride in the time they spent together during the first five years of Sean's life. He believed the next generation would be happier if more parents could do likewise. But he resented Mick Jagger for suggesting that John had sacrificed his music to stay at home, as if it were not possible to do both.

Among the pearls of wisdom that John passes on to his son is the famous line, "Life is what happens to you while you're busy making other plans." According to the British astrologer Patric Walker, this was a precept of the Islamic creed Sufi that he shared with John "over coffee in New York one morning". John first used it in a 1979 song, "My Life", which he later abandoned. In the light of impending events, it's a line that still leaps out with unwelcome force.

As far as Julian was concerned, John felt guilty about his lack of active parenting: "It's not the best relationship between father and son, but it is there... I hadn't seen Julian grow up at all, and now there's a seventeen-year-old on the phone about motorbikes." Julian Lennon later said, "The last year, I would say, was the best. I was growing older, I began to understand things a lot more and understand Dad too... Towards the end, we were definitely getting closer."

In 1995, Paul McCartney recalled a holiday with John and Julian in Greece. Paul was playing happily with the boy, which made John curious: "He said, 'How do you do that?' Well, luckily towards the end of his life, John had found out how to do that."

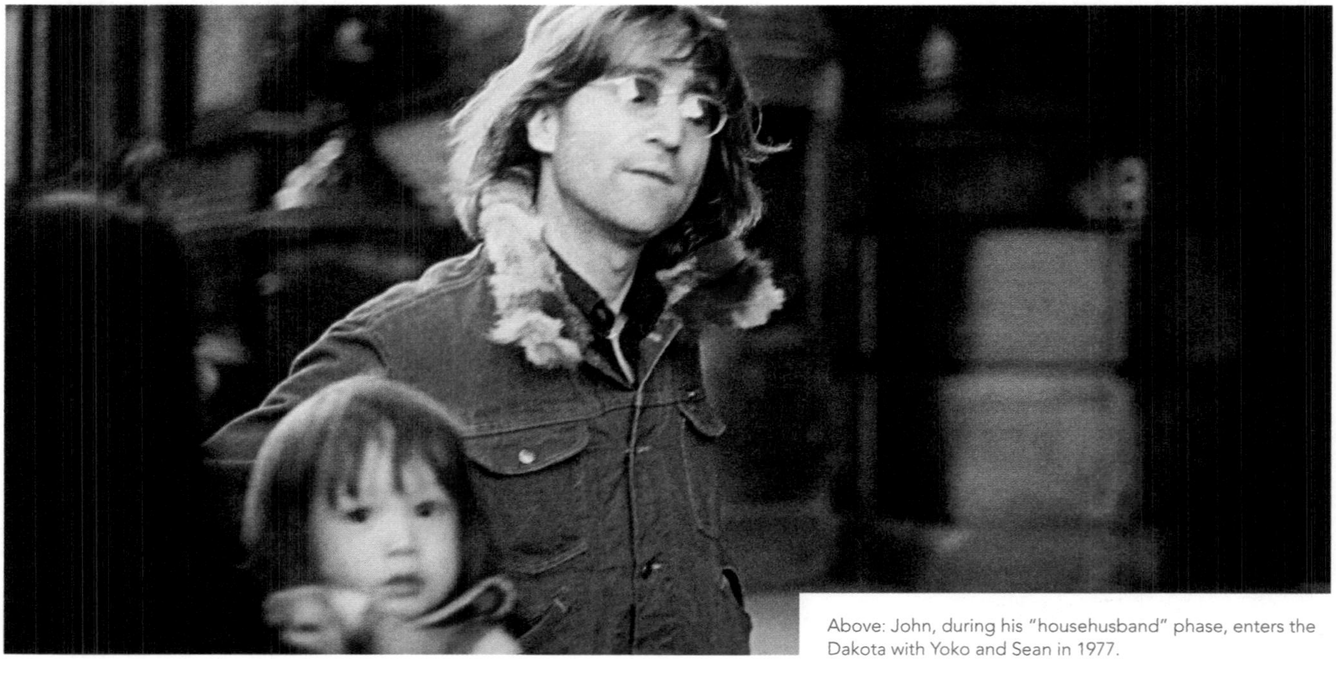

Above: John, during his "househusband" phase, enters the Dakota with Yoko and Sean in 1977.

BEAUTIFUL BOY (DARLING BOY)

Close your eyes
Have no fear
The monster's gone
He's on the run and your daddy's here

Beautiful, beautiful, beautiful
Beautiful boy
Beautiful, beautiful, beautiful
Beautiful boy

Before you go to sleep
Say a little prayer
Every day in every way, it's getting better and better

Beautiful, beautiful, beautiful
Beautiful boy
Beautiful, beautiful, beautiful
Beautiful boy

Out on the ocean sailing away
I can hardly wait
To see you come of age
But I guess we'll both just have to be patient
'Cause it's a long way to go
A hard row to hoe
Yes, it's a long way to go
But in the meantime

Before you cross the street
Take my hand
Life is what happens to you while you're busy making other plans

Beautiful, beautiful, beautiful
Beautiful boy
Beautiful, beautiful, beautiful
Beautiful boy

Before you go to sleep
Say a little prayer
Every day in every way, it's getting better and better

Beautiful, beautiful, beautiful
Beautiful boy

Darling, darling, darling
Darling Sean

WATCHING THE WHEELS

In 1972, three years before his own disappearance from public life, Lennon had defended Bob Dylan from those who criticised the singer for opting out of his role as spokesman for the counterculture: "Dylan exists with or without The Movement. We owe him a great deal of things…"

He continued: "It does not matter that Dylan has done nothing for six months or that he chooses to rest for a year, or that he is going through a psychological crisis, or that he has had an accident, or that he wants to live with his children and his family. Dylan has done what he has done and he continues. We ought to let him have a little time to breathe."

The words were remarkably prophetic of John's position in the five-year hiatus leading up to the release of *Double Fantasy*. Yet his almost total absence from the scene was really without parallel in a rock star of such magnitude. When Elvis Presley joined the Army for two years in 1958, his career was kept on the boil with photo calls, a Hollywood movie, reissues, and even new records cut while he was on leave. Bob Dylan was only a true recluse for eighteen months, following a motorbike accident in 1966. In the late Seventies, Bruce Springsteen, John's nearest rival as rock standard-bearer, had a lengthy layoff in between *Born To Run* and *Darkness On The Edge Of Town*, but continued touring in the interim.

Meanwhile Lennon's profile was authentically low, and despite his previous words of encouragement, he was privately scornful of "company men" like Dylan, Jagger, and McCartney, who all contrived to keep the product coming. When his EMI deal expired in January 1976, he was out of contract for the first time since the Beatles signed up fourteen years earlier. He was the only member of the group not to carry on: Paul renewed his deal, George went to A&M, and Ringo signed with Polydor and Atlantic.

In "Watching The Wheels", John explained how content he had been "just sitting here… watching shadows on the wall" while the outside world deplored his apparent lethargy. We know that he was not the Howard Hughes character of legend—he traveled extensively and enjoyed a fairly active social life. Nor did he abandon music completely, in spite of his subsequent suggestions to the contrary—in fact, he wrote numerous songs and made many demo recordings. But he used the five-year holiday to balance out the excessive publicity of his earlier life, to take stock, and to recover from an existence as turbulent as anyone had ever known.

Media pleadings and the consternation of his fans had little effect. Doubtless he was aware of the *New Musical Express* cover story of january 14th, 1978, which demanded, "Where the hell are you, John Lennon?" His absence was felt especially keenly in Britain: "John, plenty of us here have found your reluctance to use your green card to at least pay us a courtesy call less than excusable." The journalist, Neil Spencer, went on to note how much the UK's punk revolution owed to Lennon's influence: "They started the revolution without you, mate. But then you started it without waiting for anyone else. It took the rest of us a long time to catch up—but that's no reason to opt out now."

Even his peers among the rock aristocracy were bemused by John's inactivity. "I couldn't believe it," he said. "They were acting like mothers-in-law." He told *Newsweek* that the comments he read reminded him of his teachers' reports. On one of several visits to Japan, Lennon held a press conference to explain his inactivity. "We've basically decided, without a great decision, to be with our baby as much as we can until we feel we can take the time off to indulge ourselves creating things outside the family. Maybe when he's three, four, or five, then we'll think about creating something else other than the child."

On May 27th, 1979, the Lennons placed a full-page ad in papers in London, New York, and Tokyo. Entitled "A love letter from John and Yoko", it was addressed "to people who ask us what, when and why". Within its text, the couple described "the spring-cleaning of our minds! It was a lot of work" and once more aired their old belief in the power of wishes. Their conclusion was: "We are all part of the sky, more so than of the ground. Remember, we love you." Having begun in demo form (as "I'm Crazy") that same year, "Watching The Wheels" was John's musical version of the "love letter" that he had placed in the newspapers.

A hankering for the quiet life was not new to John's thinking. He'd often spoken wistfully of a peaceful retirement with Yoko, perhaps in a cottage in Ireland. As early as 1969, at the height of his media-saturated peace campaigning, John told interviewer Barry Miles about a TV documentary he'd just watched about a man training a falcon at some remote retreat in Cornwall: "And I thought, 'God almighty, it's all I want, really...' I always have this dream of being the artist in a little cottage and I didn't do any of this publicity or anything; my real thing is just write a little poetry and do a few oils. It just seemed like such a dream, living in a cottage and wandering in the trees."

WATCHING THE WHEELS

People say I'm crazy doing what I'm doing
Well they give me all kinds of warnings to save me from ruin
When I say that I'm ok they look at me kind of strange
Surely you're not happy now you no longer play the game

People say I'm lazy dreaming my life away
Well they give me all kinds of advice designed to enlighten me
When I tell that I'm doing fine watching shadows on the wall
Don't you miss the big time boy you're no longer on the ball?

I'm just sitting here watching the wheels go round and round
I really love to watch them roll
No longer riding on the merry-go-round
I just had to let it go

People asking questions lost in confusion
Well I tell them there's no problem
Only solutions
Well they shake their heads and they look at me as if I've lost my mind
I tell them there's no hurry...
I'm just sitting here doing time

I'm just sitting here watching the wheels go round and round
I really love to watch them roll
No longer riding on the merry-go-round
I just had to let it go
I just had to let it go
I just had to let it go
I just had to let it go

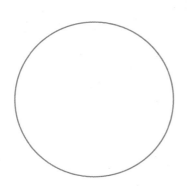

WOMAN

On its simplest level, "Woman" was another in Lennon's series of apologies to Yoko for the most oafish excesses of his past. But he was also keen that people read the song as being dedicated to womankind in general.

The track opens with an adaptation of Mao Tse-Tung's adage that women and men are complementary halves of the sky—or, as John put it, "Without each other, there's nothing." At the *Double Fantasy* sessions, John explained "Woman" to his musicians as being "early Motown/Beatles '64. It's for your mother or your sister, anyone of the female race. That's who you're singing to."

Among the most enduring and most accessible recordings of his last year, John always thought of "Woman" as the album's "Beatle track". He described it as an Eighties update of his 1965 *Rubber Soul* song "Girl", the only Beatle song that Cynthia Lennon believed that he had written specifically about her. Although he'd expressed pro-feminist feelings in earlier songs, John said he had only recently "put my body where my mouth was" by acting out his beliefs. "Woman Is the Nigger of the World", he confessed, was no more than an intellectual position. Not until the late Seventies had he made much effort to put the theory into practice. Of the books which influenced him, John acknowledged *The First Sex* by Elizabeth Gould Davis.

There were many examples of Lennon's jealous cruelty, and even outright violence, in his dealings with Yoko, May Pang, and Cynthia, as well as with the innumerable girls and women who had crossed his path in the last forty years. He was a man, he considered, who had been waited on by women all his life, and had often responded with abominable ingratitude. "My history of relationships with women is a very poor one," he told *Playboy*. "Very macho, very typical of a certain type of man, I suppose, which is very sensitive and insecure but acting aggressive and macho. You know, trying to cover up the feminine side, which I still have a tendency to do… I tend to put on my cowboy boots when I'm insecure, whereas now I'm in sneakers and it's comfy."

In the same interview, though, he angrily denied the notion that Yoko had a tendency to dominate him: "Rubbish… The only one who controls me is me, and that's just barely possible." But he went on to say of feminism, "The real changes are coming. I am the one who has come a long way. I was the pig. And it is a relief not to be a pig." As to his recent "househusband" phase, it was "the wave of the future, and I'm glad to be in on the forefront of that too".

Opposite: The Lennons, on November 2nd, 1980, in one of John's final photo sessions.

For the other half of the sky

Woman, I can hardly express
My mixed emotion at my thoughtlessness
After all I'm forever in your debt

And woman, I will try to express
My inner feelings and thankfulness
For showing me the meaning of success
Ooh, well, well, do do do do
Ooh, well, well, do do do do

And, woman, hold me close to your heart
However distant don't keep us apart
After all it is written in the stars
Ooh, well, well, do do do do
Ooh, well, well, do do do do

Woman, please let me explain
I never meant to cause you sorrow or pain
So let me tell you again and again and again

I love you (yeah, yeah) now and forever
I love you (yeah, yeah) now and forever
I love you (yeah, yeah) now and forever
I love you (yeah, yeah)

DEAR YOKO

Kicking off with a playful Buddy Holly gurgle, "Dear Yoko" closes John's contribution to *Double Fantasy* (the album's last words went to Yoko in "Every Man Has a Woman Who Loves Him" and "Hard Times Are Over").

It shares the same spirit of throwaway gaiety as "Oh Yoko!", which had concluded *Imagine* nine years previously. This song was written while John was in Bermuda, "miles at sea" and missing his absent wife. So it may have another parallel with "Oh Yoko!", which was originally conceived in a bout of insecurity. As "I'm Losing You" had shown, there were moments in Lennon's tropical sojourn when he feared desertion, and "Dear Yoko" sounds like another instance of John singing to keep his spirits up.

Even if "Dear Yoko" fails to match its predecessor's infectious gusto, John declared himself well satisfied. "It says it all," he told *Playboy*. "The track's a nice track and it happens to be about my wife, instead of 'Dear Sandra' or some other person that another singer would sing about who may or may not exist." In other words, whatever its musical merits, the song has the virtue of having sprung out of real life. And for John Lennon that was what mattered. Everything else was mere "craftsmanship".

For all we know, he might have come to disown the song. He never looked back at his music as anything more than work in progress. He'd even dreamed of rerecording "Strawberry Fields Forever", but he never got the opportunity: On December 8th, 1980, a half-crazy character named Mark Chapman stood with those die-hard fans outside the Dakota, harboring thoughts of Lennon's "dishonesty". At 10:49 that evening, the Lennons' automobile pulled up at Number 1, West 72nd Street, and Chapman committed the act that would, however temporarily, make him as famous as the man he had once worshipped.

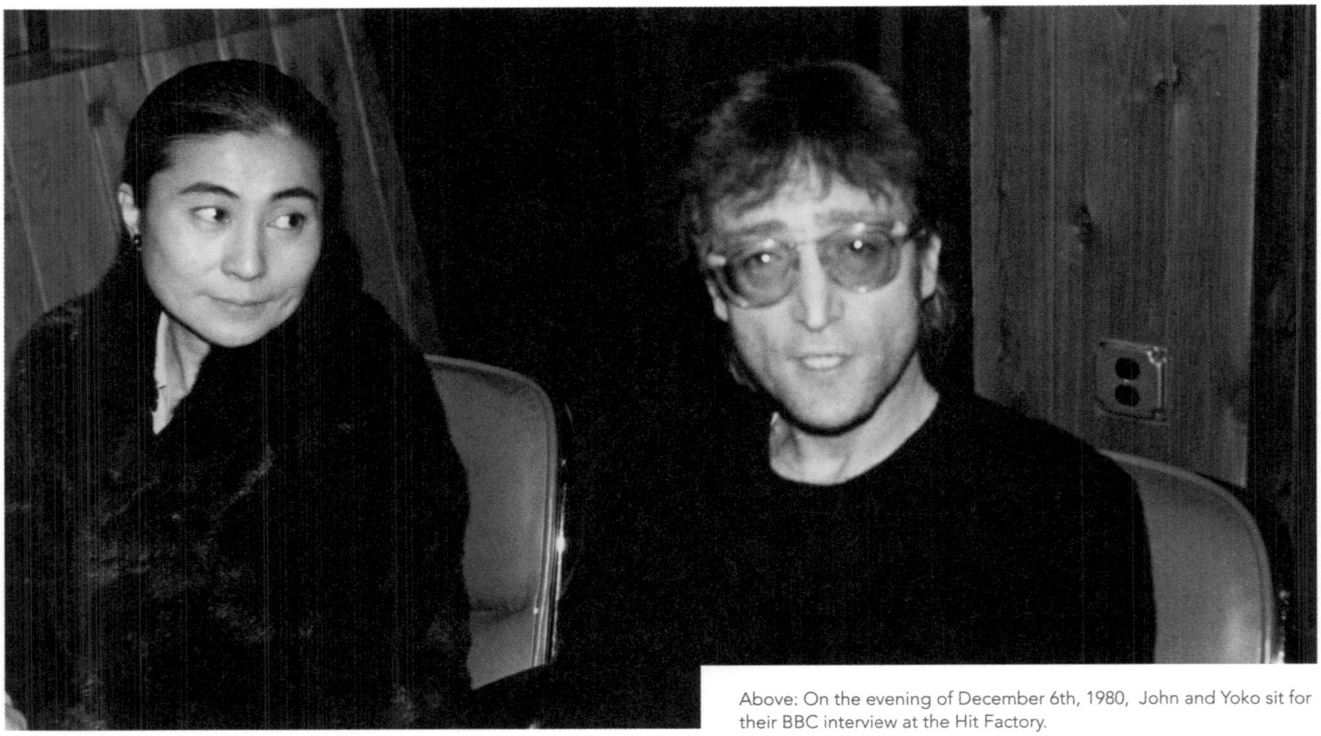

Above: On the evening of December 6th, 1980, John and Yoko sit for their BBC interview at the Hit Factory.

DEAR YOKO

Even after all these years
I miss you when you're not here
I wish you were here my dear Yoko
Even if it's just a day
I miss you when you're away
I wish you were here today dear Yoko
Even if it's just one night
I miss you and it don't feel right
I wish you were here tonight dear Yoko
Even if it's just one hour
I wilt just like a fading flower
Ain't nothing in the world like our love dear Yoko

Oh Yoko!
I'll never ever ever ever gonna let you go
Oh Yoko!
I'll never ever ever ever gonna let you go

Even when I'm miles at sea
And nowhere is the place to be
Your spirit's watching over me dear Yoko
Even when I watch T.V.
There's a hole where you're supposed to be
There's nobody lying next to me

Oh Yoko!
I'll never ever ever ever gonna let you go
Oh Yoko!
I'll never ever ever ever gonna let you go

Even after all this time
I miss you like the sun don't shine
Without you I'm a one track mind dear Yoko
After all is really said and done
The two of us are really one
The goddess really smiled upon our love dear Yoko

Chapter 8

MILK

19 84

AND HONEY

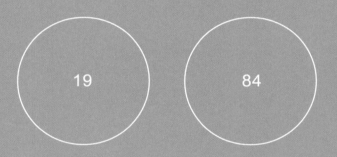

"I'm Stepping Out"
"I Don't Wanna Face It"
"Nobody Told Me"
"Borrowed Time"
"(Forgive Me) My Little Flower Princess"
"Grow Old With Me"

Recorded
August/September 1980 (with additions by Yoko up to 1983), at Hit Factory, New York City.

Produced by
John Lennon, Yoko Ono.

Musicians
John Lennon (vocals, guitar), Yoko Ono (vocals), Earl Slick (guitar), Hugh McCracken (guitar), John Tropea (guitar), Elliot Randall (guitar), Steve Love (guitar), Tony Levin (bass), Neil Jason (bass), Wayne Pedziwiatr (bass), Andy Newmark (drums), Yogi Horton (drums), Allan Schwartzberg (drums), George Small (piano), Paul Griffin (piano), Arthur Jenkins Jr (percussion), Jimmy Maelen (percussion), Pete Cannarozzi (synthesizer), Ed Walsh (percussion), Howard Johnson (saxophone), Gordon Grody, Kurt Yahjian, Carlos Alomar, Billy and Bob Alessi, Pete Thom (backing vocals).

OO

"Do you mean that he is sleeping?" said Yoko Ono to the medical staff at Roosevelt Hospital. Her husband had been shot, with five bullets to the chest, as he was entering the Dakota less than half an hour before. Now, in her bewilderment, she could not believe that he was dead. The time was around 11:15 pm, December 8th, 1980, and John Lennon's murderer, Mark Chapman, was already under arrest, having submitted himself to the police without a struggle.

"THE LAND OF MILK AND HONEY IS WHERE YOU GO WHEN YOU DIE. VERY INTERESTING THAT I THOUGHT OF THAT TITLE."

—Yoko Ono

In the days that followed John's assassination, Yoko's grief and disbelief were shared in some measure by many millions of people. Lennon's place in the collective imagination went deeper than mere celebrity; his life had touched a lot of people. His sudden loss brought a sense of bereavement with an almost spiritual dimension. He had embodied the soul of his times, and most who shared those times discovered that they loved him more than they knew.

In other ways, life went on. A mortuary assistant took a sneak photograph of John on the slab, selling it to newspapers for $10,000. Still, as Yoko noted, John at least looked peaceful in the picture, which was strangely reminiscent of the profile portrait on *Imagine*. Media tributes proliferated, while the news stands were clogged by hastily written souvenirs—the majority displaying a peculiar blend of sincerity and opportunism. On December 14th, there were simultaneous vigils in Lennon's two hometowns, Liverpool and New York City, attended by thousands of mourners. Within a year, Mark Chapman would be sentenced to twenty years to life.

By the standards of the music industry, the treatment of John Lennon's catalogue has been reasonably tasteful. The market was not bombarded with shoddy compilations, and his unfinished tracks have appeared only slowly: in the case of "Free As A Bird"—a "new" Beatles single built around one of John's poorly recorded 1977 demos—it took fifteen years. "Tribute" records are another tradition in pop music, and normally range from the cynical to the mawkish. Lennon raised the whole standard of pop, so it's fitting he inspired some tribute records of the highest order.

To begin with, though, there are the tracks that he began recording in the *Double Fantasy* sessions, presumably intending to finish them off at some later date. In January 1984, Yoko released six of John's songs on *Milk And Honey*. Alternating with tracks of her own (most of which, she says, John had heard in some form), they were subtitled "A Heart Play", in the dialogue tradition of *Double Fantasy* itself. Although they're unrefined recordings—after all, they were works in progress—they are nonetheless complete John Lennon songs. And, as ever, they diarize his hopes and fears with compelling honesty.

According to Yoko: "John thought of *Double Fantasy*, the title, and I thought of *Milk And Honey*. Of course, all the immigrants think, 'Oh, America is milk and honey.' But also, in the Scriptures, milk and honey is 'beyond'. The land of milk and honey is where you go after you die. So it's very interesting that I thought of that title. I wasn't cognisant of it, but..."

Opposite: John, in Beverly Hills in 1979. His loss provoked a global sense of bereavement.

I'M STEPPING OUT

On its initial release all of *Milk And Honey* was credited to John and Yoko as co-writers. But "I'm Stepping Out" has a rough good humour that was distinctively more Lennon than Ono.

Clearly, its theme of joyous escape remained close to his heart, and it was the very first number attempted at the *Double Fantasy* sessions. As such, the official Lennon comeback is simply bursting with the pent-up energies of five years spent away from a recording studio. It also reminds us he was not the total "homebody" of cherished myth.

Practically gabbling with excitement, John sets out his stall at the very beginning. This is the story of a "househusband" who's gone stir-crazy at home, looking after kids and cats and watching summer repeats on the TV. For the sake of his own sanity, he's going to beat his cabin fever, dress up tonight and paint the town red. Oh, and don't worry, he'll "be in before 1… or 2 … or 3."

Such a merry manifesto of independence is a happy contrast to his many songs of meek contrition, and tends to suggest that he was never really the Hermit of West 72nd Street. Sections of the song date back to 1977; it had eventually reached the demo stage in Bermuda. Even by the end, it was a fairly knockabout recording that he might have improved upon later, but it skips along in high spirits and it's packed with persuasive little details. Thus, he decides he'll kick over the traces and leave a rude message on his answering machine. Then, with baby and cats pacified, he'll treat himself to a longed-for cigarette. A devout smoker, Lennon trusted that his macrobiotic regime would protect him against cancer. "Of course," he added, casually, "if we die, we're wrong."

"AFTER ALL IS SAID AND DONE, YOU CAN'T GO PLEASING EVERYONE."

—John Lennon

One, two
One, two, three, four
This here is the story about a househusband who
You know, just has to get out of the house, he's been looking
At the, you know, the kids for days and days, he's been watching
The kitchen and screwing around watching
Sesame Street till
He's going crazy!

Woke up this morning blues around my head
No need to ask the reason why
Went to the kitchen and lit a cigarette
Blew my worries to the sky

I'm stepping out
I'm stepping out
I'm stepping out
I'm stepping out

If it doesn't feel right you don't have to do it
Just leave a message on the phone and tell them to screw it
After all is said and done, you can't go pleasing everyone
So screw it

I'm stepping out
I'm stepping out
I'm stepping out, baby
I'm stepping out

Baby's sleeping, the cats have all been blessed
Ain't nothing doing on TV (summer repeats)
Put on my space suit I got to look my best
I'm going out to do the city

I'm stepping out
I'm stepping out
I'm stepping out, babe
I'm stepping out
Boogie

(One more)

I'm stepping out
Hold it down
I'm stepping out
I'm stepping out
Gotta, gotta, gotta, gotta get out
I'm stepping out, babe
Just a while
Ain't been out for days

Gotta do it tonight
Gimme a break, gimme a break
Gotta get out, gotta get out
Just for a while, just for the night
I'll be in before one or two

I DON'T WANNA FACE IT

Another Bermuda demo with its roots in 1977, "I Don't Wanna Face It" was never quite perfected at the Hit Factory sessions. Then again, it provides a telling insight into Lennon's Dakota years.

Plenty of people criticized John Lennon, but he usually got there first, and did it better. The litany of putdowns is, in this case, clearly self-directed. He is the man who looks in the mirror and sees nobody there. Like the classically self-righteous radical, he proclaims his love of humanity (it's just people he can't stand), and he sings for a supper that he doesn't know how to make. Here is John, still "with one eye on the Hall of Fame", coming to realize that his ambitions no longer lie in that arena. At any rate, not for now.

"John had periods when he renounced the whole thing," says Paul McCartney, who was in touch with Lennon during the late Seventies. As with any new kick he'd discovered, John was passionately evangelical: "I remember him phoning me and saying, 'Look, lad, it's the most difficult thing to renounce our fame. We're so hooked on fame, but it's great, you should kick it over.' And I'm going, 'Hmm, do tell me, what do you mean here?' I listened to him but after about a year of that he was back. And what was his famous line? 'This housewife wants a job.'"

Un ... deux
Ein, zwei, hickle pickle

Say you're looking for a place to go
Where nobody knows your name
You're looking for oblivion
With one
Eye on the Hall of Fame

I don't want to face it oh no
I don't want to face it no, no, no, no
Well, I can dish it out
But I just can't take it

Say you're looking for some peace and love
Leader of a big old band
You want to save humanity
But it's people that you just can't stand

I don't want to face it oh no
I don't want to face it no, no, no, no
Well, I can sing for my supper
But I just can't make it

Well, now you're looking for a world of truth
Trying to find a better way
The time has come to see yourself
You always look the other way

I don't want to face it no, no
I don't want to face it no, no, no, no
Well, I can see the promised land
And I know I can make it

I don't want to face it I know
I don't want to face it oh no
I don't want to face it oh no
I don't want to face it
I don't want to face it

I just can't face it no more
Every time I look in the mirror
I don't see anybody there

NOBODY TOLD ME

When Lennon first sketched this song it was called "Everybody's Talkin', Nobody's Talkin'", perhaps inspired by the title of Harry Nilsson's hit. The verse words present a string of paradoxes—"There's always something happening / And nothing going on"—until, at the chorus, John throws up his hands in exasperation. "Nobody Told Me" is fine, sturdy rock 'n' roll, and proof that his cynical wit was not extinct.

With its catalogue of daily frustrations, "Nobody Told Me" is another signal that John's last years were not so blissfully mellow as he suggested. (Another demo from the same era, called "You Save My Soul", actually implies he was nearly driven to suicide.) During his career, Lennon learned to his cost that it's foolish to be totally open with the media. His "bigger than Jesus" quote brought endless trouble; talking about drugs invited more problems with the authorities; references to his family would often cause them pain. By 1980, John was adept at setting his interviewers' agenda, painting the picture which he and Yoko had agreed upon. But the songs he wrote seemed immune to this self-censorship. Their candor is like something he cannot help. Yoko's song, "O Sanity", follows and offers a glimpse of her own moments of doubt in the unreal period post-1980.

There's some evidence that John intended to give "Nobody Told Me" to Ringo. If that's true, it would have been one of Lennon's better presents to his old drummer, who'd been the recipient of less-than-classic compositions. As recently as 1976, John had donated the lackluster "Cookin' (In The Kitchen Of Love)" to Ringo's *Rotogravure* album. In 1974, he contributed the title track to *Goodnight Vienna*. And, a year before that, he offered Ringo "I'm the Greatest"—a song he'd originally written for himself, before deciding that Mohammed Ali's famous line might sound less arrogant coming from Ringo Starr than from John Lennon.

Possibly the oddest line in "Nobody Told Me" concerns "the little yellow idol". In fact, it's a near-quote from a 1911 poem, "The Green Eye Of The Yellow God" ("There's a one-eyed yellow idol to the north of Kathmandu") written by J. Milton Hayes, who died in the year of Lennon's birth. Like Rudyard Kipling's work, this poem was familiar to people of John's parents' generation, a staple of pub and parlor recitations in John's formative years.

Above: In their last year together, the Lennons take a break in Central Park.

NOBODY TOLD ME

...Three, Four!

Everybody's talking
And no-one says a word
Everybody's making love
And no-one really cares
There's Nazis in the bathroom
Just below the stairs
Always something happening
And nothing going on
Always something cooking
And nothing in the pot
They're starving back in China
So finish what you've got

Nobody told me there'd be days like these
Nobody told me there'd be days like these
Nobody told me there'd be days like these
Strange days indeed
Strange days indeed

Everybody's running
And no-one makes a move
Everyone's a winner
And nothing left to lose
There's a little yellow idol
To the north of Kathmandu
Everybody's flying
And no-one leaves the ground
Everybody's crying
And no-one makes a sound
There's a place for us in movies
You've just got to lay around

Nobody told me there'd be days like these
Nobody told me there'd be days like these
Nobody told me there'd be days like these
Strange days indeed
Most peculiar mama

Everybody's smoking
And no-ones getting high
Everybody's flying
And never touch the sky
There's a UFO over New York
And I ain't too surprised

Nobody told me there'd be days like these
Nobody told me there'd be days like these
Nobody told me there'd be days like these
Strange days indeed
Most peculiar mama, woah

BORROWED TIME

While the island of Bermuda is not actually in the Caribbean, the old British colony had a sufficiently West Indian feel to put John in the mood for reggae. He whiled away the 1980 summer trip listening to Bob Marley, the superstar of Jamaican music, whose iconic status and crusading role made him, in effect, John Lennon's black counterpart.

The two men never met—in fact, Marley was to die just six months after John—but their paths would surely have crossed in the Eighties, had they not both met such premature ends. John was always fond of Marley's *Burnin'*, the 1972 album which brought the Wailers to global attention, especially when John's friend Eric Clapton covered "I Shot The Sheriff". It was another *Burnin'* track, "Hallelujah Time", which gave John the idea for "Borrowed Time".

Bearing in mind that his song never got beyond the band rehearsal stage, we can forgive the faux-tropical accent John attempts. "Borrowed Time" is an evocative piece of writing; it's a pity we'll never hear it in definitive form. That said, it's less reggae than generic, West Indian easy listening. Lennon spent the last years trying to widen his horizons: He enjoyed Muzak because there were no words to distract him; he explored Japanese folk music and Indian music; and he defended disco from detractors who thought it too simplistic and repetitive—those were the very qualities that had turned him on to Little Richard.

Reggae was a style John had championed since the Sixties. In its earlier forms—ska, bluebeat, and rocksteady—the music thrived in British clubs, imported by Caribbean immigrants, then taken up by London tastemakers such as the Beatles. The group made a few facetious stabs at it, including "Ob-La-Di, Ob-La-Da" and the *Anthology II* take of "You Know My Name (Look Up The Number)". But John was frustrated in his efforts to make convincing reggae on his solo albums, finding his American musicians unused to it, and the American audience unready for it. Nor was he the only white rocker to find that loving reggae was not the same as mastering it.

It's the optimism and contentment of "Borrowed Time" which make it such an endearing song. With a poignancy we need not labor, John reflects on life's brevity. He's outgrown the confusion of youth and believes it's "good to be older". The wisdom of age has shown him how little he really knows, but he's free, at least, of illusions and distractions: "The future is brighter and now is the hour." John's life was cruelly abbreviated, but it's satisfying that his body of work should contain this song. Complementing the frank unhappiness of earlier works, it introduces a final note of wholeness and fulfilment.

Lennon had only contempt for the supposed glamor of early death. He was scornful of Neil Young's 1979 *Rust Never Sleeps* song "My My Hey Hey", which extolled the Sex Pistols' Johnny Rotten and the notion that it's "better to burn out than to fade away". Referring to the recent death of Rotten's sidekick, Lennon retorted, "Sid Vicious died for what? So that we might rock? It's garbage."

Below: Bob Marley, whose "Hallelujah Time" inspired John's "Borrowed Time".

"I ALWAYS LOOK FORWARD TO BEING OLD, JUST REMEMBERING EVERYTHING."

—John Lennon

(FORGIVE ME) MY LITTLE FLOWER PRINCESS

It's understandable that Yoko should be partial to John's most abject songs of submission, but there is a case for saying that "(Forgive Me) My Little Flower Princess" ought to have been left in peace. John recorded this tale early in the *Double Fantasy* sessions and did not return to it. Even had he done so, it's difficult to see how it might be salvaged.

One, two, one, two, three, four

Forgive me, my little flower princess
For crushing your delicateness
Forgive me, if you could forgive me

Forgive me, my little flower princess
For crushing your delicateness
Forgive me, if you could forgive me

Well, I know there is no way to repay you
Whatever it takes I will try to
The rest of my life I will thank you
Thank you, thank you, my little

Forgive me, my little flower princess
For crushing your delicateness
Forgive me, if you could forgive me

Time is on our side
Let's not waste another minute
Because I love you, my little friend
I really love you

Give me just one more chance
And I'll show you
Take up the dance where we left off
The rest of our life is the, my little

I'm home

GROW OLD WITH ME

John's "Grow Old with Me" is preceded by a companion Yoko song, "Let Me Count the Ways", which she can remember playing to him when he was in Bermuda.

Her title quotes Elizabeth Barrett Browning's *Sonnets from the Portuguese* ("How do I love thee?/Let me count the ways..."), while John responds with a song derived from another poem, "Rabbi Ben Ezra", by Elizabeth's husband Robert Browning: "Grow old along with me! The best is yet to be." Ono and Lennon apparently identified with the Brownings, a devoted couple who wrote some of the most admired poetry in 19th-century English literature. Yoko's next track, the album's finale, "You're the One", offers a few more analogies: to the mocking world, she and John were Laurel and Hardy; in their own imaginations, they were the storm-tossed lovers of *Wuthering Heights*, Cathy and Heathcliff.

The chorus of "God bless our love", and John's simple piano part, gives "Grow Old with Me" the Sunday School air of a Victorian hymn. The sad irony of its central image ("man and wife together, world without end") echoes its inspiration: Browning's poem first appeared in 1864, three years after his wife's death. John once told interviewer Barry Miles of his dreams for the future. "I really can't wait to be old," he said. "You do your best and then there is a time when you do slow down and it seems nice. I always look forward to being an old couple of about sixty, just remembering everything. I suppose we'll still be cursing because we're in a wheelchair."

Grow old along with me
The best is yet to be
When our time has come
We will be as one
God bless our love
God bless our love

Grow old along with me
Two branches of one tree
Face the setting Sun
When the day is done
God bless our love
God bless our love

Spending our lives together
Man and wife together
World without end
World without end

Grow old along with me
Whatever fate decrees
We will see it through
For our love is true
God bless our love
God bless our love

Chapter 9

LONG

LOST JOHN

Albums

Live In New York City

Menlove Ave.

Lennon Legend

John Lennon: Anthology

Wonsaponatime

Acoustic

"Signature" Box Set

Power To The People: The Hits

John Lennon's legacy
Tribute records
The 1994/1995 Beatles sessions
Rarities
Posthumous compilations

For the five years before those last recording sessions, John's had been the empty chair at the rock 'n' roll banquet. He'd been far from idle, but was not especially attentive to new trends. Though he approved of London's new punk scene, he was unexcited by it; as far as he was concerned, he'd sung that stuff himself at the Cavern and in Hamburg.

He took no more than a passing interest in the New York acts who were reinvigorating rock in the late Seventies—Television, Talking Heads, Blondie, the Ramones, Patti Smith. From his Dakota window, he could perhaps see across to the Bronx, where hip-hop—the next decade's most vibrant genre—was busy being born. Had he lived longer, he might have loved rap as much as reggae. Just before he died, he made an effort to update his tastes by checking out the Manhattan dance clubs. Some of that contemporary edge is heard in "Walking on Thin Ice", the Yoko single he helped to complete on the night of his murder.

There would be no new Lennon music, but his death sent others into the studios. Roxy Music's version of "Jealous Guy", recorded just after the murder, was a moving epitaph, catching the universal mood of bittersweet nostalgia. Paul Simon wrote "The Late Great Johnny Ace", a skilfully constructed elegy that weaves in John's demise with those of John F. Kennedy and the original Johnny Ace, a Fifties R&B star who shot himself while playing Russian roulette. George Harrison was joined by Paul and Ringo on his own tribute, "All Those Years Ago". Yoko's next album, *Season Of Glass*, was naturally by way of an ode to John, even reenlisting Phil Spector for part of the production. But its cover was hard to take—a photo of John's bloodstained spectacles on a window-ledge of the Dakota apartment.

McCartney's personal memorial came in a track on 1982's *Tug Of War* album. Called "Here Today", he describes it as "a song saying, 'Well, if you were here today, you'd probably say what I'm doing is crap. But you wouldn't mean it, cos you like me really.' It's one of those 'come out from behind your glasses, look at me' kind of things. It was a love song about my relationship with him. I was trying to exorcise the demons in my own head, because it's tough when you have somebody like John slagging you off in public... He was a major influence on my life, as I suppose I was on his. But the great thing about me and John was that it was me and John, end of story. Everyone else can say, 'Well, he did this and so-and-so...', but when we got in a little room, it was me and John who

Right: John performs for the Rolling Stones' TV special *Rock and Roll Circus*, on December 11th, 1968. His one-off band, The Dirty Mac, featured Eric Clapton, Mitch Mitchell, and Keith Richards.

"'HERE TODAY' WAS A LOVE SONG ABOUT MY RELATIONSHIP WITH HIM."

—Paul McCartney

wrote it, not any of these other people who think they all know about it. I was the one in the room with him."

In 1983, Yoko authorized *Heart Play—Unfinished Dialogue*, recordings of the 1980 *Playboy* interviews. Three years later came *Live In New York City*, a souvenir of John's 1972 charity shows in Madison Square Garden. It's a good, rough rock disc, but posterity might prefer a few more Beatles songs and less from Lennon's album of the moment, *Some Time In New York City*. Arguably the first essential Lennon record to appear after *Milk And Honey* was *Menlove Ave*. Named after the Liverpool road where John lived with his Aunt Mimi in later childhood, this 1986 set comprises some mid-Seventies outtakes and unused songs. From the Spector *Rock 'n' Roll* sessions, it has John and Phil's collaboration, "Here We Go Again", which is lavishly Spectoresque, but lyrically next door to despair, reflecting the pessimistic trough of his "lost weekend"; "Angel Baby" was a 1960 hit for Rosie & the Originals ("one of my all-time favorite songs," announces John, proudly); "My Baby Left Me" revisits early Elvis; "To Know Her Is to Love Her" adapts the old Spector hit. From the *Walls and Bridges* time came John's own song, "Rock and Roll People", understandably left off the album but given to Johnny Winter, and alternative versions of "Steel and Glass", "Scared", "Old Dirt Road", "Nobody Loves You (When You're Down and Out)", and "Bless You". Shorn of all embellishments, the latter tracks are as hauntingly gaunt as the *John Lennon/Plastic Ono Band* album.

Below: The Stones' Brian Jones and The Who's Roger Daltrey join Yoko, Julian, John, and Eric at the *Rock and Roll Circus*.

What nobody foresaw was that John Lennon's solo legacy would one day be reclaimed by the Beatles. When Paul and Yoko met in New York in 1994 to induct John into the Rock & Roll Hall of Fame as a solo artist, they discussed the unfinished songs that John had written in the Dakota. With the band's *Anthology* films about to be produced, there was a symbolic need for input from all four members. It was decided that Paul, George and Ringo would take away tapes of "Real Love" and "Free as a Bird", both begun around 1977 as part of a projected musical, *The Ballad Of John And Yoko*. At Paul's studio in Sussex, producer Jeff Lynne was summoned to help turn John's mono tapes into virtual band recordings.

For the surviving Beatles, there were difficulties in the task, both technical and emotional. McCartney recalls, "I said to Ringo, 'Let's pretend that we've nearly finished the recordings and John is just going off to Spain on holiday.' He's rung up saying, 'Look, there's one more song I wouldn't mind getting on the album; it's a good song but it's not finished. Take it in the studio, have fun with it, and I trust you.' And with that scenario in place, Ringo said, 'Oh, this could even be joyous!' And it was... The good thing about 'Free as a Bird' for us was that it was unfinished. The middle eight didn't have all the words, so that was like John bringing me a song and saying, 'Do you want to finish it?'"

Ringo concurs. "We got over it by feeling that he'd gone for lunch, he'd gone for a cup of tea… It's a sadness because the three of us got pretty close again, and still there's that empty hole, you know, that is John." And George Harrison added: "Maybe I'm peculiar—but to me he isn't dead. When I never saw him for years before he died, I thought, 'Oh well, he's living in New York and I just haven't seen him in a while.' It's kind of still like that. I don't believe that death is a terminal thing. The soul lives on. We are going to meet again. Life is just shadows; we are shadows on this sunny wall... I miss John in as much as we could have a good laugh and, also, I think he was a good balance. I miss him in the context of the band because he wouldn't take any shit. I want truth. John was good at that."

"Free as a Bird" and "Real Love" were released to an enormous media fanfare, and charted worldwide, as did the *Anthology* CDs and video series. Nearly thirty years after their demise, the Beatles were once again the planet's highest-grossing entertainers.

The *Anthology* project spurred Yoko to check out the heaps of unreleased Lennon tapes that languished in the Dakota and elsewhere. A lot of this material had appeared on bootlegs; some received a legitimate airing in the long-running US radio series, *The Lost Lennon Tapes*. There were likewise some rare Lennon tracks scattered around on various compilations. Thus, the 1982 *John Lennon Collection* found room for another *Walls and Bridges* outtake, "Move Over Ms. L", a rather throwaway cut that was previously the B-side to "Stand By Me". In 1988, on the

"WE GOT OVER IT BY FEELING THAT HE'D GONE FOR A CUP OF TEA."

—Ringo Starr

Above: Ringo Starr in 1974, when the Beatles' legacy was still proving burdensome to him.

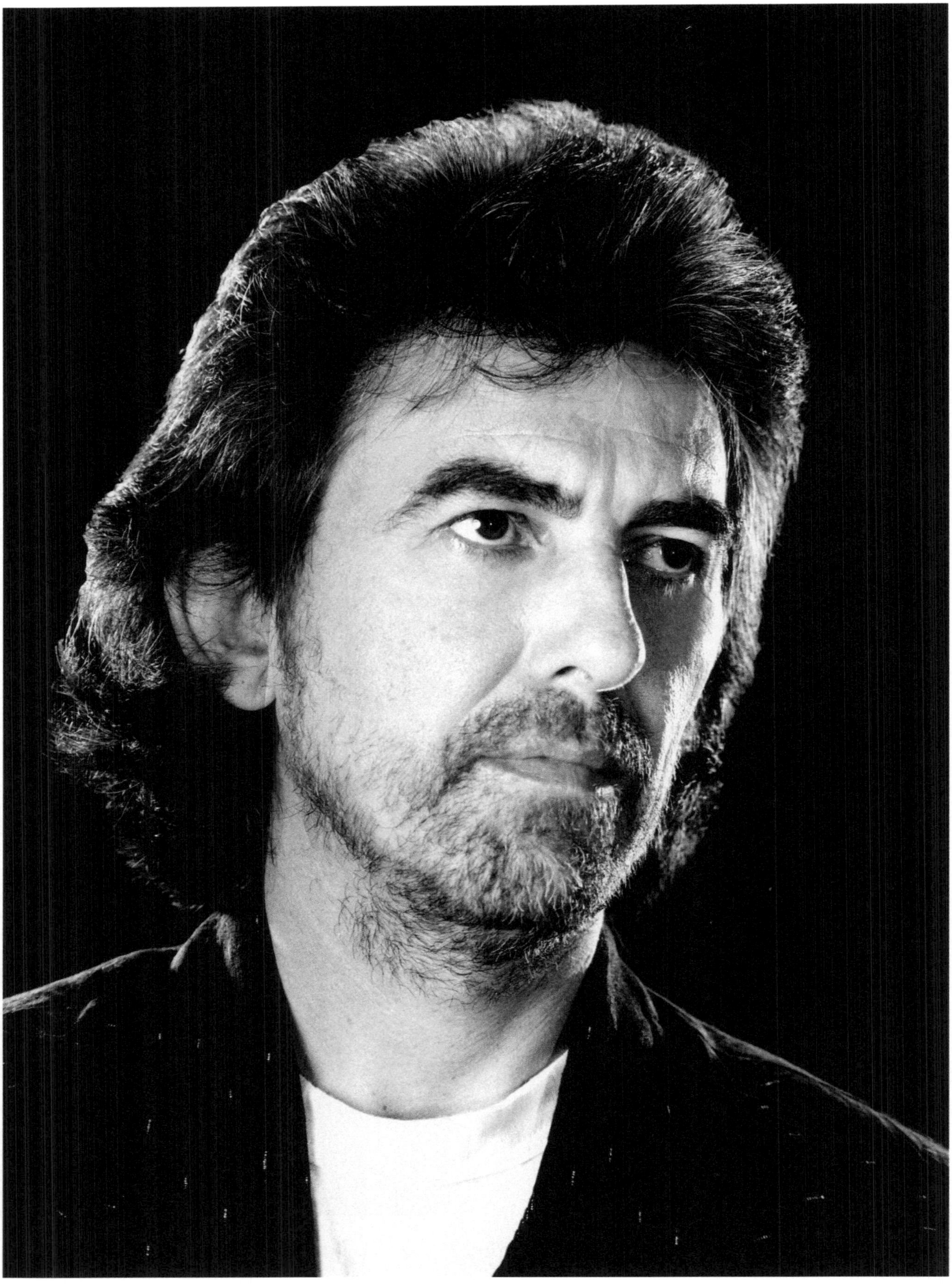

"TO ME HE ISN'T DEAD. THE SOUL LIVES ON. WE ARE GOING TO MEET AGAIN."

—George Harrison

documentary soundtrack CD *Imagine: John Lennon*, there were demo versions of "Imagine" and the then-unknown "Real Love". In 1990 a four-CD box, *Lennon*, included his duets with Elton John at Madison Square Garden.

The full fruit of Yoko's endeavors arrived in 1998. A four-CD boxed set, *John Lennon Anthology*, collects around 100 songs and snippets of tape from the post-Beatle years, and presents them under four headings: "Ascot", "New York City", "The Lost Weekend", and "Dakota". In all, they form a great companion to the musical journey we've followed in this book, while the less obsessive fan can buy a single CD digest of the set, called *Wonsaponatime*. *Anthology* offers alternative versions ("Imagine" with a harmonium, "Hold On'"as rockabilly, and so on) that illustrate John's progress towards the definitive takes. We trace the transition of "Mind Games" from a piano blues, "I Promise", to "Make Love Not War". "Stranger's Room" and "My Life" are a basis for "I'm Losing You" and "(Just Like) Starting Over", respectively. There is the original Dakota take of "Real Love", a song that Yoko was keener for the Beatles to record than Paul was, and the beautiful "Grow Old With Me" receives a graceful new setting from the Beatles' producer, George Martin.

Of the live tracks, "Attica State" stands out for the sheer emotional charge of that show before the grieving families in the Harlem Apollo. There are some knockabout cover versions as well, like the traditional "Long Lost John", which Lennon would remember as a hit for the British skiffle king, Lonnie Donegan. Elsewhere, a studio run-through is interrupted with a parody of Paul's "Yesterday": "Suddenly I'm not half the man I used to be/Cos now I'm an amputee." And the mixing-desk repartee between Lennon and Phil Spector only confirms the legends of inebriated chaos surrounding those "lost weekend" sessions in California.

"God Save Oz" carries John's guide vocal for the track released in 1971 as "God Save Us" by Bill Elliot & The Elastic Oz Band. With its original B-side "Do The Oz" (also included here), it was Lennon's gesture of solidarity with radical freakdom. *Oz* magazine was a London publication, whose editors were facing prosecution for obscenity thanks to a special issue aimed at school students. In fact, the line "Let us fight for Rupert Bear" refers to an *Oz* page portraying the much-loved cartoon character, suddenly gifted with a giant penis.

Probably Lennon's most renowned 'lost' song is "Serve Yourself", a waspish riposte to Bob Dylan's "Gotta Serve Somebody" from the 1979 album *Slow Train Coming*. In a comedy Liverpool accent, Lennon ridicules the singer's new religious fervour. While he was careful, in his interviews, not to criticize the Jewish-born Dylan's conversion to Christianity, John does not pull punches here, taking swings at every belief system from Buddhism to Marxism, much as he'd done ten years before on "God". Another of his Dylan skits selects "Knockin' on Heaven's Door", beginning, "Lord, take this make-up offa me."

"Mr. Hyde's Gone (Don't Be Afraid)" and "Dear John" are underworked Dakota tracks, though the latter has the poignant distinction of being John's last attempted song, a tenderly self-forgiving number—he sniggers at one point when his melody turns into the vintage standard "September Song"—which closes with the words, "The race is over. You've won." Meanwhile, "Life Begins at 40" is a jokey Country-and-Western number, reminiscent of Hank Williams' more deeply felt "Cold, Cold Heart". Taped as John approached that particular milestone, it turns his own self-pity to comic effect. It's a joy to hear, but would he have released the song had he lived? Perhaps, as has been suggested, he intended giving it to country-loving Ringo.

The *Anthology* box contains the blueprints of three other numbers recorded for Ringo: there is the mock-bombast of "I'm the Greatest"; a version of "Only You", made famous by vocal group The Platters in 1956 and a hit for Ringo in 1974; and the title track of that year's album, *Goodnight Vienna*, which was the last big hit the drummer achieved.

From a 1980 demo, "The Rishi Kesh Song" (usually known as "The Happy Rishi Kesh Song") is a true curio. Its origins lay in the Beatles' 1968 trip to Rishikesh, in India, to visit the Maharishi. Typically of John, he would become the most passionate convert to a cause and start to doubt it moments afterwards. "Rishi Kesh" captures this transition from certainty to scepticism, likening the guru's spiritual prescription—the mantra—to a drugstore panacea. The words "Something is missing" connect the lyric to "Serve Yourself", addressed to the same theme of not trusting in belief systems; darkness closes in on Lennon as he halts the rhythm to murmur thoughts of suicide, echoing an old Rishikesh composition, "Yer Blues". It's a strange track, all in all, plunging from gentle satire to authentic anguish. At least one Beatle kept his faith in the Maharishi, but in another tape from the Dakota era, John remarks sardonically: "Sometimes I wish I was just George Harrison, with all the answers."

Even the *Anthology* box was not the last word in unreleased Lennon material, which remains considerable. Some CD reissues of his solo albums have carried bonus tracks; the 2001 *Double*

Opposite: George Harrison in 1987. Six years earlier he'd enlisted Paul and Ringo for his tribute song to John, "All Those Years Ago".

Fantasy, for instance, offered the unreleased 1980 track "Help Me to Help Myself", wherein John looks for some balance of voluntary self-improvement and divine assistance. A less convincing addition to the canon came in the shape of 2004's *Acoustic* album, compiled by Yoko from assorted demo sessions and packaged with chord diagrams to inspire budding guitarists. There were no new compositions, only some minor variants, though a 1969 run-through of "Cold Turkey" suggests that John was taken with the vocal mannerisms of London's rising star of that time, Marc Bolan.

In 2010 there came a "stripped-down" version of *Double Fantasy*: Yoko and the album's co-producer Jack Douglas remixed its tracks to throw new emphasis on John's vocal performance. "It's almost like a different album," Yoko says. "I mean, his voice now comes across so powerfully. There's no other rocker who can come near him."

In that same year, all of John's original 1970s albums were remastered and repackaged in the "Signature" series (with liner notes by the writer of this book, based on new interviews with Yoko). In the series' box set version, we find a bonus disc of home tapes and studio outtakes that offers unfamiliar angles on familiar songs (including Carl Perkins' "Honey Don't", a rockabilly favorite of the young Beatles). There are also two John Lennon songs that get a first airing: "One of the Boys" and "India, India". The latter was another composition for the never-completed *Ballad of John and Yoko* musical, a gently strummed memory of being in Rishikesh. Rather harshly for his wife Cynthia, who had accompanied him, he reports he is homesick for England and "the girl I left behind", namely Yoko. And 1977's "One of the Boys" is John's response to people's perplexity at his Gatsby-like disappearance from the pop party. I'm still around, he seems to say, even in low profile, and I'm doing fine.

Opposite: Julian and Sean together in March 2019 at a New York launch for the *Captain Marvel* movie.

Below: Sean, Yoko and Paul came together in New York for the 1994 Rock and Roll Hall of Fame ceremony, at which John was inducted as a solo artist.

"HE WAS THE FATHER I LOVED WHO LET ME DOWN."

—Julian Lennon

In between these carefully rationed releases, there were contributions from other members of the dynasty. His son Julian Lennon launched a musical career in 1984, initially with great chart success. (Even his mother, Cynthia, who passed away in 2015, made one single, the avowedly nostalgic "Those Were the Days".) In 2005, Julian said of his father: "I have always had very mixed feelings about Dad. He was the father I loved who let me down in so many ways. Who knows how our relationship might have developed if he had not been murdered?"

Despite his early fears of a "Here comes the son" syndrome, Yoko's son Sean Lennon became a musician too. Under the sponsorship of the Beastie Boys' Grand Royal label, he made a well-received debut in 1998 and has continued as a solo artist, band member, and producer ever since.

"People have always wanted me to make a record," Sean says, "because I'm an extension of my dad, physically, biologically, genetically. It would fulfill some kind of need they have for my dad. But I can't fulfill that need, because that's not my purpose. I remember giving this interview when I was six years old, when my dad had just died, and I was 'I don't wanna be a musician! I wanna be a toothpick-maker!'"

Sean puts up a vigorous case for John's solo work: "That's what I admire most about my dad. He came out with *Two Virgins* after *Sgt. Pepper*. Think about the balls it takes to do that; it's unbelievable! Listen to *McCartney*, that was Paul's first record after the Beatles. It's a great record, but it's definitely not such a drastic fuck-you. I mean, my dad made *Two Virgins* and then he made *Plastic Ono Band*, which I think is one of the top three albums of all time. That's an insanely brilliant record, so raw and stripped down and so exactly not what the Beatles were doing. It's like punk before there was punk."

But he's even more forthright in defence of Yoko. "My mom is the whole reason he did that work. When he met my mom, he was basically this macho superstar and she fucking changed his life. Boom! It was, 'Oh my God, this woman is smarter than anyone I've ever met.' Those Beatles came from the macho Liverpool world, and my mom comes in, this incredibly intelligent woman, and she's gorgeous and he became completely

obsessed with her and that's what made them make *Two Virgins* and *Plastic Ono Band*.

"Let's not forget that his greatest record is called 'Plastic ONO Band' and there's a reason for that, not just because he was in love with my mom but because he was infatuated with her artistically. Her ideas are what gave him the inspiration to make 'Mother' and 'God' and 'Imagine'. 'Imagine' is an inspiration from Yoko Ono and anyone who would deny that is retarded.

"Let's be honest here. It was my mom who gave him those ideas, and he wouldn't deny it. If he was sitting here today, he'd be like, 'Yes, Sean, you're right.' He went from being Paul's partner to being Yoko's partner. It's important to me to wake people up to how cool she was and how she influenced my dad in such a cool way."

Yoko Ono, meanwhile, has continued to record and perform through the four decades since 1980, and often with Sean. *Season of Glass*, her first album after John's death, affirmed she was neither rock chick nor noise merchant, nor can she be confined to either American or Japanese reference points. Frequently she echoes the European art-cabaret tradition—of Jacques Brel, Kurt Weill, and others—that David Bowie and Scott Walker would have recognized. The messages remain uncompromising, but the music is more welcoming than weaponized. Dance remixes by artists such as Pet Shop Boys have kept her within the commercial orbit promised by "Walking on Thin Ice", the most enduring of Yoko's solo tracks.

Above: Yoko is joined by Sean for the launch of her *To The Light* exhibition at London's Serpentine Galleries, June 2012.

Opposite: Yoko in July 2016, at Las Vegas for the tenth anniversary of Cirque du Soleil's show The Beatles: Love.

"HIS GREATEST RECORD IS CALLED PLASTIC ONO BAND AND THERE'S A REASON FOR THAT."

—Sean Lennon

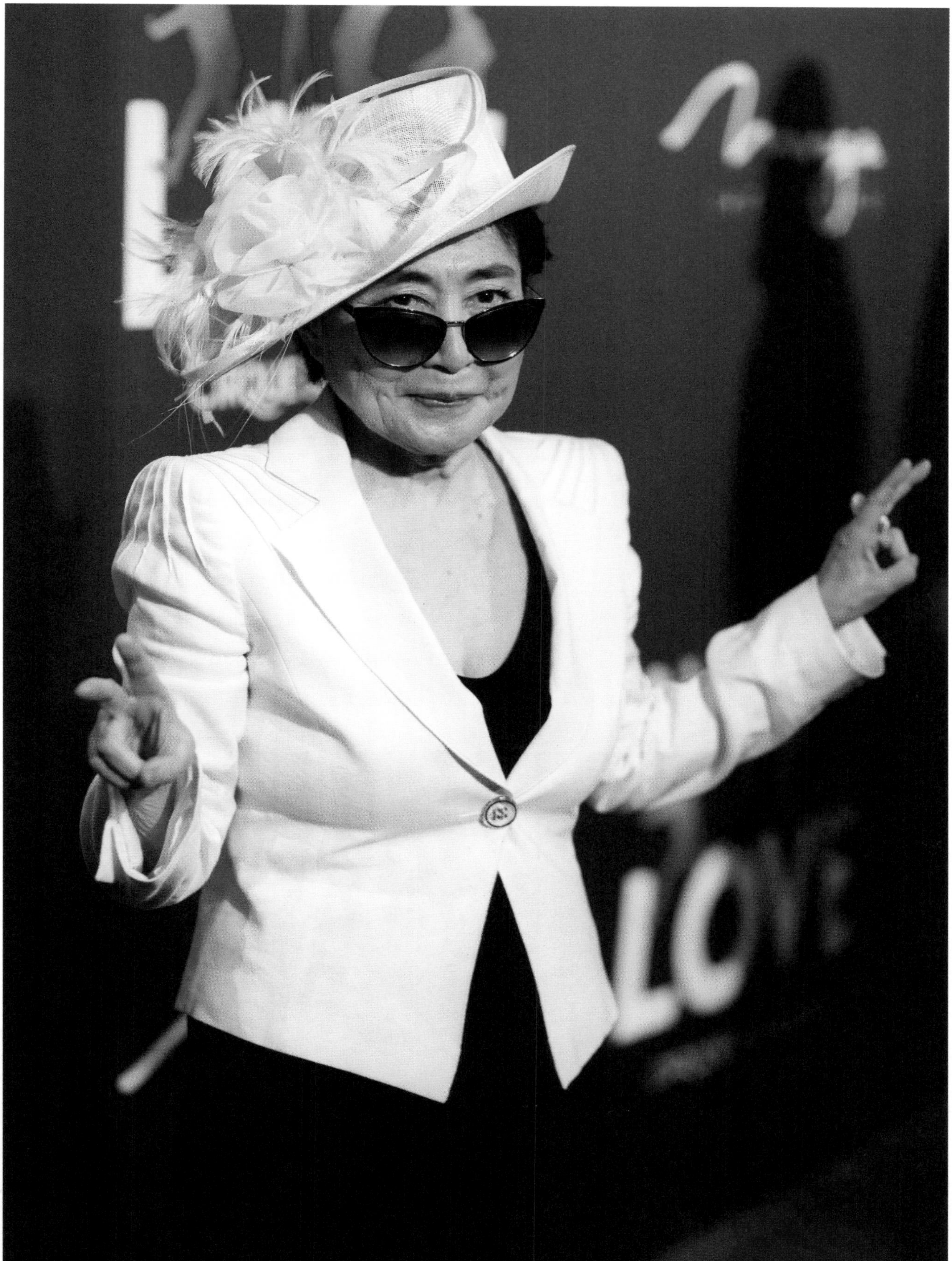

What are the essential solo Lennon records? The discography at the end of this book indicates what's out there, while the formats now stretch from vinyl to online, according to taste. Various compilations (the latest being *Power to the People: The Hits*) provide a decent introduction to the final decade of his life, especially to the chart singles. As for the original albums, *Walls and Bridges* is perhaps the most undervalued. Serious fans of his music tend, like Sean Lennon, to favor the naked vulnerability of *John Lennon/Plastic Ono Band*. But the wider world's favorite is still *Imagine*, its popularity reflected by the near-reverence accorded to the title track. In a spate of media polls conducted for the 2000 millennium, John was voted Artist of the Century and "Imagine" as the Best-Loved Lyric. In Britain, the track was rereleased and became a Top 5 hit all over again.

Whose solo work was better, John's or Paul's? Comparisons are unfair in that McCartney has lived—and recorded—for far longer. But then McCartney has had to compete with the mystique surrounding his martyred partner. The one solid judgement we can reach is that they were most effective when they worked as a team. We need look only to *Sgt. Pepper*'s plangent finale, "A Day in the Life": its two components might have made fine listening in their own right, but John and Paul's songs wedded together are on a higher plane. The explanation isn't merely musical. It has to do with the melding of two distinct sensibilities.

Their old producer George Martin told me, "In the beginning they were inseparable; they were so excited by each other. As they went on, they tended to write more of their own songs. But it was a collaboration of competition. If one wrote something really good, then the other would say, 'Shit, I wish I could do as well as that,' and they'd write something better."

Of their solo music, Martin said, "I followed it, but I wouldn't say I was a great fan. Yoko actually said years later, 'I wish you'd recorded *Double Fantasy*,' and I said, 'Well, you never asked me.' I think *Imagine* was very good. I think John did a lot of good stuff, and Paul did too, but it wasn't as good as when they were together and I think they have to accept that.

"Paul had a stronger sense of melody and harmony which appealed to the main mass of the public, and John had a kookier way of dealing with lyrics, but they influenced each other enormously. I doubt if Paul would have written 'Eleanor Rigby' unless he'd met John. And I doubt that John would have written something like 'Imagine' without Paul's influence. I think the talents were equal. They were different but equal. And I still marvel at what they did."

Below: The Georges Harrison and Martin, at Abbey Road Studios in September 1993 for the CD launch of the Beatles' "Red" and "Blue" compilation albums.

Opposite: John and Yoko in France, 1979. They stayed at the exclusive Hotel du Cap-Eden-Roc in Antibes.

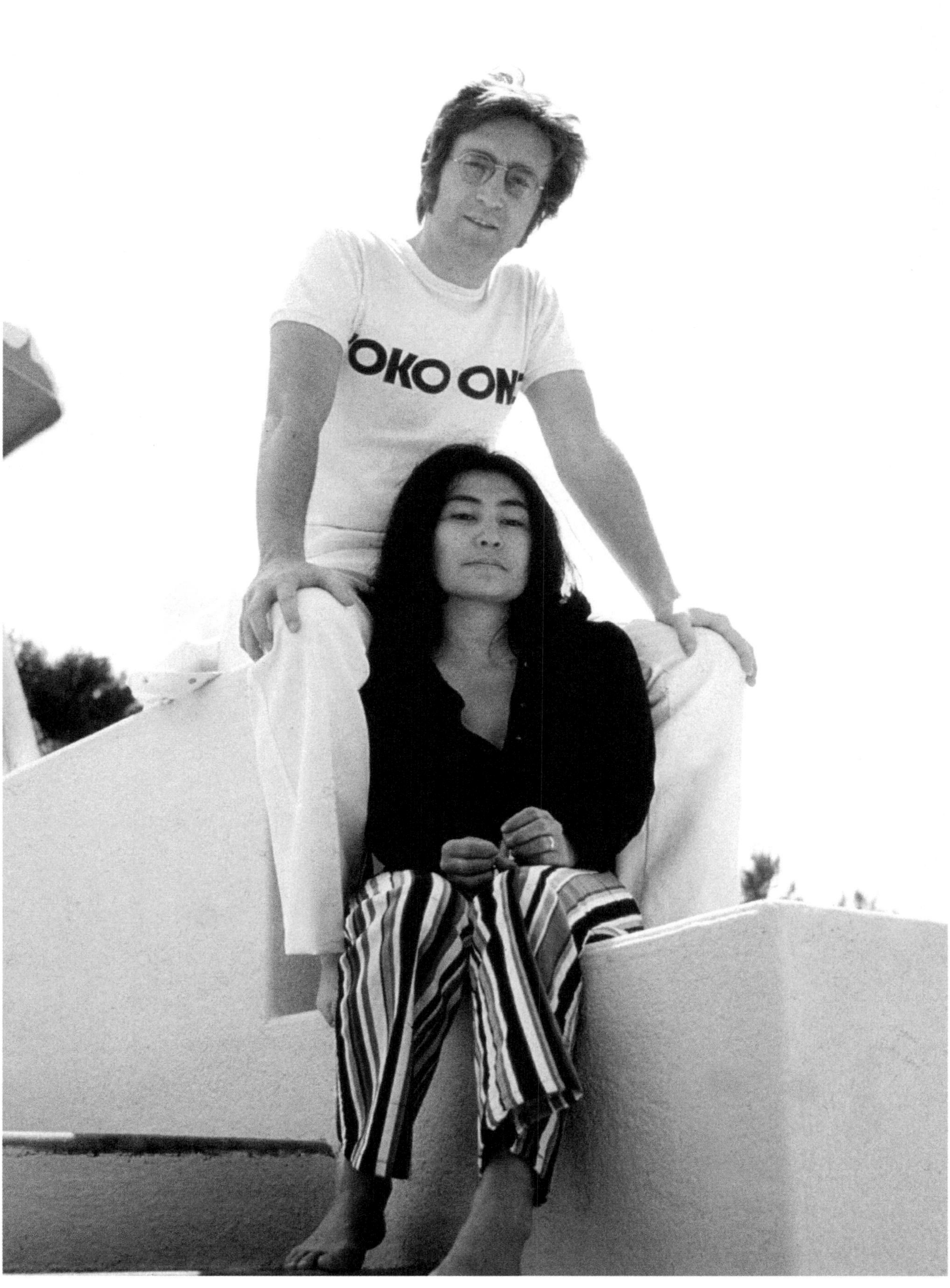
YOKO ON

Right up to the end of his life, John resented living in the Beatles' shadow. Whenever they were mentioned it was, by implication, always to the detriment of his solo work, but it seems likely that he would eventually have made his peace with history. "He would have loved being back with us now," claims Ringo. "A lot of the footage of John is angry because that's where he was in the Seventies. He was sort of putting the Beatles down. Now he'd have felt differently… You're talking about the ex-Beatles, and it's something we'll never get away from. When I was thirty, I thought, 'Well, what about "me"? Just "me", you know?' Now you realize it doesn't matter what you do; it's gonna be related to the Beatles, so you just live with that. And that isn't bad now, because the music is well worth it. You can forget the personalities and just listen to the records, and that's what it was all about."

Would there have been a Beatles reunion? Lennon's nostalgia for Britain was growing in 1980, and there were plans for a world tour that would have brought him home. If John had grown reconciled to Paul, there seems no reason why the process could not have culminated in some musical collaboration. The Live Aid concert of 1985 might have been the perfect occasion for all concerned. As it happened, it was left to Paul to end the Wembley event and seal the Beatles' symbolic position as pop's preeminent artists. And the *Anthology* project, a decade later, would have been another opportunity. It was made possible by the resolution of the Beatles' remaining legal conflicts; John would surely have got involved. More than all the Beatles, he itched to go back and tamper with the songs he'd rushed through the first time.

The death of George Harrison in 2001 left Paul and Yoko even more exposed as the custodians of Beatle history. While Ringo has maintained the affable neutrality that has been his lot since the beginning, the Lennons and the McCartneys became rival dynasties. They are like the Houses of Montague and Capulet, without a redeeming love story. Whereas Paul tours constantly, and places Beatle songs at the core of his live repertoire, Yoko has nurtured an iconic image of the solo John, loving husband, caring father, and figurehead for peace. In between, the two sides have been known to snipe at each other. At an awards speech in 2005, Yoko offered this calculated putdown: "Sometimes, in the middle of the night, John would ask, 'Are you awake?' and I would say, 'Yes, yes'. And he said, 'You know, they always cover Paul's songs and never mine, and I don't know why.' I said, 'You're a good songwriter—it's not 'June' with 'Spoon' that you write. You're a good singer, too, and most musicians are probably a little bit nervous about covering your songs.'"

Her care for Lennon's memory is exemplified by John's childhood home, Mendips, on Liverpool's Menlove Avenue, which she acquired and gave to Britain's conservation body, the National Trust. "You go inside John's bedroom there," she said to me 2003, "and it seems so tiny. But then you think, 'what big dreams he must have had.'" Mendips' many visitors have included one surprise guest in the form of Bob Dylan. As the house's guide Colin Hall recalls, Bob was struck by its similarity to the place he'd grown up in back in Duluth, Minnesota. He was fascinated also by a typical 1950s book displayed in John's bedroom: "Uh, who's *Just William*?" he asked. William was, of course, the schoolboy hero of Richmal Crompton's novels: a rebellious suburban scamp with permanently muddy knees who was doubtless a formative influence on the young Lennon.

In our world, Lennon's legacy is lived and felt by the millions who love his music. New listeners discover his songs each day, and respond to the beauty they hear in them, to the honest and vulnerable humanity. He held almost nothing back in his songs and he craved the same level of candour from others: "Gimme Some Truth". No system of thought ever won his enduring allegiance; he was never an ideological man. The only consistent strand in his work is the quest for some transcendent answer. His unelected status left him free to follow his restless instincts. He was free to discard yesterday's ideas in a manner that no politician ever could.

Above: Richmal Crompton's *Just William*, perhaps the first of John Lennon's role models.

Opposite: Yoko and Ringo are joined by New York mayor Bill de Blasio and actor Jeff Bridges for a September 2018 event featuring the John Lennon Educational Tour Bus.

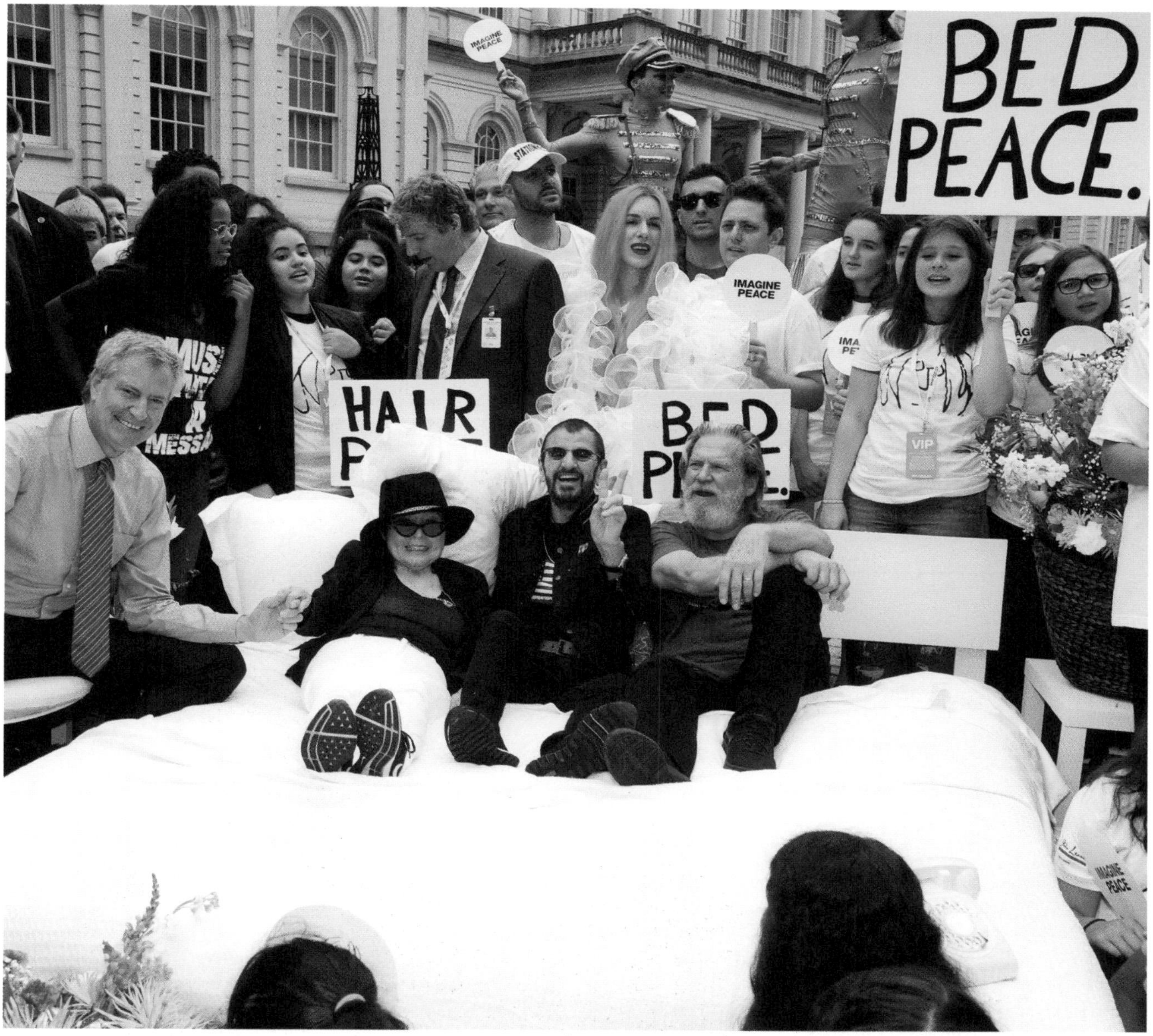

"HE WOULD HAVE LOVED BEING BACK WITH US NOW. A LOT OF THE FOOTAGE OF JOHN IS ANGRY. NOW HE'D HAVE FELT DIFFERENTLY."

—Ringo Starr

"HOW IN THE WORLD YOU GONNA SEE, LAUGHING AT FOOLS LIKE ME?"

—John Lennon

(By 1978, he considered "Power to the People" "embarrassing".) And he could embrace new possibilities with reckless glee.

He grasped intuitively and articulated the emerging moods within society. Sometimes he distilled them into campaign slogans with unforgettable pop hooks attached. Lots of people opposed the Vietnam War, but it took John Lennon to create "Give Peace A Chance". His unconscious talent was to represent the undercurrents of his era, both good and bad: the blurring of gender roles, the demand for racial and cultural equality, the primacy of youth over age, the decline of deference, the tolerance of narcotics, the clash of material wealth and spiritual need, the repudiation of patriotism, the taste for instant gratification. Whatever was going on in Western life, whether above or below the surface, Lennon was drawn to the point of conflict. Both in his life and his art he made the tensions manifest.

There is no knowing where life might have taken Lennon had he survived the assassin's bullets. Domesticity or debauchery? Radicalism or reaction? Mysticism or mischief? The only thing of which we can be certain is that his art would have hidden nothing. Yoko expressed regret in 2005 that John did not live to experience the internet. Such an opportunity to communicate, and to learn from others in return, would have had him hooked. And the temptation to wade in on social media would surely have proved irresistible. As the decades pass, John Lennon's achievements do not fade from our memories. If anything, they seem even more substantial. He is undiminished.

Above: Aftershock. Outside the Dakota, December 9th.

Opposite: John Lennon, 1940–1980.

Overleaf: "Sitting in an English garden." The Lennons at their last London home, Tittenhurst Park, in 1971. Before the year's end they would move to New York City, and John would never see England again.

CHRONOLOGY

1940
October 9th: John Winston Lennon is born in Oxford Street Maternity Hospital, Liverpool.

1946
John's mother Julia puts him in the care of her sister, Mimi. His father Freddie offers to take him away to New Zealand, but John decides to stay.

1957
March: John forms his first band, the Black Jacks, later named the Quarry Men.
July 6th: Paul McCartney watches the Quarry Men at a summer fete. He jams with the band and John invites him to join.
September: John becomes a student at Liverpool College of Art.

1958
July 15th: Julia Lennon is killed in a road accident.
Also in this year, the Quarry Men, now with George Harrison, pay to make their first recording, "That'll Be The Day".

1960
August: Renamed the Beatles, John's group play their first residency in Hamburg.

1962
August 23rd: John marries art school girlfriend Cynthia Powell, who is pregnant with their son Julian.
September 4th: The Beatles record their first single for EMI, 'Love Me Do'.

1963
August 29th: Beatles' single "She Loves You" tops the UK chart for seven weeks.
November 4th: The Beatles appear before the Queen at the Royal Command Performance.

1964
February 9th: Following a riotous welcome in New York, the Beatles play Ed Sullivan's TV show to an audience of 73 million.

1965
August 15th: The Beatles' first show at Shea Stadium.

1966
March 4th: John's comment that the Beatles are "more popular than Jesus" stirs controversy in the US.
August 29th: The Beatles play their last concert, in San Francisco.
November 9th: John meets Japanese artist Yoko Ono at the Indica Gallery in London.

1967
June 1st: Release of the Beatles' *Sgt. Pepper's Lonely Hearts Club Band.*

1968
May 20th: In Cynthia's absence, Yoko and John record *Two Virgins* and become lovers.
October 18th: Police raid the London flat that John has borrowed from Ringo. John pleads guilty to possessing cannabis.
November 21st: Yoko suffers the first in a series of miscarriages.

1969
March 20th: John and Yoko marry in Gibraltar. After visiting Paris, they fly on to Amsterdam, turning their honeymoon into a seven-day "bed-in" for world peace.
April 22nd: John changes his middle name (Winston) to Ono.
May 26th: Montreal bed-in begins, eventually producing "Give Peace a Chance".
September 13th: Recording of *Live Peace in Toronto.*
October 24th: UK release of "Cold Turkey".
November 25th: John returns his MBE to the Queen in an antiwar protest.

1970
January 27th: John writes and records "Instant Karma!".
April 10th: Paul McCartney announces that the Beatles have disbanded.
April 23rd: To Los Angeles for course in Primal Therapy with Dr. Arthur Janov.
December 9th: Release of *John Lennon/Plastic Ono Band.*

1971

March 22nd: US release of "Power to the People" single.
September 3rd: John travels to New York, in search of Yoko's daughter Kyoko. He never returns to the UK.
September 9th: Release of *Imagine*.
December 1st: US release of "Happy Xmas (War Is Over)".
December 10th: Appears at the John Sinclair benefit concert in Ann Arbor, Michigan.

1972

March 16th: John is served with a US deportation order. He lodges an appeal.
June 12th: US release of *Some Time In New York City*.
August 30th: Afternoon and evening concerts at Madison Square Garden in support of the One To One children's charity.

1973

April 1st: At a New York press conference, John and Yoko announce the state of Nutopia.
September 18th: Ringo buys John's home, Tittenhurst Park.
October: John separates from Yoko. With May Pang, he leaves for LA and attempts to record an album of rock 'n' roll cover versions with Phil Spector.
November 2nd: Release of *Mind Games*.

1974

March 12th: Drunk and disorderly, John is ejected from the Smothers Brothers show at the Troubadour club, Los Angeles.
July 12th: John is ordered to leave the US within 60 days. He lodges another appeal.
August 31st: In the New York federal court, John accuses the Nixon administration of tapping his phone and wishing to deport him for political reasons. His accusations will later be vindicated.
September 26th: US release of the *Walls And Bridges* album.
November 16th: "Whatever Gets You Thru the Night" becomes John's first solo Number 1 hit in the States.
November 28th: John keeps a promise by joining Elton John onstage at Madison Square Garden. This will prove to be his last public concert appearance. Yoko and John meet again after the show.

1975

January: John returns to live with Yoko at the Dakota Building in New York. Yoko becomes pregnant.
February 17th: Release of the *Rock 'n' Roll* album.
March 1st: John and Yoko appear together in public at the Grammy awards.
April 18th: John appears on stage for last time, at the filming of TV special, *Salute to Lew Grade*.
October 9th: On John's thirty-fifth birthday, Yoko gives birth to the couple's only son, Sean.

1976

April 1st: Death of John's father, Freddie Lennon.
July 27th: Issued with his "Green Card", John is finally granted right of US residency.

1977

January 20th: John attends inauguration gala of President Jimmy Carter.
October 4th: John and Yoko hold press conference in Japan, announcing their plan to raise Sean before returning to work.

1978

John divides his time between travelling, recording home demo tracks, acting as "househusband", learning Japanese, and writing the autobiographical essay *The Ballad Of John And Yoko*, intended as program notes for a proposed musical of that name. The essay will later appear in his posthumous book *Skywriting by Word of Mouth*.

1979

May 27th: Full-page advert, "A love letter from John and Yoko", appears in newspapers around the world.

1980

July: John takes a boat trip to Bermuda, where he will develop the songs for *Double Fantasy*.
August 4th: John begins his first studio recordings for five years.
November 17th: UK release of *Double Fantasy*.
December 8th: John is shot five times outside the Dakota Building. He dies shortly afterward, at New York's Roosevelt Hospital.

DISCOGRAPHY

This list is selective: It's designed to reflect Lennon's output during his lifetime, and the gradual availability of extra material thereafter. Most of the posthumous compilations and reissues are therefore omitted. All the albums here were released under John Lennon's name except where noted. Likewise, all the songs were written by John except where noted in the square brackets. A few songwriting credits have been officially amended over the years, notably for "Give Peace a Chance" and "Imagine".

Lennon's solo records were originally released in vinyl (and often cassette) form, mostly on the Apple label. Reissues and CDs have generally been on EMI/Parlophone in the UK, and Capitol in the US. Nowadays, of course, the majority of John's catalogue can also be found online. Whichever route you take, I hope you will find much to love.

SINGLES

Give Peace a Chance [Lennon/Ono]
B/W Remember Love [Yoko]
(PLASTIC ONO BAND)
UK: July 4th, 1969
US: July 7th, 1969
APPLE

Cold Turkey
B/W Don't Worry Kyoko [Yoko]
(PLASTIC ONO BAND)
UK: October 24th 1969
US: October 20th 1969
APPLE

Instant Karma! (We All Shine On)
B/W Who Has Seen the Wind? [Yoko]
UK: February 6th, 1970
US: February 20th 1970
APPLE

Power to the People
B/W Open Your Box [Yoko]
(Replaced in the US by another Yoko Ono song, "Touch Me")
UK: March 12th, 1971
US: March 22nd, 1971
APPLE

Imagine [Lennon/Ono]
B/W Working Class Hero
UK: October 24th, 1975
US: October 11th, 1971
APPLE

Happy Xmas (War Is Over) [Lennon/Ono]
B/W Listen, the Snow Is Falling [Yoko]
UK: November 24th, 1972
US: December 1st, 1971
APPLE

Woman Is the Nigger of the World [Lennon/Ono]
B/W Sisters O Sisters [Yoko]
US: April 24th, 1972
APPLE

Mind Games
B/W Meat City
UK: November 16th, 1973
US: October 29th, 1973
APPLE

Whatever Gets You Thru the Night
B/W Beef Jerky
UK: October 4th, 1974
US: September 23rd, 1974
APPLE

#9 Dream
B/W What You Got
UK: January 31st, 1975
US: December 16th, 1974
APPLE

Stand by Me [King/Leiber/Stoller]
B/W Move Over Ms. L
UK: April 18th, 1975
US: March 10th, 1975
APPLE

(Just Like) Starting Over
B/W Kiss Kiss Kiss [Yoko]
UK: October 24th, 1980
US: October 27th, 1980
GEFFEN

Woman
B/W Beautiful Boys [Yoko]
UK: January 16th, 1981
US: January 12th, 1981
GEFFEN

Watching the Wheels
B/W Yes, I'm Your Angel [Yoko]
UK: March 27th, 1981
US: March 13th, 1981
GEFFEN

Nobody Told Me
B/W O'Sanity [Yoko]
UK: January 9th, 1984
US: January 6th, 1984
POLYDOR

Borrowed Time
B/W Your Hands [Yoko]
UK: March 9th, 1984
US: May 11th, 1984
POLYDOR

I'm Stepping Out
B/W Sleepless Night [Yoko]
UK: July 15th, 1984
US: March 19th, 1984
POLYDOR

ALBUMS

UNFINISHED MUSIC NO. 1 TWO VIRGINS (JOHN LENNON & YOKO ONO)
Two Virgins 1–10 [with Yoko]
UK: November 29th, 1968
US: November 11th, 1968
APPLE

UNFINISHED MUSIC NO. 2: LIFE WITH THE LIONS (JOHN LENNON & YOKO ONO)
Cambridge 1969
No Bed for Beatle John
Baby's Heartbeat
Two Minutes Silence
Radio Play
[all tracks Lennon/Ono]
UK: May 9th, 1969
US: May 26th, 1969
APPLE

WEDDING ALBUM (JOHN LENNON & YOKO ONO)
John And Yoko [with Yoko]
Amsterdam [with Yoko]
UK: November 7th, 1969
US: October 20th, 1969
APPLE

LIVE PEACE IN TORONTO 1969 (THE PLASTIC ONO BAND)
Blue Suede Shoes [Perkins]
Money [Bradford/Gordy]
Dizzy Miss Lizzy [Williams]
Yer Blues [Lennon/McCartney]
Cold Turkey
Give Peace a Chance [with Yoko]
Don't Worry Kyoko (Mummy's Only Looking for Her Hand in the Snow) [Yoko]

John, John (Let's Hope for Peace) [Yoko]
UK & US: December 12th, 1969
APPLE

JOHN LENNON/PLASTIC ONO BAND

Mother
Hold On
I Found Out
Working Class Hero
Isolation
Remember
Love
Well Well Well
Look at Me
God
My Mummy's Dead
UK & US: December 11th, 1970
APPLE

IMAGINE

Imagine [with Yoko]
Crippled Inside
Jealous Guy
It's So Hard
I Don't Want to Be a Soldier
Gimme Some Truth
Oh My Love [with Yoko]
How Do You Sleep?
How?
Oh Yoko!
UK: October 8th, 1971
US: September 9th, 1971
APPLE

SOME TIME IN NEW YORK CITY (JOHN & YOKO/PLASTIC ONO BAND)

Woman Is the Nigger of the World [with Yoko]
Sisters, O Sisters [Yoko]
Attica State [with Yoko]
Born in a Prison [Yoko]
New York City
Sunday Bloody Sunday [with Yoko]
The Luck of the Irish [with Yoko]
John Sinclair
Angela [with Yoko]
We're All Water [Yoko]
Cold Turkey
Don't Worry Kyoko [Yoko]
Well (Baby Please Don't Go) [Ward]
Jamrag [with Yoko]
Scumbag [with Yoko and Frank Zappa]
Au [with Yoko]
UK: September 15th, 1972
US: June 12th, 1972
APPLE

MIND GAMES

Mind Games
Tight A$
Aisumasen (I'm Sorry)
One Day (at a Time)
Bring on the Lucie (Freda Peeple)
Nutopian International Anthem
Intuition
Out the Blue
Only People
I Know (I Know)
You Are Here
Meat City
UK: November 16th, 1973
US: November 2nd, 1973
APPLE

WALLS AND BRIDGES

Going Down on Love
Whatever Gets You Thru the Night
Old Dirt Road [with Harry Nilsson]
What You Got
Bless You
Scared
#9 Dream
Surprise Surprise (Sweet Bird of Paradox)
Steel and Glass
Beef Jerky
Nobody Loves You (When You're Down and Out)
Ya Ya [Robinson/Dorsey/Lewis]
UK: October 4th, 1974
US: September 26th, 1974
APPLE

ROCK 'N' ROLL

Be-Bop-A-Lula [Davis/Vincent]
Stand By Me [King/Leiber/Stoller]
Rip It Up [Blackwell/Marascalco]
Ready Teddy [Blackwell/Marascalco]
You Can't Catch Me [Berry]
Ain't That a Shame [Domino/Bartholomew]
Do You Wanna Dance [Freeman]
Sweet Little Sixteen [Berry]
Slippin' and Slidin' [Penniman/Bocage/Collins/Smith]

Peggy Sue [Holly/Allison/Petty]
Bring It on Home to Me [Cooke]
Send Me Some Lovin' [Price/Marascalco]
Bony Moronie [Williams]
Ya Ya [Robinson/Dorsey/Lewis]
Just Because [Price]
UK: February 21st, 1975
US: February 17th, 1975
APPLE

DOUBLE FANTASY (JOHN LENNON & YOKO ONO)

(Just Like) Starting Over
Kiss Kiss Kiss [Yoko]
Cleanup Time
Give Me Something [Yoko]
I'm Losing You
I'm Moving On [Yoko]
Beautiful Boy (Darling Boy)
Watching the Wheels
Yes, I'm Your Angel [Yoko]
Woman
Beautiful Boys [Yoko]
Dear Yoko
Every Man Has a Woman Who Loves Him [Yoko]
Hard Times Are Over [Yoko]
UK & US: November 17th, 1980
GEFFEN

MILK AND HONEY (JOHN LENNON & YOKO ONO)

I'm Stepping Out
Sleepless Night [Yoko]
I Don't Wanna Face It
Don't Be Scared [Yoko]
Nobody Told Me
O'Sanity [Yoko]
Borrowed Time
Your Hands [Yoko]
(Forgive Me) My Little Flower Princess
Let Me Count the Ways [Yoko]
Grow Old with Me
You're the One [Yoko]
UK: January 23rd, 1984
US: January 19th, 1984
POLYDOR

LIVE IN NEW YORK CITY

New York City
It's So Hard
Woman Is the Nigger of the World [with Yoko]
Well Well Well
Instant Karma! (We All Shine On)
Mother
Come Together [Lennon/McCartney]
Imagine [with Yoko]
Cold Turkey
Hound Dog [Leiber/Stoller]
Give Peace a Chance [with Yoko]
UK & US: January 24th, 1986
PARLOPHONE (UK)/CAPITOL (US)

MENLOVE AVE.

Here We Go Again [with Phil Spector]
Rock and Roll People
Angel Baby [Hamlin]
Since My Baby Left Me [Crudup]
To Know Her Is to Love Her [Spector]
Steel and Glass
Scared
Old Dirt Road [with Harry Nilsson]
Nobody Loves You (When You're Down and Out)
Bless You
UK: November 3rd, 1986
US: October 27th, 1986
PARLOPHONE (UK)/CAPITOL (US)

COMPILATIONS AND BOX SETS

SHAVED FISH

Give Peace a Chance [with Yoko]
Cold Turkey
Instant Karma! (We All Shine On)
Power to the People
Mother
Woman Is the Nigger of the World [with Yoko]
Imagine [with Yoko]
Whatever Gets You Thru the Night
Mind Games
#9 Dream
Happy Xmas (War Is Over) [with Yoko]
Reprise: Give Peace a Chance [with Yoko]
UK and US: October 24th, 1975
APPLE

JOHN LENNON: ANTHOLOGY

(4-CD Box Set)

CD1: ASCOT

Working Class Hero
God
I Found Out
Hold On
Isolation
Love
Mother
Remember
Imagine (take 1) [with Yoko]
"Fortunately"
Baby Please Don't Go [Ward]
Oh My Love [with Yoko]
Jealous Guy
Maggie Mae [Traditional, arranged Lennon/McCartney/Harrison/Starkey]
How Do You Sleep?
God Save Oz [with Yoko]
Do the Oz [with Yoko]
I Don't Want to Be a Soldier
Give Peace a Chance [with Yoko]
Look at Me
Long Lost John [Traditional]

CD2: NEW YORK CITY

New York City
Attica State [with Yoko]
Imagine (live) [with Yoko]
Bring on the Lucie (Freda Peeple)
Geraldo Rivera—One to One Concert
Woman Is the Nigger of the World (live) [with Yoko]
It's So Hard (live)
Come Together (live) [Lennon/McCartney]
Happy Xmas (War Is Over) [with Yoko]
The Luck of the Irish (live) [with Yoko]
John Sinclair (live)
The David Frost Show
Mind Games (I Promise)
Mind Games (Make Love, Not War)
One Day (at a Time)
I Know (I Know)
I'm the Greatest
Goodnight Vienna
Jerry Lewis Telethon
"A Kiss Is Just a Kiss" (as Time Goes By) [Hupfeld]
Real Love
You Are Here

CD3: THE LOST WEEKEND

What You Got
Nobody Loves You When You're Down and Out
Whatever Gets You Thru the Night (home)
Whatever Gets You Thru the Night (studio)
Yesterday (parody) [Lennon/McCartney]
Be-Bop-A-Lula [Davis/Vincent]
Rip It Up/Ready Teddy [Blackwell/Marascalco]
Scared
Steel and Glass
Surprise Surprise (Sweet Bird of Paradox)
Bless You
Going Down on Love
Move Over Ms. L
Ain't She Sweet [Yellen/Ager]
Slippin' and Slidin' [Penniman/Bocage/Collins/Smith]
Peggy Sue [Allison/Holly/Petty]
Bring It on Home to Me/Send Me Some Lovin' [Cooke/Price/Marascalco]
Phil and John 1
Phil and John 2
Phil and John 3
"When in Doubt, Fuck It"
Be My Baby [Barry/Greenwich/Spector]
Stranger's Room
Old Dirt Road [with Harry Nilsson]

CD4: DAKOTA

I'm Losing You
Sean's "Little Help" [Lennon/McCartney]
Serve Yourself
My Life
Nobody Told Me
Life Begins at 40
I Don't Wanna Face It
Woman
Dear Yoko
Watching the Wheels
I'm Stepping Out
Borrowed Time
The Rishi Kesh Song
Sean's "Loud"
Beautiful Boy
Mr Hyde's Gone (Don't Be Afraid)
Only You [Rand/Ram]
Grow Old with Me
Dear John
The Great Wok
Mucho Mungo
Satire 1

Satire 2
Satire 3
Sean's "In the Sky"
It's Real
UK: November 2nd, 1998
US: November 3rd, 1998
CAPITOL

WONSAPONATIME (Selections From Lennon Anthology)

I'm Losing You
Working Class Hero
God
How Do You Sleep?
Imagine (take 1) [with Yoko]
Baby Please Don't Go [Ward]
Oh My Love [with Yoko]
God Save Oz [with Yoko]
I Found Out
Woman Is the Nigger of the World (live) [with Yoko]
"A Kiss Is Just a Kiss" (as Time Goes By) [Hupfeld]
Be-Bop-A-Lula [Davis/Vincent]
Rip It Up/Ready Teddy [Blackwell/Marascalco]
What You Got
Nobody Loves You When You're Down and Out
I Don't Wanna Face It
Real Love
Only You [Rand/Ram]
Grow Old with Me
Sean's "In the Sky"
Serve Yourself
UK: November 2nd, 1998
US: November 3rd, 1998
CAPITOL

ACOUSTIC

Working Class Hero
Love
Well Well Well
Look at Me
God
My Mummy's Dead
Cold Turkey
The Luck of the Irish [with Yoko]
John Sinclair
Woman Is the Nigger of the World [with Yoko]
What You Got
Watching the Wheels
Dear Yoko
Real Love
Imagine [with Yoko]
It's Real
UK: November 1st, 2004
US: November 2nd, 2004
PARLOPHONE (UK)/CAPITOL (US)

JOHN LENNON "SIGNATURE" BOX SET

(a) Remastered CDs of the eight original albums (also available individually): John Lennon/Plastic Ono Band; Imagine; Some Time In New York City (double-CD); Mind Games; Walls and Bridges; Rock 'n' Roll; Double Fantasy; Milk and Honey.
(b) The "Singles" CD: Power to the People; Happy Xmas (War Is Over) [with Yoko]; Instant Karma! (We All Shine On); Cold Turkey (single version); Move Over Ms. L; Give Peace a Chance [with Yoko].
(c) The "Studio Outtakes/Home Recordings" CD: Mother; Love; God; I Found Out; Nobody Told Me; Honey Don't [Carl Perkins]; One of the Boys; India, India; Serve Yourself; Isolation; Remember; Beautiful Boy (Darling Boy); I Don't Wanna Be a Soldier Mama I Don't Wanna Die.
UK & US: October 4th, 2010
EMI

POWER TO THE PEOPLE: THE HITS

Power to the People
Gimme Some Truth
Woman
Instant Karma! (We All Shine On)
Whatever Gets You Thru the Night
Cold Turkey
Jealous Guy
#9 Dream
(Just Like) Starting Over
Mind Games
Watching the Wheels
Stand by Me [King/Leiber/Stoller]
Imagine [with Yoko]
Happy Xmas (War Is Over) [with Yoko]
Give Peace a Chance [with Yoko]
UK & US: October 4th, 2010
EMI

INDEX

SONG CREDITS

"GIVE PEACE A CHANCE" Words and Music by John Lennon © 1969,
Reproduced by permission of Sony/ATV Music Publishing, London W1F 9LD

"COLD TURKEY"
Written by JOHN WINSTON LENNON
© 1969 Lenono Music (GMR)

"INSTANT KARMA!"
Written by JOHN WINSTON LENNON
© 1970 Lenono Music (GMR)

"POWER TO THE PEOPLE"
Written by JOHN WINSTON LENNON
© 1971 Lenono Music (GMR)

"HAPPY CHRISTMAS (WAR IS OVER)"
Written by JOHN WINSTON LENNON and YOKO ONO
© 1971 Lenono Music (GMR)/ Ono Music (GMR)

"MOTHER" from the album *John Lennon/Plastic Ono Band*
Written by JOHN WINSTON LENNON
© 1970 Lenono Music (GMR)

"HOLD ON" from the album *John Lennon/Plastic Ono Band*
Written by JOHN WINSTON LENNON
© 1970 Lenono Music (GMR)

"I FOUND OUT" from the album *John Lennon/Plastic Ono Band*
Written by JOHN WINSTON LENNON
© 1970 Lenono Music (GMR)

"WORKING CLASS HERO" from the album *John Lennon/Plastic Ono Band*
Written by JOHN WINSTON LENNON
© 1970 Lenono Music (GMR)

"ISOLATION" from the album *John Lennon/Plastic Ono Band*
Written by JOHN WINSTON LENNON
© 1970 Lenono Music (GMR)

"REMEMBER" from the album *John Lennon/Plastic Ono Band*
Written by JOHN WINSTON LENNON
© 1970 Lenono Music (GMR)

"LOVE" from the album *John Lennon/Plastic Ono Band*
Written by JOHN WINSTON LENNON
© 1970 Lenono Music (GMR)

"WELL WELL WELL" from the album *John Lennon/Plastic Ono Band*
Written by JOHN WINSTON LENNON
© 1970 Lenono Music (GMR)

"LOOK AT ME" from the album *John Lennon/Plastic Ono Band*
Written by JOHN WINSTON LENNON
© 1970 Lenono Music (GMR)

"GOD" from the album *John Lennon/Plastic Ono Band*
Written by JOHN WINSTON LENNON
© 1970 Lenono Music (GMR)

"MY MUMMY'S DEAD" from the album *John Lennon/Plastic Ono Band*
Written by JOHN WINSTON LENNON
© 1970 Lenono Music (GMR)

"DO THE OZ" from the album *John Lennon/Plastic Ono Band*
Written by JOHN WINSTON LENNON and YOKO ONO
© 1970 Lenono Music (GMR)/Ono Music (GMR)

"IMAGINE" from the album *Imagine*
Written by JOHN WINSTON LENNON
© 1971 Lenono Music (GMR)

"CRIPPLED INSIDE" from the album *Imagine*
Written by JOHN WINSTON LENNON
© 1971 Lenono Music (GMR)

"JEALOUS GUY" from the album *Imagine*
Written by JOHN WINSTON LENNON
© 1971 Lenono Music (GMR)

"IT'S SO HARD" from the album *Imagine*
Written by JOHN WINSTON LENNON
© 1971 Lenono Music (GMR)

"I DON'T WANT TO BE A SOLDIER" from the album *Imagine*
Written by JOHN WINSTON LENNON
© 1971 Lenono Music (GMR)

"GIMME SOME TRUTH" from the album *Imagine*
Written by JOHN WINSTON LENNON
© 1971 Lenono Music (GMR)

"OH MY LOVE" from the album *Imagine*
Written by JOHN WINSTON LENNON and YOKO ONO
© 1971 Lenono Music (GMR)/Ono Music (GMR)

"HOW DO YOU SLEEP?" from the album *Imagine*
Written by JOHN WINSTON LENNON
© 1971 Lenono Music (GMR)

"HOW?" from the album *Imagine*
Written by JOHN WINSTON LENNON
© 1971 Lenono Music (GMR)

"OH YOKO!" from the album *Imagine*
Written by JOHN WINSTON LENNON
© 1971 Lenono Music (GMR)

"WOMAN IS THE NIGGER OF THE WORLD" from the album
Some Time in New York City
Written by JOHN WINSTON LENNON and YOKO ONO
© 1972 Lenono Music (GMR)/Ono Music (GMR)

"ATTICA STATE" from the album *Some Time in New York City*
Written by JOHN WINSTON LENNON and YOKO ONO
© 1972 Lenono Music (GMR)/Ono Music (GMR)

"NEW YORK CITY" from the album *Some Time in New York City*
Written by JOHN WINSTON LENNON
© 1972 Lenono Music (GMR)

"SUNDAY BLOODY SUNDAY" from the album *Some Time in New York City*
Written by JOHN WINSTON LENNON and YOKO ONO
© 1972 Lenono Music (GMR)/Ono Music (GMR)

"THE LUCK OF THE IRISH" from the album *Some Time in New York City*
Written by JOHN WINSTON LENNON and YOKO ONO
© 1972 Lenono Music (GMR)/Ono Music (GMR)

"JOHN SINCLAIR" from the album *Some Time in New York City*
Written by JOHN WINSTON LENNON
© 1972 Lenono Music (GMR)

"ANGELA" from the album *Some Time in New York City*
Written by JOHN WINSTON LENNON and YOKO ONO
© 1972 Lenono Music (GMR)/Ono Music (GMR)

"MIND GAMES" from the album *Mind Games*
Written by JOHN WINSTON LENNON
© 1973 Lenono Music (GMR)

"TIGHT A$" from the album *Mind Games*
Written by JOHN WINSTON LENNON
© 1973 Lenono Music (GMR)

"AISUMASEN (I'M SORRY)" from the album *Mind Games*
Written by JOHN WINSTON LENNON
© 1973 Lenono Music (GMR)

"ONE DAY (AT A TIME)" from the album *Mind Games*
Written by JOHN WINSTON LENNON
© 1973 Lenono Music (GMR)

"BRING ON THE LUCIE (FREDA PEOPLE)" from the album *Mind Games*
Written by JOHN WINSTON LENNON
© 1973 Lenono Music (GMR)

"INTUITION" from the album *Mind Games*
Written by JOHN WINSTON LENNON
© 1973 Lenono Music (GMR)

"OUT THE BLUE" from the album *Mind Games*
Written by JOHN WINSTON LENNON
© 1973 Lenono Music (GMR)

"ONLY PEOPLE" from the album *Mind Games*
Written by JOHN WINSTON LENNON
© 1973 Lenono Music (GMR)

"I KNOW (I KNOW)" from the album *Mind Games*
Written by JOHN WINSTON LENNON
© 1973 Lenono Music (GMR)

"YOU ARE HERE" from the album *Mind Games*
Written by JOHN WINSTON LENNON
© 1973 Lenono Music (GMR)

"MEAT CITY" from the album *Mind Games*
Written by JOHN WINSTON LENNON
© 1973 Lenono Music (GMR)

"GOING DOWN ON LOVE" from the album *Walls and Bridges*
Written by JOHN WINSTON LENNON
© 1974 Lenono Music (GMR)

"WHATEVER GETS YOU THRU THE NIGHT" from the album *Walls and Bridges*
Written by JOHN WINSTON LENNON
© 1974 Lenono Music (GMR)

(50%) "OLD DIRT ROAD" from the album *Walls and Bridges*
Written by HARRY NILSSON and JOHN WINSTON LENNON
© 1974 Lenono Music (GMR)

(25%) "OLD DIRT ROAD"
Words by Harry Nilsson and JOHN WINSTON LENNON, Music by JOHN WINSTON LENNON
© 1974 Golden Syrup Music (BMI)
All rights on behalf of Golden Syrup Music administered by Warner-Tamerlane Publishing Corp.

(25%) "OLD DIRT ROAD"
Words and Music by John Lennon and Harry Nilsson © 1974 Reproduced by permission of EMI Blackwood Music Inc, London W1F 9LD

"WHAT YOU GET" from the album *Walls and Bridges*
Written by JOHN WINSTON LENNON
© 1974 Lenono Music (GMR)

"BLESS YOU" from the album *Walls and Bridges*
Written by JOHN WINSTON LENNON
© 1974 Lenono Music (GMR)

"SCARED" from the album *Walls and Bridges*
Written by JOHN WINSTON LENNON
© 1974 Lenono Music (GMR)

"#9 DREAM" from the album *Walls and Bridges*
Written by JOHN WINSTON LENNON
© 1974 Lenono Music (GMR)

"SURPRISE SURPRISE (SWEET BIRD OF PARADISE)" from the album *Walls and Bridges*
Written by JOHN WINSTON LENNON
© 1974 Lenono Music (GMR)

"STEEL AND GLASS" from the album *Walls and Bridges*
Written by JOHN WINSTON LENNON
© 1974 Lenono Music (GMR)

"BEEF JERKY" from the album *Walls and Bridges*
Written by JOHN WINSTON LENNON
© 1974 Lenono Music (GMR)

"NOBODY LOVES YOU (WHEN YOU'RE DOWN AND OUT)" from the album *Walls and Bridges*
Written by JOHN WINSTON LENNON
© 1974 Lenono Music (GMR)

"(JUST LIKE) STARTING OVER" from the album *Double Fantasy*
Written by JOHN WINSTON LENNON
© 1980 Lenono Music (GMR)

"CLEANUP TIME" from the album *Double Fantasy*
Written by JOHN WINSTON LENNON
© 1980 Lenono Music (GMR)

"I'M LOSING YOU" from the album *Double Fantasy*
Written by JOHN WINSTON LENNON
© 1980 Lenono Music (GMR)

"BEAUTIFUL BOY (DARLING BOY)" from the album *Double Fantasy*
Written by JOHN WINSTON LENNON
© 1980 Lenono Music (GMR)

"WATCHING THE WHEELS" from the album *Double Fantasy*
Written by JOHN WINSTON LENNON
© 1980 Lenono Music (GMR)

"WOMAN" from the album *Double Fantasy*
Written by JOHN WINSTON LENNON
© 1980 Lenono Music (GMR)

"DEAR YOKO" from the album *Double Fantasy*
Written by JOHN WINSTON LENNON
© 1980 Lenono Music (GMR)

"I'M STEPPING OUT" from the album *Milk and Honey*
Written by JOHN WINSTON LENNON
© 1984 Lenono Music (GMR)

"FACE IT (I DON'T WANNA FACE IT)" from the album *Milk and Honey*
Written by JOHN WINSTON LENNON
© 1984 Lenono Music (GMR)

"NOBODY TOLD ME" from the album *Milk and Honey*
Written by JOHN WINSTON LENNON
© 1984 Lenono Music (GMR)

"BORROWED TIME" from the album *Milk and Honey*
Written by JOHN WINSTON LENNON
© 1984 Lenono Music (GMR)

"LITTLE FLOWER PRINCESS" from the album *Milk and Honey*
Written by JOHN WINSTON LENNON
© 1984 Lenono Music (GMR)

"GROW OLD WITH ME" from the album *Milk and Honey*
Written by JOHN WINSTON LENNON
© 1984 Lenono Music (GMR)

CREDITS

The publishers would like to thank the following sources for their kind permission to reproduce the pictures in this book.

Alamy: 129, 174

Getty Images: /Jorgen Angel/Redferns 87; /Apic 107; /Bob Aylott/Keystone/ Hulton Archive 20; /Dick Barnatt/Redferns 13; /Dave M. Benett 170; / Bettmann 42, 45, 57, 90, 101; /Michael Brennan 153; /Paul Bruinooge/Patrick McMullan 169; /Frederick R. Bunt/Evening Standard 110; /Tom Copi/Michael Ochs Archives 58; /Anthony Cox/Keystone 38; /Richard Creamer/Michael Ochs Archives 125; /Cummings Archives/Redferns 27; /Daily Herald Archive/ SSPL 14; /John Downing 28; /Frank Edwards/Fotos International 112, 113; / Evelyn Floret/The LIFE Images Collection 76; /Fotos International 116-117; /Ron Galella/Ron Galella Collection 124, 133; /Gijsbert Hanekroot 54, 64, 98; /Mark and Colleen Hayward 148; /Jeff Hochberg 165; /Ron Howard/ Redferns 10-11, 25, 33, 34; /Hulton Archive 41, 164; /Hulton-Deutsch Collection/Corbis 62, 82, 134; /Keystone/Hulton Archive 68; /JB Lacroix 171; /Bernd Lubowski/ullstein bild 83; /Andrew Maclear/Redferns 162-163; / Marka/Universal Images Group 177; /Kevin Mazur/Getty Images for The John Lennon Educational Tour Bus 175; /David McGough/DMI/The LIFE Picture Collection 95; /Jack Mitchell 146; /Steve Morley/Redferns 119; /Oliver Morris 85; /Michael Ochs Archives 16, 36, 48, 120, 158; /New York Times Co. 126; /Larry C. Morris/Popperfoto 26; /Michael Putland 59, 61; /Brian Rasic 172; /John Rodgers/Redferns 122; /Rolls Press/Popperfoto 15; /SSPL 44; / Thomas Monaster/NY Daily News Archive 72; /Robin Platzer/IMAGES 168; /Popperfoto 77; /Aaron Rapoport/Corbis 166; /Silver Screen Collection 103; /Leni Sinclair/Michael Ochs Archive 89; /Dennis Stone/Mirrorpix 73; /Three Lions 78; /Votava/Imagno 19; /Tom Wargacki 111; /Watford/Mirrorpix 80; / Art Zelin 141; /Vinnie Zuffante/Michael Ochs Archives 96, 138, 142

Lipinski via Wikimedia Commons: 129 (main)

Shutterstock: AP 9, 137, 176; /John Barrett/Photolink 136; /Antonio Di Filippo 173; /Fairchild Archive/Penske Media 105; /Globe Photos/Mediapunch 55; /Mikhail Kolesnikov 6-7 /George Konig 46, 178-179; /Pacific Press 156; /SIPA 53

Every effort has been made to acknowledge correctly and contact the source and/or copyright holder of each picture and Welbeck Publishing apologises for any unintentional errors or omissions, which will be corrected in future editions of this book.